URBAN OPEN SPACES

URBAN OPEN SPACES

Helen Woolley

London and New York

Spon Press

First published 2003 by Spon Press
11 New Fetter Lane, London EC4P 4EE

Simultaneously published in the USA and Canada
by Spon Press
29 West 35th Street, New York, NY 10001

Spon Press is an imprint of the Taylor and Francis Group

© 2003 Helen Woolley

Typeset in Gill Sans by Ninety Seven Plus
Printed and bound in Hong Kong by Everbest Printing Company

British Library Cataloguing in Publication Data
A catalogue record for this book is available from the British Library

Library of Congress Cataloging in Publication Data
A catalog record for this book has been requested

ISBN 0-419-25690-3

Contents

Foreword

At the beginning of the twenty-first century, urban theory and policy throughout the world is returning to the issue of public space. The widespread flight from traditional urban centres in the developed world, whether to the suburbs or to new greenfield settlements, along with a rising fear of urban street crime, has alerted politicians of all political shades to the cultural importance which good quality public environments play in restoring popular confidence in urban living.

In the UK there have been a number of report and parliamentary select committees looking into the role which parks and green spaces can play in urban regeneration, culminating in the Urban Green Spaces Taskforce report, *Green Spaces, Better Places* (May 2002), which laid out a set of policies and recommendations to government to bring Britain's parks and public spaces back into good repair and improved future management. Helen Woolley was one of the key academics commissioned to undertake the research for this government enquiry, and her work and that of her colleagues played a large part in convincing government of the vital role played by public space in so many people's lives.

In this book Helen Woolley provides detailed evidence for her claim that urban open spaces play a vital role in creating healthier, more sociable communities, and extends her vision to include many of the rather more marginal places which provide so much meaning in local life – the small play areas, allotments and city farms which architects and landscape architects too frequently ignore in their preoccupation with more prestigious city centre spaces. The case studies which form the concluding section of this book reveal a range of recent landscape design initiatives which show that the art of place-making is slowly being rediscovered again in city planning. This is most notable, perhaps, in the astonishing success of Birmingham's Victoria Square and the adjacent improvements, which has signalled a dramatic change in the fortunes of the city centre and its perception by outsiders.

The author also brings to the subject a strong focus on the 'people benefits' of public investment in good quality urban design, in terms of better public morale, as well as some of the specific benefits which particular kinds of landscapes and gardens can bring to those recovering from illness or forms of mental distress – reminding us that our physical environment is as important a determinant of our mental well-being as our physical health. Finally she insists that ecologcal arguments are likely to play an even more important role in urban investment for our future, as it becomes clear that trees, plants, green corridors, pocket parks and urban natural settings can create much healthier micro-climates in the city, humanising it and reclaiming it for the walker and the child at play, as much as for the motorist or shopper.

Helen Woolley's work as a teacher, researcher and practising landscape architect has been quietly influential in recent urban thinking about public spaces and places, and this book is likely to consolidate that influence. It is very welcome.

Ken Worpole

Preface

From my early days as a child, born and brought up in Bournville next to Cadbury's chocolate factory, I was lucky enough to have a system of open spaces that could be called upon for recreation and relaxation. Some of these experiences were daily, some seasonal such as the conker tree, opposite the Green, on the way to school. Other experiences were less frequent, such as playing Pooh Sticks on the bridge in the first park or ice-skating on the Valley Pool in the winter of 1962–63. There are three parks, linked together, that we used regularly. The first not only offered the opportunity for Pooh Sticks, nature trails from school and conker hunting in the autumn but also watching old people playing bowls and anybody playing tennis. The second park in the series was somewhat smaller, almost linking the other two parks, with more trees planted along the edge of the Bourn Brook – very much a space linking the other two and mainly for walking through. The third park was, and still is, the Valley Park. In character this was somewhat open but still with tree planting along the brook and elsewhere. The Valley Pool was the attraction here. This was where toy sailing ships and motor boats could be found – sometimes in abundance, especially on a Sunday afternoon. There was a story that when my father and his brother were playing there once their sailing boat got stuck in the middle, with not a puff of wind to return it to the shore (a bland concrete edge). One of them got out a ball of string and they each held on to one end of the string, and, walked around the edge of the pond as they did so. Thus they were able to catch the boat by its keel and return it to shore. Across generations of families the daily and annual experiences of Bournville included seasonal changes to the lime trees in the streets, the brightness of the laburnum trees in Laburnum Road when they were in full flower, and the dullness of the eight foot high holly hedges in Holly Grove, until they were cut down. Annual events in open spaces included carol singing on the Green to the now famous carillon on top of the junior school, the delight at seeing the Christmas lights in the conifer tree on the Green and the school sports day and the annual Bournville Village Festival on the 'Men's Recreation Ground'. All of these are now treasured memories.

These experiences influenced my decision to choose Landscape Architecture as a career. There was too much wrong with architecture to put it right, so I discarded this as a career option, and felt that everyone should have the opportunity to grow up in the pleasant environment that I had done – hence landscape architecture was my choice from the age of 16. Yet what frustrations there are in grown-up life! Not everyone thought open spaces as important as I did; and still, in many situations, this is the case. My frustration with the lack of importance given to the provision, funding, planning, good design and management of open spaces for communities continues to concern me. Thus this book.

Perhaps if it can be proved by scientific and social scientific research that open spaces do benefit daily urban living, then attitudes, policies and actions might change. I do live in hope – especially because during the time that I have been writing this book there have been some changes. The government's Environment Select Committee into Town and Country Parks of 1999 (House of Commons, 1999) received evidence from over 60 individuals and organisations and confirmed that the overwhelming benefits of parks were not being supported by financial resources. The Urban White Paper of 2000 (Department of the Environment, Transport and the Regions, 2000) began to address some of the issues relating to parks and began to raise the importance of parks and open spaces. The latter has initiated a programme of research, funding for the Urban Parks Forum and a government advisory committee (or Taskforce) about urban parks, play areas and green spaces. What the outcome of the latter is we do not know at the time of writing – but we will know by the time of publication. I hope that it will be a tool for confirming the importance of urban open spaces to people's quality of daily life and put in place policies, strategies and funding mechanisms to regenerate and sustain these important contributors to peoples' urban life.

A particular event in the autumn of 1998 became the conception of this book. I was asked to speak in the first Urban Design Alliance week in London at the event that was sponsored by the Landscape Institute. After preparing for this

presentation two issues came to mind. First, the content of what I really wanted to say on this topic really was too long for the twenty minutes or so that I had been allocated. Second, I had put a considerable amount of work into the preparation of the presentation. I did not want this effort and what I was trying to say through it to go to waste, and I considered options for publication. It was evident that there was a clear structure to the presentation and that its length did not suit itself to a paper in a journal. Thus I approached a publisher, who accepted the proposal very quickly. The rest, as they say, is history.

Acknowledgements

I would like to thank a range of students who from time to time helped with practical issues related to the literature searches for the book. These include Silvia Hahn and Anja Fanghaenel from The University of Halle, Jamileh Hafezian, Mohsen Faizi and Rebecca Hey. Nick Gibbins also gave valuable technical help in the compilation of the book.

I am grateful to a range of people who provided me with written information – these include the staff at Sport England and the British Heart Foundation, Sheila Harvey, librarian at the Landscape Institute, Peter Taylor, from the Department of Leisure Studies at the University of Sheffield, Nigel Dunnett from the Department of Landscape at the University of Sheffield and Carys Swanwick, Head of the Department of Landscape who provided advice on parts of the text. In addition three colleagues from Sheffield City Council helped by reading sections of the text, providing information or spending time in conversations with me – my thanks go to Martin Page, Liz Neild-Banks and David Cooper.

Fifty landscape practices were willing to provide case study information. I would like to thank them and in particular the Landscape Architects of the selected case studies for their help with the individual text for each case study. Thanks also go to most of these practices for sponsoring the colour reproduction of the supporting illustrations for the case studies.

Throughout the process of researching and writing the book unstinting support and encouragement was given by my research colleague and friend Dr Christopher Spencer, from the Department of Psychology at the University of Sheffield. I am very grateful to him for this moral and academic support, which took the form of reading the text and providing occasional copies of journal articles and discussions – usually over lunch in the café at Weston Park Museum, conveniently located in the park between our two departments.

Finally I am eternally grateful to Mike, my husband, who has tolerated all the ups and downs of the lengthy process of book writing together with the taking over of our dining room by relevant, and sometimes irrelevant, books and papers. On the days when I worked at home Mike also learnt to cope with the exclamations when the computer did something that I had not purposely asked it to! Our son, James, has also been patient of the process, while Emma's arrival somewhat delayed the end product. Yet both of our children have taught me more about the importance of our urban open spaces through their own experiences and enjoyment of them.

Urban Open Spaces

I am grateful to the following individuals and organisations for providing photographs for the main text in sections one and two:
Nigel Dunnett: 5.2, 5.3.
Federation of City Farms and Community Gardens: 2.3, 4.3, 6.13, 6.14.
Learning Through Landscapes: 1.1, 6.8, 6.9.
National Urban Forestry Unit: 7.5, 7.6.
Panni Poh Yoke Loh at Green City Action, Abbeyfield Park, Sheffield: 1.4, 1.6.
Larraine Worpole: 1.8, 5.4, 7.2.
The remainder of the illustrations were provided by the author.

The following landscape practices are due many thanks for providing information and illustrations for the case studies. I am also grateful that most of these organisations were able to contribute to the cost of colour reproduction of the illustrations supporting the case studies.

Neighbourhood and recreational urban open spaces

Sherwood, Longsands and Cottam, Preston, Lancashire: Trevor Bridge, Trevor Bridge Associates, Ashton-under-Lyne, Lancashire. Photograph copyright: Trevor Bridge Associates.

Northwestern Gardens, Llandudno: Bridget Snaith and Richard Peckham, Bridget Snaith Landscape Design, Chester. Photograph copyright: Christian Smith.

Stormont Estate Playpark, Belfast, Northern Ireland: Henry Irwin, Department of Finance and Personnel, Northern Ireland. Photograph copyright: Department of Finance and Personnell, Northern Ireland.

Redgates School Sensory Garden for Children with Special Educational Needs, Croydon: Robert Petrow, Robert Petrow Associates, New Malden, Surrey. Photograph copyright: Robert Petrow Associates.

Spring Gardens, Buxton, Derbyshire: Andrew Harland, Landscape Design Associates, Peterborough. Photograph copyright: Landscape Design Associates.

Stockley Golf Course, London: Bernard Ede, Bernard Ede Associates, Warminster. Photographs copyright Bernard Ede Associates. Photograph 1 copyright: Marcus Taylor.

Civic urban open spaces

Victoria Square, Birmingham: Adrian Rourke, The Landscape Practice Group, Birmingham City Council, Birmingham. Photographs by Gareth Lewis. Photograph copyright: Birmingham City Council.

The Peace Gardens, Sheffield: Richard Watts, Development, Environment and Leisure, Sheffield City Council, Sheffield. Photograph copyright: Sheffield City Council, Communication Service.

Edinburgh Park, Edinburgh: Ian White, Ian White Associates, Edinburgh. Photograph copyright: Ian White Associates.

Mold Community Hospital: Nigel Ford of Capita Property Services Limited. Photographs by Clwydian Community Healthcare Trust (now North East Wales NHS Trust), Cardiff. Photograph copyright: Capita Property Services.

Heriot-Watt University, Riccarton Campus, Edinburgh: Mike Browell, Weddle Landscape Design, Sheffield, South Yorkshire. Photograph copyright: Weddle Landscape Design.

Curzon Street Courtyard: Lionel Fanshawe, The Terra Firma Consultancy, Petersfield, Hampshire. Photograph copyright: The Terra Firma Consultancy.

Marie Curie 'Garden of Hope', Finchley, London: Rupert Lovell, David Huskisson Associates, Tunbridge Wells, Kent. Photograph copyright: David Huskisson Associates.

Chatham Maritime Regeneration: David Comben, Gibberd Landscape Design, London. Photograph copyright: Gibberd Landscape Design.

Black Country Route Sculptures, Wolverhampton: David Purdie, Landscape Section, Regeneration and Environment, Wolverhampton City. Photograph copyright: Wolverhampton City Council.

Victoria Quays, Sheffield Canal Basin, Sheffield: Judy Grice and Susan Smith, British Waterways, Rugby. Photograph copyright: Destination Sheffield and British Waterways.

Introduction

Urban living

The importance of cities has increased significantly over the centuries, and the current dramatic growth of urban populations is seen as critical to the future of Earth by some. The development from village and rural life to urban 'civilisation' has had both social and environmental impacts; the growth of urban populations and associated industrialisation has resulted in a range of detrimental and often dehumanising outcomes. In 1800 London was the only city in the world with a population of a million people, while the 100 largest cities altogether had a population of only 20 million. By 1990 the world's largest 100 cities had a combined population of 540 million people with 220 million of these living in the twenty largest cities (Girardet, 1996). By 1991, in England alone, over 80 per cent of the population was living in towns and cities of over 10,000 people (OPCS, 1993).

It is expected that by the year 2025 half of the global population, anticipated at some three billion people, will be living in cities (UNCHS, 1996). Thus the city and the urban environment will become extremely important in the daily lives of increasing numbers of people across the world. The quality of that urban environment will have an impact on a wide range of elements of daily life including housing, education, health, crime, employment and leisure, both for individuals and communities or populations as a whole. In different countries of the world the quality of life in cities will be determined by factors affecting each individual country as human needs and physical and economic conditions vary. A framework of needs – physiological, safety, affiliation, esteem, actualisation and cognitive and aesthetic – has been suggested by Maslow (1954). The former needs in this framework, physiological, safety and affiliation, are suggested as being the strongest and therefore more basic needs, while the latter, cognitive and aesthetic, are the weakest. Thus it is likely that in different parts of the world different communities will exist at different levels of this framework. For instance, in developing countries effort is more likely to be concentrated on achieving the strongest needs, while in many developed countries the luxury of the weaker needs can be expressed in ways such as the appreciation of beauty in the external environment. This is of course a somewhat simplistic analysis of the situation, but it is possible to imagine that someone without food and shelter is unlikely to concentrate on the finer things of life. Having said this, if some of the detrimental impacts of industrialisation and increasing populations are not addressed in the more developed countries, we may also experience some of the stronger elements of the hierarchy in forthcoming years.

These significant increases in populations together with the mobilisation towards urban centres have been accompanied by highly significant changes in energy use, consumption of food, energy and materials and associated pollution. The increase in total world energy consumption, together with the change in types of fuel used – especially the dramatic increase in the consumption of fossil fuels – has resulted in increased levels of pollution during the last 150 years (Rayner and Malone, 1998a). The Organisation for Economic Co-operation and Development (OECD) has summarised the range of environmental problems that urban areas are facing as that of air pollution, water pollution, waste, noise generation, pressure on land for urban development, a deterioration in the quality of urban life and the degradation of the urban landscape (OECD, 1990).

Open spaces are one aspect of the urban environment that is of great importance in daily life for people who live in urban areas. Often the importance of urban open spaces is forgotten in the debate about architecture and the built form. Open space might be considered as non-essential in the less developed countries, although this is debatable – but the importance of urban open spaces lies in the many different benefits and opportunities that they can provide. This is confirmed by the large numbers of people who use urban open spaces and the value that people attribute to them.

This book focuses on the importance and relevance of open spaces to peoples' everyday urban lives, whether this is on an individual basis or as a member of a community in the developed Western countries. Perhaps few people reading this book will need to be persuaded of the importance of open spaces in urban areas. Still it is likely that many readers will have to argue for the creation, preservation and resourcing of urban open spaces in fora and debates with clients, politicians and funding bodies, where such opinions do not hold sway. So, instead of resting on a comfortable, shared assumption about the importance of urban open spaces, this book provides both professionals and students with evidence to back up assertions that urban open spaces are important at the personal, community and civic levels. Most landscape professionals do not have ready access to such evidence, many having trained before much of the work referred to was written: one purpose of this book is to offer a brief guide to the kind of evidence which might back up assertions about the benefits and opportunities that urban open spaces can provide. There are many varieties of open spaces in the urban context, so different open spaces are also discussed from the view of the user. Each of the different types of urban open spaces discussed may be important at different times of life. Case studies are used as illustrations for some of the types of urban open spaces that are available for people to use.

What is open space?

It might be assumed that the answer to this question is obvious, but this is not the case. A variety of different authors and thinkers have used a range of definitions relating to open space. Open space can be defined as land and water in an urban area that is not covered by cars or buildings, or as any undeveloped land in an urban area (Gold, 1980). On the other hand Tankel (1963) has suggested that open space is not only the land, or the water on the land in and around urban areas, which is not covered by buildings, but is also the space and the light above the land. Cranz (1982) argued that open spaces are wide-open areas that can be fluid to the extent that the city can flow into the park and the park can flow into the city.

Open space has also been described from a user's point of view as being an arena that allows for different types of activities

encompassing necessary, optional and social activities (Gehl, 1987). Necessary activities are 'almost compulsory' and include going to school or work, shopping and waiting for a bus. They have to take place and therefore their existence is not dependent upon the physical environment; though how much improved people's daily quality of life might be if the spaces that these activities take place in are well conceived, designed and managed cannot be fully estimated. Optional activities are described as taking place 'if there is a wish and time' and may take the form of walking for fresh air, standing, sitting or sun-bathing. Being optional these activities only take place if the weather or place make the setting desirable for any particular individual. These activities are thus very dependent upon the external environment and the quality of that environment. Social activities are considered to be an evolution from necessary and optional activities. These depend upon the presence of at least one other person and may include children's play, greetings and conversations, communal activities and the passive activities of watching and hearing other people. The design and management of the physical environment can clearly have an impact upon the opportunities that might arise for such social activities.

Many researchers have shown that there is a relationship between environment and behaviour. This relationship may be conscious or unconscious and it may have a beneficial or detrimental impact on both individuals and society as a whole. Environment is not the only factor determining behaviour, but it is a contributing factor that we ignore at our peril. I would suggest, even, that the more deprived areas of our country, which the government is now targeting for an holistic approach to regeneration, possibly have the greatest need for a sensitively designed and managed variety of open spaces.

Open spaces can, of course, be defined physically by their legal ownership and boundaries but the *perception* of who owns a space is also important. Some open spaces are exclusively used by one person or a few individuals, while other spaces are shared with more people. Still other open spaces are seen as being available, or belonging, to everyone. Thus feelings of inclusion and exclusion can be experienced by people. The most well known of definitions related to use was developed some thirty years ago with the categories of public, semi-public, semi-private and private open space being suggested (Newman, 1972). Private open space is possibly the easiest to understand and includes individual gardens to homes. Public open space can be identified as spaces such as parks and plazas. Semi-private open spaces include those where a limited number of people use the space but where the ordinary public would generally not be welcomed. Such open spaces might include courtyards to houses or flats and communal gardens and play spaces. Semi-public open spaces might include spaces with limited opening times to the public or be generally accessed and used by particular groups within society – spaces such as school playgrounds.

A definition of different types of public space, both indoor and outdoor, has also been described by Walzer (1986) who suggests that:

Public space is space where we share with strangers, people who aren't our relatives, friends or work associates.

It is space for politics, religion, commerce, sport; space for peaceful coexistence and impersonal encounter.

Its character expresses and also conditions our public life, civic culture, everyday discourse.

Two types of public space – single-minded space and open-minded space – are suggested by Walzer. The former, he suggests, is designed, planned, built and used with only one activity in mind. Such an example might be a zoned central business district and the use of such spaces is not only single minded, but often associated with hurrying. Open-minded space, on the other hand, includes spaces such as squares or plazas, where a variety of buildings provide a context of mixed use and where the space itself is more likely to be used for activities of a less hurried nature, such as watching, walking, talking, eating lunch and discussing politics and world affairs. These single-minded and open-minded spaces reflect, to some extent, the necessary, optional and social activities of Gehl (1987), discussed above.

Urban open spaces

So as cities become home to increasing numbers of people as we move further into the twenty-first century, the quality of life for people in those cities is important. However open spaces are defined, or whatever state they are in, there can be no doubt that each urban conurbation has many of them. How can such open spaces affect the quality of life for city dwellers? What are the benefits and opportunities of such open spaces to people? How might such open spaces be used? Are such open spaces important to people's lives? Surely people who use these spaces do not spend hours discussing definitions of the types of spaces they are using, neither do they debate the benefits provided by urban open spaces, rather they experience the benefits and sometimes take the open spaces for granted. But they do value and 'own' such spaces and use them as part of their daily life, thus these spaces contribute greatly to an individual's and a community's quality of life in the urban context.

The book is divided into three sections, because that is how the text best sits. Each section is then further broken down into chapters. The sections are urban open spaces – benefits and opportunities, urban open spaces – spaces for all and urban open spaces – case studies.

The first section seeks to draw upon research from different academic and professional sources to show that open spaces can provide many opportunities and benefits to people's everyday life in the city. However, it is not a comprehensive literature search and those of you who read it coming from any one background will, I am sure, know of much more literature that could be referred to. If all the literature had been addressed this would have made the book on the tedious side and less accessible to the breadth of readership that I hope will be interested in the publication. The idea is to show that open spaces are important for a very wide range of reasons in people's daily lives in the city. Perhaps the significance is not so readily acknowledged by some because numbers of users are not recorded and people do not have to pay to use the facilities, but this should not allow

us to deny the vital role that open spaces play in everyday urban life. Chapter one discusses social benefits and opportunities, themed as children's play, passive recreation, active recreation, community focus, cultural focus and educational opportunities. Chapter two discusses health benefits and physical health – opportunities for exercise, mental health – the restorative effects of nature, the experience of 'near nature' and the aesthetic importance of nature in the city. Chapter three focuses on the environmental benefits and opportunities of urban open spaces, discussing the urban climate and environment and how trees and green spaces can ameliorate this. In addition wildlife is discussed with the opportunities that open spaces provide for wildlife habitats. Chapter four discusses the economic benefits and opportunities of urban open spaces. There is limited evidence in this subject area but the impact of trees and open spaces on property values, employment opportunities, crop production and tourism are briefly discussed.

Hierarchies of open space have been suggested by different authors over the years, but section two addresses urban open spaces as spaces for all. At different stages of our life we may have access to and use different types of open spaces, all of which enhance our quality of life experiences. As children, gardens and parks may be important, when in hospital the environment there is significant, if working in the city oppor-

tunities for lunchtime breaks in plazas, squares or green spaces may help relieve the daily boredom. Transport corridors become increasingly important to those who spend too many hours a day travelling and cemeteries are not only a resting ground at the end of our physical life but may be a place where we can come to terms with our grief for the loss of others. Thus this second section is structured into three chapters: domestic urban open spaces, neighbourhood urban open spaces and civic urban open spaces.

Landscape architecture as a profession is still not as fully recognised within the United Kingdom as it might be. We have not been very good at talking ourselves up or influencing the movers and shakers in our society, locally, regionally or nationally. Yet it is an important profession for it is the prime one for planning, designing and managing our external urban environment. I believe that there are many good examples of landscape architecture, applied to urban open spaces, within our own country and the third section of the book moves away from the theoretical into a more practical section of case studies. The studies are related to the domestic, neighbourhood and civic urban open spaces and are all examples of external environments that have been facilitated by a team that includes a Chartered Landscape Architect. They cover a range of types and sizes of sites, designs, funding opportunities and city users.

The Benefits and Opportunities of Open Spaces

Introduction

The Council for Europe identifies open space and its importance thus:

> Open space is an essential part of the urban heritage,
> a strong element in the architectural and aesthetic form of a city,
> plays an important educational role,
> is ecologically significant,
> is important for social interaction
> and in fostering community development
> and is supportive of economic objectives and activities.
> In particular it helps reduce the inherent tension
> and conflict in deprived parts of urban areas of Europe;
> it has an important role in providing for
> the recreational and leisure needs of a community
> and has an economic value in that of environmental enhancement.
> (Council of Europe, 1986)

Many benefits and opportunities are provided by the existence of open spaces in urban areas. Benefits can be understood to be something that gives advantage to a person, and are positive, while an opportunity, according to the *Oxford English Dictionary*, is a 'favourable occasion' or 'opening offered by circumstances'. Thus urban open spaces provide opportunities, or openings, for certain activities, such as play, watching and walking, while the benefits associated with such activities might relate to improved mental or physical health.

Although authors vary somewhat in their terminology, there is agreement that open spaces are of benefit in the urban situation. Thus for example Collins (1994) reports that the Ontario Federation of Parks and Recreation identifies four categories of benefits of parks and recreation as being personal, social, economic and environmental. Following a significant review of literature that was available at the time, Driver and Rosenthal (1978) identified social benefits of green spaces, including trees and other features, as:

- Developing, applying and testing skills and abilities for a better sense of worth;
- Exercising to stay physically fit;
- Resting, both physically and mentally;
- Associating with close friends and other users to develop new friendships and a better sense of social place;
- Gaining social recognition to enhance self-esteem;
- Enhancing a feeling of family kinship or solidarity;
- Teaching and leading others, especially to help direct the growth, learning and development of one's children;
- Reflecting on personal and social values;
- Feeling free, independent and more in control than is possible in a more structured home and work environment;
- Growing spiritually;
- Applying and developing creative abilities;
- Learning more about nature, especially natural processes, man's dependence upon them and how to live in greater harmony with nature;
- Exploring and being stimulated, especially as a means of coping with boring, undemanding jobs and to satisfy curiosity and the need for exploration;
- Replenishing adaptive energies and abilities by temporarily escaping adverse social and physical conditions experienced in home, neighbourhood and work environments. Needs include factors such as noise, too many things to do, demands of others, time pressures, crowdedness, insufficient green or open space, lack of privacy, pollution, unsafe environments and demanding jobs.

The Department of the Environment grouped the benefits of open spaces and greening urban areas into three main categories – economic regeneration, environmental and educational and social and cultural (Department of the Environment, 1996). The Council of Europe describes open space as 'a public living room for the locality' (Council of Europe, 1986). It also states that open space has an educational role, is of ecological significance, is important for social interaction and provides opportunities for community development through individuals having management responsibilities, creates community pride and has a recreational and leisure role.

The Benefits and Opportunities of Open Spaces

More recently the Department of Transport, Local Government and the Regions has affirmed the benefits of open spaces in urban areas in the interim report of the Urban Green Spaces Taskforce: "by enhancing the quality of life for people living in towns and cities, transforming the environment, especially in high density urban areas and encouraging inward investment in formerly run-down areas" (Department of Transport, Local Government and the Regions, 2001).

These benefits are increasingly being accepted as social, environmental and economic and will be discussed in this order in this section of the book. Chapter one discusses some of the social benefits that are important in people's daily lives where urban open spaces are valued for play or watching children play, for walking the dog, meeting friends or just watching the world go by. Such benefits may be experienced by an individual, a friendship group, an organisation within a community or an entire neighbourhood. Research recently completed for the Department of Transport, Local Government and the Regions (Dunnett *et al.*, 2002) has illuminated the fact that in addition to social benefits and opportunities urban open spaces provide specific opportunities relating to both physical and mental health, and these are discussed in chapter two. Environmental benefits are there for everyone, whether they realise it or not: chapter three discusses the urban climate and environment, together with some of the benefits to this climate that can be derived from urban open spaces. In addition this chapter also discusses the environmental benefit of the presence of wildlife in the city. The economic benefits of urban open spaces are discussed in chapter four and, as will be seen, there is less evidence about these benefits than the others, especially in the United Kingdom. However, issues such as the impact on property values, employment opportunities that open spaces can provide and the opportunities for crop production and tourism are all briefly discussed, together with recent and developing evidence that urban open spaces can play an important role in urban regeneration.

CHAPTER ONE

Social benefits and opportunities

Introduction

Perhaps the most obvious benefits and opportunities that urban open spaces provide for city living are social benefits – that is opportunities for *people* to do things, take part in events and activities or just to be. Sometimes these opportunities are undertaken in a solitary capacity and sometimes as part of a familiar or friendship group. On other occasions such opportunities will be as part of a neighbourhood, community or interest group. This chapter discusses social benefits and opportunities under the headings of children's play, passive recreation, active recreation, community focus, cultural focus and educational opportunities.

The importance of children's play in child development can sometimes be overlooked. Therefore, this will be discussed at some length because the evidence reveals the importance of play as one of the building blocks of life. Some of this evidence is significant because it puts children first or seeks to understand the urban environment from the child's perspective, rather than the adult's. When considering play with other benefits we can see that there is a clear connection between play and health benefits – this is discussed in chapter two – and play can help children to obtain and keep a healthier approach to life.

There is now repeated evidence to show that passive activities are the most frequently undertaken activities in urban open spaces, despite a lingering perception that active activities – particularly football – are the main use of urban open spaces. These passive activities include watching – children, vegetation, water, wildlife, activities, other people – reading, meeting friends or visiting the café. Such passive activities can be linked with the mental health benefits of the restorative opportunities that urban open spaces provide. These benefits have been clearly expressed as opportunities for rest, relaxation and getting away from it all.

Active recreation often takes place in groups and may include sports such as football, basketball, rounders, bowls or tennis. There is concern that the benefits of some of these activities are being restricted to organised clubs and groups of users while casual use of tennis courts or bowling greens is being discouraged in some urban locations (Dunnett *et al.*, 2002). Some active recreation, such as jogging, may take place as an individual activity or in small groups, while walking may be undertaken by individuals or in familial or friendship groups. Increasingly organised walking groups exist in some locations for disabled people, women or through 'walking for health' schemes. All of these activities link very strongly with health issues and consolidate the opportunities that urban open spaces can provide for such benefits.

The fact that urban open spaces can be a focus for the community is evident because the events that do take place, whether they be small or large, attract large numbers of people to them – in fact the numbers of people attending events across the country is estimated to be more than those taking part in sporting activities in urban open spaces (Dunnett *et al.*, 2002). These events may be organised by rangers – perhaps as walks for women or as educational events for children in school holidays – by community groups – such as plant sales, religious gatherings and fêtes – by local authorities – such as shows, firework displays and music events – or by commercial organisations – such as circuses, fairs and larger music events. These events help to enhance the value that a community attributes to its urban open spaces.

There is less evidence of the importance of urban open spaces as a cultural focus – especially in the UK, although there is increasing research being undertaken in this field. Local authorities do keep records of events and these, however, reveal that many events have a focus for a particular cultural or religious group. There is evidence from the US about the use patterns of different cultural groups and these are briefly discussed, but such accounts are sparse in the UK.

Educational opportunities and benefits of open spaces are discussed not only with respect to school grounds, which are perhaps the most obvious urban open space for these opportunities, but also with respect to other organisations who have promoted these opportunities in different types of urban open spaces over the years.

Of course these different social benefits and opportunities are often not discrete experiences and the use of an urban open space for one primary reason may result, and perhaps usually will result, in a secondary benefit. This can perhaps most readily be understood when people take children to play in an urban open space – often time spent in this way can provide an opportunity, away from the hustle and bustle of domestic or work issues, or the stress of unemployment, for mental restoration or catching up with community news from other adults and children met along the way.

Children's play

'Modern civilization interferes with a heavy hand in the spontaneous play of children'
(Hurtwood, 1968)

Separate from the very active pursuits of sports such as football, tennis and cricket, children's play is a very important activity in urban open spaces. It has been confirmed that taking children to play is one of the main reasons for visiting urban open spaces for many people (Greenhalgh and Worpole, 1995; Dunnett *et al.*, 2002). The importance of play for a child's development is proven by a wide range of research and is now increasingly accepted not only by professionals but also by ordinary people, not trained in these areas of expertise. Play is shown to be important for social development including collaborative skills, negotiating skills, confrontation and resolution of emotional crises, management of conflicts and development of moral understanding (see an extensive review of research on children by Taylor, 1998). Play is also important for the develop-ment of cognitive skills such as language and language compre-hension, experimentation and problem solving techniques. In addition the importance of opportunities for creative play are important.

Imitation of adults' activities is also considered to be a significant aspect of play as a means of bringing children closer to the adult world and helping children to construct their own identity, separate from their parents or other adults whom they might mingle with (Noschis, 1992).

The National Playing Fields Association (NPFA) (2000) also assert the importance of play in the outdoor environment in providing opportunities for freedom, large-scale physical activities and different challenges for children, while confirming that 'play provision benefits parents and carers because their children are enjoying themselves, are active and will be learning at the same time'. Thus the NPFA has suggested seven play objectives that they feel should apply to any provision aiming to offer children good play opportunities.

The type of play that children participate in varies with age, and sometimes with how they are feeling on any particular day. One of the most comprehensive studies of children's play both in the street and the playground was undertaken by Peter and Iona Opie. From casual observation, starting in 1960 through to regular weekly visits to the playground from 1970 until 1983 they observed many different aspects of children's play – the games, the interactions, the rhymes. During the 1960s the Opies observed that children across the country play different types of games – chasing, catching, seeking, hunting, racing, duelling, exerting, daring, guessing, acting and pretending games. On top of this is the experience of starting a game – gathering people to join in – which can in itself become a game (Opie and Opie, 1969). A further record of games, rhymes and jokes was made following Iona Opie's weekly visits to a playground (Opie, 1993). A more recent discourse of events in the playground is provided by Bishop and Curtis (2001) whose exploration discusses games, folklore and, to some extent, attitudes in the playgound in the latter part of the twentieth century.

In his pioneering work about children's play Hart (1979) discusses how children explore the environment and only by developing an understanding of that exploration can other people, namely adults, begin to design and provide environments

1.1 *Play aids the development*
     of many skills

1.1

for play that will be meaningful to children. In order to understand something of children's spatial knowledge and experience, of their environment from 'the door of their home to the fringes of their known world', Hart investigated four areas of interaction with the environment: spatial activity; place knowledge; place values and feelings and place use. Underlying this research was a fundamental belief that children experience the landscape in a very personal way. Discarding the traditional laboratory approach Hart chose to undertake his study in a small compact town, in America, with a relatively stable population that included 86 children. Initial model making with the children in school was well received and initiated the development of positive relationships not only with the children but also with the parents.

Relationships with the children were further developed when Hart joined the children in the exploration of their local environment, to the extent that when interviewing parents Hart was treated as the child's guest and as part of the children's 'gang'. Discussions with the children were positive, although there were times when the children just preferred to share the experience of what they were doing, rather than talk about it. This was an important part of understanding aspects of children's play. Observations, interviews, diaries, mapping, questionnaires with parents and activity surveys with the children were some of the methods used during the project that lasted nearly two years. Children's favourite places were identified by interviews and child-led expeditions, with the expeditions in

The Benefits and Opportunities of Open Spaces

1.2   *Water is liked by all*

1.2

the environment leading to many more places than were recalled in the classroom interviews. These places were valued for a variety of reasons: the uses children put them to in their play; a social reason such as an activity taking place; something being bought from a place or the feel or the look of the place being liked. Some of the uses that children put these places to included the 'ballfield' where activities included games and the annual fair; 'rivers' where 'fishing and dabbling' were enjoyed, child-built forts and houses; and lots of places that gave opportunities for activities such as climbing, sliding, hiding and cycling. This

innovative work revealed that the children involved in this study did indeed have a good understanding of their local environment and the opportunities for play that it provides. Some of the qualities identified as important to the children, were 'sand/dirt, small shallow ponds or brooks, slight elevations in topography, low trees and bushes and tall unmanicured grass'. Yet these are not the types of elements that designers or providers of play facilities usually include in play areas or in housing estates, despite the fact that these are elements that really can facilitate a child's development. Hart concludes that one very important factor is that the environment should be able to be modified by children in order to facilitate play.

In addition this pioneering work instigated some of the early discussions about what is now termed 'home range', that is how far from home children are allowed to travel without supervision in order to play and explore their urban environment. This work reveals that the farthest distance that a child was allowed to go from home related to both their age and their gender; boys were allowed to go further than girls and the allowed distance increased with age. It should be noted that Hart clearly describes how the 'allowed' distance or destination of travel was in fact an issue that was negotiated between parent, usually mother, and child, with the child understanding the reasons for the constraint (Hart, 1979). Is the home range of children today, some twenty years later, still negotiated? Or is it more prescribed because of the increase of cars and parental fear about strangers, often fuelled by media reports?

What else might be of value to the child in their experience of play in the city? Places to hide, vegetation and water are three elements of the landscape that children can benefit from in their play activities and they are highlighted below.

A study of the use that pre-school aged children made of a particular play area of Washington revealed the importance for children of the opportunity for play in a 'refuge' setting (for prospect/refuge theory see Appleton, 1996) or places to hide or see out from, as the children might describe it; what adults might call enclosure. Of all the play observed, 47 per cent was of this type, which is of particular interest because only 10 per cent of the land take of this play area was designed for this type of play. This work also studied the different types of play in which children participated in the three refuge locations, and categorised these activities as dramatic – including domestic and adventure play – other non-verbal and verbal play. Two of the refuge areas were vegetated corners of the playground, while the third was a built refuge. Dramatic play in each of these refuge areas accounted for 68, 63 and 42 per cent of all the recorded play respectively. Thus it was clear that the provision of refuge opportunities was very supportive of dramatic play (Kirkby, 1989). Opportunities for shelter and privacy while playing in private gardens have also been identified as favourite elements that are well remembered as childhood experiences by adults (Francis, 1995).

A summary of the varying play behaviours of different aged children has been suggested for practitioners. One to three-year olds are described as playing alongside each other, not with each other and enjoy fantasy and role play, while pre-school children, continuing these activities, also try new skills such as running, climbing and digging. In their primary school years children like animals and plants, further exploring their environment, playing with sand, water and clay, and construction play. Early secondary years are when children become more competitive and more particular about organising activities. Adolescents become more focused in their activities, enjoying music, dancing, hobbies and in some instances becoming more rebellious and boisterous (Coffin, 1989).

Two pieces of research in the United Kingdom examined children's play on housing estates. In the first of these studies, parents, adults without children and children were interviewed over twelve housing estates built since 1950. Observations were also undertaken and some children wrote essays. One finding was that 50 per cent of children had left the playground within fifteen minutes of arriving. Sitting, standing, talking and wandering, sometimes looking for a friend, all took up a significant amount of the play time. In addition it was observed that, for all pieces of equipment, the maximum number of children grouped round the equipment was the same as or more than the number of children using the piece of equipment. Thus the equipment could be seen to be providing a social focus (Hole, 1966). In a second study 50,000 observations were made of children's outdoor activities on sixteen housing estates and in one adventure playground. Irrespective of building form or density three-quarters of the children were observed playing near to home and this was particularly the case with under five-year olds. Two-fifths of the children played on roads, in front of garages, or on adjoining pavements – a figure significantly higher than for those who played in gardens, play areas or on paved areas. This research also identified that the most frequent activities were running and walking and sitting/standing/lying. Playing with bicycles and wheeled toys was the next most frequent activity, followed by ball games, and playground equipment (Department of the Environment, 1973).

From time to time there has been debate among professionals about the value, or not, of planting around children's play areas and whether such planting affords opportunities for play. A negative approach to the existence of planting around play areas has related to concerns about safety, the possibilities that strangers may be hiding among such vegetation and the fact that vegetation can collect litter. One option is to design the vegetation in such a way that prospect can be afforded from within, thus giving children a sense of control over their own play experience. Children's experiences of vegetation as a play object, food, a task, an obstacle, an ornament or as adventure were identified in a research project involving over 800 children aged 8 to 11 in the south of England (Harvey, 1989). Girls and boys both experienced vegetation as often as each other and enjoyed these experiences equally. Some differences were found between boys and girls with respect to the type of experience that they had. Experiences of play and adventure, that is climbing a tree, playing in tall grass, playing hide and seek among bushes, playing in the park, walking through a forest and camping in the countryside, were recalled significantly more by boys than girls. On the other hand the experience of vegetation as food and ornament, that is, picking fruits and vegetables, tasting leaves, flowers or berries, planting seeds and watching them grow, growing a houseplant, putting flowers in a vase and pressing leaves or flowers were recalled significantly more by girls than boys. Enjoyment of these specific activities was also recalled in a similar way between the genders. Girls were generally more positive in their attitude towards vegetation than boys. When asked about preference between trees, bushes and flowers girls liked flowers most, boys liked trees most and they both liked bushes least. Differences in experiences by age were small, with a suggestion being made that differences

would be greater if a younger age group were studied. When the results were analysed according to socio-economic status, the twenty-one schools involved in the research being on a continuum from inner city to rural, some differences were identified. Children from a higher socio-economic status had more varied and frequent experiences of nature, while more of these children identified that they appreciated this contact with vegetation. Thus when spaces, whether formal or informal, are being designed for children's play or even considered as affording opportunities for play the provision of vegetation, particularly trees and flowers, should be considered in the light of these findings.

Plants can themselves be designed into a space for the purposes of play. At the Austin, Texas, Center for Battered Women bamboo hedges have been used not only for adding richness to a play area but also to provide materials for construction. In Dougherty in the US, a play cottage nestles amongst mature pecan trees, while swings and a hammock hang in nearby trees. A three-level tree fort is built around a dead ash juniper in the Mink Playspace (also in the US). Wisterias were planted for flowers and foliage, while a bird feeder hangs from a branch. These are just a few examples of how vegetation can be directly used for play opportunities (Talbot, 1989). Perhaps in the UK willow could be used instead of bamboo and there are many trees that can provide opportunities for tree houses.

Vegetation was identified as making a significant contribution to children's play in research undertaken in a public housing scheme in Chicago (Taylor et al. 1998). Nearly twice as many children were observed playing in outdoor common spaces with 'many' trees as in spaces with 'few' trees. In addition more creative play was observed in spaces with higher levels of trees than in spaces with lower levels of trees. Interaction with adults is also seen as important to a child's social and cognitive development, and thus access to adults was also observed as part of this research project. Of the groups of children observed having access to, or interacting with, one or more adults, twice as many groups had such access in common outdoor spaces with high

1.3 *Passive recreation
is very important*

1.3

levels of vegetation than with low levels of vegetation. Thus vegetation was clearly identified as having both play and social importance in the common outdoor spaces within this housing scheme.

Thus we have seen that play is important for child development in many ways and that urban open spaces provide ideal opportunities for a variety of play opportunities, often overlooked when schemes are being developed. The importance of play is also confirmed by the fact that there is an increasing conviction that play deprivation can have negative impacts on child development. The following are some of the ways that children can be negatively affected by play deprivation:

• Poorer ability in motor tasks
• Lower levels of physical activity
• Poorer ability to deal with stressful and traumatic situations and events
• Poorer ability to assess and manage risk
• Poorer social skills, leading to difficulties in negotiating social situations such as dealing with conflict and cultural difference
(National Playing Fields Association, 2000).

Despite the importance of play for a child's development, there are some issues in the urban context that restrict the opportunities for play in the external environment for many children. Such constraints relate to the following issues, identified by research undertaken by Barnardo's (McNeish and Roberts, 1995):

• Parental anxiety about children's safety – especially when children are playing outside
• Parental fear of strangers, traffic, drugs, bullying and dogs
• Parental concern about safety
• Poor provision of play facilities – no playground or a badly maintained playground.

Some of these issues that concern parents, such as fear of strangers and concerns about safety, can be exaggerated by the way the media reports individual incidents – both locally and nationally. Other issues – such as the poor provision of play facilities and lack of spaces for play – can be addressed by increased resources and are surely a challenge to our society as we move further into the twenty-first century.

Passive recreation

Open space for recreation and amenity accounts for 14 per cent of the land take of the urban environment in Britain (Morgan, 1991). Such open space is used for a range of recreational and amenity purposes which we will consider under the groupings of passive and active recreation. Active recreation is usually taken to mean activities such as football, cricket, hockey and other games, whereas passive recreation is taken to mean activities such as watching – children or others or wildlife – looking at views, reading, resting or meeting friends.

The importance of open spaces and parks in the urban situation for both active and passive recreation has been accepted since the instigation of parks in the nineteenth century, when public walks were seen as part of the recreational package of these spaces (Walker and Duffield, 1983).

Research in both the US and the UK has provided information of the recreational use to which urban parks are put. A range of activities and times of use have been identified as part of urban life. Parks are well used at lunchtimes (Whyte, 1980) and in the early afternoon on weekdays (More, 1985). The cyclical nature of leisure activities of a Cleveland, Ohio park, as a result of the increasing segregation between work and nonwork, is discussed by Scott (1997).

Earlier research in America studied the use of two city parks in Boston and Hartford where data about 20,000 users was recorded over twenty-four hour periods at different times and on different days of the week. The study identified that the two parks provided opportunities for 300,000 hours of use over two summer months. Different groups of people within society exhibited different patterns of use at different times of the day and week. The findings revealed a clear pattern of use of the

1.4

parks throughout the day, with single male adults using the parks in the early hours of the morning giving way to the morning rush hour when adult males predominated with passive activities such as walking, looking, reading and photography. The morning shopping period involved women and children in social and individual activities of reading, looking, feeding wildlife and play. In both of the parks studied the lunch time period showed 'tremendous' levels of activity. During this time social activities and the level of women users peaked. Eating and conversing were the dominant activities. The levels of activity initiated in this time lingered into the afternoon and although the levels of use declined from the lunchtime high, activities such as conversing, looking, feeding wildlife and photography were frequent. The afternoon rush hour revealed lower levels of activity, with play, of children and after work adults, being an important activity alongside conversing and consuming behaviour. The levels of use in the early evening were lower and the main behaviours included affection (e.g. holding hands, kissing), consuming and conversing. In addition music and dance were

observed during this time period. The numbers of users declined into the evening with similar patterns of behaviour to the early evening. Night time was, not surprisingly, the time period of the least use of the parks. This research not only studied activities undertaken but also revealed that many different types of people were using the parks – people with ethnic and socio-economic differences from each other – and yet all were using the parks and, in the main, tolerating each other. Thus the researcher identified that parks are a neutral ground where people tolerate a wide range of activities and people – a place of freedom within the city (More, 1988).

Others have identified that the use of green space in British urban parks tends to be mainly related to passive activities, yet the provision of resources and finance to support such activities does not reflect this (Bradley and Millward, 1986; Greenhalgh and Worpole, 1995). The importance of such passive activities to individual's lives has been confirmed recently by research for the Office of the Deputy Prime Minister (formerly the Department of Transport, Local Government and the Regions) (Dunnett, *et al.,*

1.4   *Chess in the park*
1.5   *Active recreation
      is more than just football*

1.5

2002) which clearly revealed that more people use urban open spaces for passive reasons, less for events and lower numbers still for active reasons.

The contemporary importance of urban parks in the United Kingdom has been clearly identified by the work of Greenhalgh and Worpole (1995) who identified that more than 40 per cent of people use their local park on a daily basis. This research included observations of 10,000 people in eight parks on Sundays in the summer of 1994 and interviews with over 1,000 park users. It provided the first clearly recorded accounts of the use of parks in the UK in recent years. For every eight people one dog was recorded, making dog walkers a large user group of our urban parks. Taking children to the park was also a main reason for adults visiting parks. Many of these adults would undertake the passive activity of watching children play while socialising themselves – perhaps discussing the weather, or school issues or other activities relating to the interests of their children.

For women, open spaces provide opportunities not only for relaxation and recreation for themselves but also for others. Although a generalisation to some extent, research has identified that the 'ethic of care', which is a model of moral development, is exhibited more by women than men. This ethic of care may relate to caring for children, older relatives, friends and even strangers (Day, 2000). A wide variety of reasons have been given as constraints to women's use of public space including limited time, money and mobility, isolation, lack of services, constrained emotions such as fear, responsibilities and social norms. The ethic of care is seen by some as one of these constraints to women's use of public spaces, including public open spaces such as parks, but this moral code can also be a positive reason for the use of public space. Many women with children only go to open spaces to take the children and while there they may engage in discussion with and caring for other parents, old people and even strangers. Thus the ethic of care can in fact have a positive impact on public open space by reducing the fear of crime and enhancing the perception of safety (Day, 2000).

It can be seen that many different passive activities take place in our urban open spaces. Some of these activities are social – being with other people, meeting friends, looking after children, conversing with strangers – and some are solitary – opportunities for contemplation away from the hurly-burly of life or even an anonymous moment. Other activities provide opportunities for social identity and inclusion at community or cultural events.

Active recreation

The government's Household Survey, an annual survey of about 12,500 people, indicated that in the three years up to 1990 up to 41 million people were involved in a range of sporting activities, including walking (Collins, 1994). Such sports include both indoor and outdoor activities and private and public sites, but Collins estimates that some 7.5 million visitors each year use public parks for these active recreational activities, while acknowledging that such users are a minority, accounting for 16 per cent or less of park users. Indoor sport numbers are more readily recorded, partly due to the fact that these are fee-paying activities, whereas the use of parks is free and users of open spaces are not regularly recorded by most local authorities. Collins asserts that the increase in machinery, as labour-saving devices in the workplace, has reduced the quantity of physical activity undertaken at work and suggests that 70 per cent of all vigorous activity is now undertaken in leisure time and is freely chosen, rather then being an obligatory or unavoidable part of the daily work situation. The benefits of exercise have now been well proven to include the reduction of the risk of heart attacks and strokes, improved weight control, reduction of blood pressure, and prevention of bone strength loss, back pain and mild depression. In addition exercise can help with self-esteem and coping with life in general. Some of the activities that can help in this way include running and jogging, cycling and walking, and parks and other open spaces have an important part to play in provision for such activities.

Almost two-thirds (29 million) of the adult population of Great Britain takes part in sport and recreation at least once a month; the figure rises to 36 million if children are included (Sports Council, 1994). The sports showing most growth between 1987 and 1990 were walking, swimming, snooker, keep fit, cycling, golf, running, weight training and soccer (football). Swimming, cycling, soccer, walking and tennis were identified as the most popular sports undertaken by young people in school time, while a fifth of young people had undertaken these sports outside of school time (English Sports Council, 1997a). In addition minority activities such as skate-boarding are important to some young people, predominantly young men, who form social ties with like-minded people while undertaking this very physical activity in outdoor spaces, some which they 'claim' as their own (Woolley and Johns, 2001). Men over 60 years of age like walking, swimming, cycling, golf and bowls, while women of this age enjoy walking, keep fit, swimming, cycling and bowls (English Sports Council, 1997a). With international predictions for the over 60-year-old population rising from 350 million in 1975 to over 1,100 million in 2025, nearly 14 per cent of the total world population, concern about the health and fitness of this section of people is increasing (Diallo, 1986). Many physical conditions that are blamed on ageing can, in fact, be considered to be the result of lack of use – 'the Disuse Syndrome' (Bortz, 1990). Encouraging older people to participate in physical activities may not only improve their physical fitness and sense of well-being but may also increase their IQ and longevity (Bortz, 1990). Other skills may also be developed during recreational activities. Social integration, spiritual expansion, contact with nature, physical mobility, creativity, camaraderie and mental development have all been observed as beneficial results of older people participating in organised camping events in Chile (Chilean National Committee on Recreation, 1986). Cycling is allowed in some urban spaces and not in others, with some parks having by-laws preventing the activity. One example worth mentioning here is the *Blue Peter* bikeathon – a sponsored bike ride, by a long-standing and popular children's television programme, to raise money for the Leukemia Research Fund, which took place in early May 2001. Due to the foot-and-mouth disease epidemic the countryside was out of bounds, so all of the tens of thousands of people who took part had to cycle in urban areas – many of them using their local parks for this event (www.bbc.co.uk/bluepeter last accessed 10 May 2001).

An alternative form of active recreation, which often makes use of open spaces, has developed in recent years and is worthy of mention. 'Urban outdoor activities' can provide opportunities for young and old to develop feelings of well-being, self-confidence, relaxation and independence (Sainsbury, 1987). These activities are considered to be of particular benefit to children from inner cities and other disadvantaged groups within the urban community. Two components are identified as being necessary for Urban Adventure, through urban outdoor activities – the agencies and the activities. The agencies are important because they facilitate the activities. Such agencies might include resource holders such as park and recreation departments, water authorities, educationalists and youth associations, working together in partnership. In addition facilitatory organisations such as social services, youth groups and community groups together with skilled experts, who might be outdoor activities staff, trained community groups or commercial organisers, are important agencies. The variety of activities that can be facilitated by such agencies are identified as indoor, water-based, outdoor, climbing/rope work and wayfinding/orienteering. Water-based activities can take place on canals, rivers or park lakes and can include raft building, sailing, canoeing and board-sailing. Outdoor activities can include camping in the park, which for some urban children is a novelty, a great adventure and a learning experience. Climbing and rope work can be undertaken on an old railway arch or on a cliff and can aid physical health by developing strength, endurance, balance and agility. Way-finding and orienteering need not be contained to a rural situation. Most parks and open spaces have features of some type which lend themselves to this activity, which is low cost in capital outlay. In addition routes can be devised that can facilitate use by people in wheelchairs or pushing pushchairs. These varied activites must be supported by staff with relevant training, but they are considered to 'foster an appreciation of the outdoors and the environment by identifying with it rather than subjecting it to some of the more anti-social excesses with which we are all too familiar' (Sainsbury, 1987).

A more recent development with respect to health and fitness opportunities in parks comes in the form of the organisation British Military Fitness. This was set up in 1998 'to offer a unique and professional method of mental and physical fitness, adventure training and team building events. We motivate and encourage our members in a fun and challenging environment to get results' (http://www.britmilfit.com last accessed 20 May 2002). Many people join health clubs each new year, perhaps due to guilt about overeating at Christmas, but the dropout rate from such health clubs is very dramatic. The dropout rate from the activities organised by British Military Fitness has been very small in comparison. The organization was initiated in Battersea, expanded to other parts of London, and is now moving northwards to other locations. It holds daily classes in parks, provides classes for novices and those with more experience and the website suggests easy exercises that can be undertaken on grass or using a park seat.

People with disabilities have been encouraged to participate in sport with outdoor activities such as individual and team ball games, athletics and camping proving to be good at providing variety, pleasure and an opportunity for personal progression (De Potter, 1981). It has been estimated that there are 6.2 million people in Great Britain who have an impairment of some kind. Cheshire County Council was one of the leaders in appointing a Sports Development Officer with responsibility for Special Needs. Training for soccer skills has been an important part of this programme, not just because of the physical skills of dexterity and co-ordination that it can help to develop but also because of the personal attributes of confidence and enthusiasm that it can inspire (Jackson, 1991). Many sporting and recreational activities can be participated in by people who have an impair-

ment. Sailing is considered to be one of the activities where people with impairments can compete on equal terms with the able-bodied at all levels. Some 3,000 visually impaired people are estimated to be involved in sport of some kind. The most popular of activities for people with visual impairment is bowling, while hang-gliding, cricket – with a large ball – and football, using a ball with a bell within it, are other outdoor sports that can readily be taken part in. Perhaps the most successful sport for people with visual impairment is athletics, where the differences in performance between sighted and partially sighted people is closing (Pinder, 1991).

A range of outdoor activities such as walking, cycling, running, tennis, soccer, golf, bowls and skateboarding are enjoyed by large numbers and different sectors of the British population. In urban areas the fact that open spaces can provide opportunities for such a wide range of active activities, that add to the health and social fabric of the nation, is therefore very important.

Active recreation – reduction of incivilities and crime

Historically it has been considered that sport in open spaces might reduce uncivil activities. This was a theme of some of the early park providers but was also echoed by the government early in the twentieth century when it was hoped that 'sport would diminish juvenile crime and improve the physical health of future conscripts of the armed forces' (Turner, 1996a). More recently involvement in sport has been considered to play a part in reducing antisocial behaviour such as vandalism and drug taking. Thus outdoor sport is increasingly being seen, by some organisations, as a meaningful alternative to crime for young people who are considered to be at risk. The numbers of young people involved in crime are staggering, with 45 per cent of crimes that result in a conviction or formal caution being undertaken by young people aged 10-21 years old (English Sports Council, 1997b). Indeed it is reported that seven million crimes a year, at a cost of £1 billion, are committed by young people aged between 10 and 17 years old (English Sports Council, 1997c).

The Benefits and Opportunities of Open Spaces

1.6 *Multicultural festival in Abbeyfield Park, Sheffield*

1.7 *Teenagers love somewhere to 'hang out'*

Following a sports counselling project in the Solent area between 1987 and 1990, a similar project was set up in West Yorkshire and monitored during the period between January 1993 and December 1995 (Nichols and Taylor, 1996). This involved people who were on probation volunteering for a programme of three hours a week over a period of twelve weeks receiving individual counselling with a sports leader. A programme of activities was drawn up for each individual with the inclusion of core elements such as awareness of local sports facilities and clubs, leisure centres and the experience of outdoor activities in everyone's programme. A control group who did not receive the sports counselling was also involved in the project. Both quantitative and qualitative measures were used to monitor the impact of the programme. The reconviction rates of the counselled group and the control group were monitored over a two year period and it was revealed that although the predicted reconviction rate was 63.8 per cent, only 49 per cent of those involved in the counselling scheme were reconvicted in that time. In addition 15 per cent of the participants obtained a sports qualification, 57 per cent a 'passport to leisure' card and 42 per cent visited a local sports club. The more qualitative benefits of the programme were identified as a series of interrelating benefits such as improved fitness, increased self-esteem, new opportunities, the positive role model of the sports leaders and the gaining of new peers in life, resulting in changed behaviour through a new self-identity. Open spaces were among the locations that were used in this programme and thus can be said to be important because of the contribution they can make to the possible reduction of the number of people on probation.

More recently Sport England (previously Sports Council England) together with the Youth Justice Board and the United Kingdom Anti-Drugs Coordination Unit launched a scheme entitled *Positive Futures*. The aim of this scheme, being undertaken in 24 locations in England, is to try to involve young people who are at risk of disengagement from society in sport and leisure activities. It is hoped that this will result in a reduction of youth offences and drug misuse among 10 to 16 year olds and an increase in regular participation in sport and physical activity. Sport, training, mentoring, educational and leadership skills programmes are all included in this scheme (Sport England, 2000a). Again many of these activities will be undertaken in our urban open spaces, thus making a contribution to society through the potential reduction of crime.

Community focus

Many writers from the planning, design and sociological disciplines have asked how a sense of community can be fostered – suggested solutions have ranged from careful siting of resources to consideration of the ideal size of population and symbolic identifiers. Research in recent years by a range of investigators has confirmed the importance of open spaces as a focus for the community, or as a place for people to meet each other, both formally and informally. For some an urban open space may be important not only for the possibilities provided for use but also because of the historic nature of the space, while for others a sense of civic pride may be fostered through not only the historic, but also the social or horticultural value an individual or community places attributes to a particular urban open space.

In the UK it has been identified that urban parks, in particular, are used for a range of events which might increase the sense of community. These have included a May Day festival in Hounslow when an estimated 50,000 people attended, a Hindu prayer meeting in Leicester where 20,000 people attended, a handicapped children's fete in Cardiff where about 1,500 people attended and an Irish festival at Peckham Rye where about 15,000 people were involved (Greenhalgh and Worpole, 1995). Many other towns have had, and in some instances continue to have, such public gatherings: for instance in Sheffield on Whit Monday Sunday schools from around the city would walk from their places of worship to the park, with their banners, for a celebration gathering (Hoyles, 1994) (an attempt to reintroduce

1.6

1.7

this 'Whit Sing' was made in one Sheffield park in 2001). In addition thousands of other activities such as school sports days, nature trails, charity galas, religious meetings, tree planting days, ethnic minority fairs, funfairs and circuses take place. Many local authorities have a calendar of events for a year based on sporting, cultural and seasonal matters. In recent years parks and squares have become popular in the UK as venues for pop and classical musical events, sometimes raising money for charity, for example The Party in The Park and Proms in the Park. It has been estimated that the numbers of people now using urban open spaces annually for events is more than the numbers using such spaces for active sport (Dunnett, Swanwick and Woolley, 2002).

It is not only large and formally organised events that are important to the community. The study by Greenhalgh and Worpole (1995) identified that about one-third of the people entering the parks went alone, while another third visited with a friend and the final third went as part of a larger group. Familial and friendship groups regularly use urban parks for meeting each other, safe cycling for children, informal games, walking and the use of children's playgrounds. Informal games and bonfires are frequently organised community activities.

Different sectors of society, in a range of countries, have been identified as valuing their urban parks as places to be in, meet in, or 'hang out' in. Teenagers in Australia value developed parks (Owens, 1994). Pakistani children in Sheffield are frequent users of their parks (Woolley and Amin, 1995), while different racial groups were identified as having different approaches to active and passive recreation in thirteen parks in Chicago (Hutchison, 1987).

On a smaller scale community focus can also be provided in small open spaces such as community gardens. In Glasgow the community were engaged in a range of activities in Elcho Gardens (McLellan, 1984). Members of the community were not only involved during the design process of the gardens and associated housing but in the post-construction phase a local gardening club was initiated in order to stimulate interest in a variety of aspects of gardening.

Acknowledging the fact that three-quarters of older Americans live in metropolitan areas, a study was undertaken to investigate the impact that green outdoor space has on neighbourhood ties and a sense of community. The location was a community of mainly African Americans in an age-integrated public housing development in Chicago incorporating three of the poorest neighbourhoods in America (Kweon et al., 1998). Life in the city can be difficult for older people at times due to limited or restricted physical mobility and the likelihood of lower levels of social interaction. Financial strain, noise, building height and dilapidated physical environments, together with the sense of distrust that such environments can engender, can all discourage older people from interacting with each other. Kweon's research was set on an estate consisting of twenty-eight architecturally identical sixteen-storey buildings, with three buildings typically grouped to form a U-shaped courtyard. Other consistent features of the ninety-one participants of the research were race, income and education. The key variable was the treatment of the U-shaped courtyards, with some having trees and grass, while others were only concrete or asphalt. Eleven buildings were involved in this particular study, five of these having courtyards with several trees and grass, while six had courtyards with few or no trees and very little grass. Questions were asked of the participants about exposure to nearby nature in outdoor common spaces, social integration and a sense of local community. The results of this research indicate that exposure to common green space, in this case only a few trees and basic provision of grass, is associated with higher levels of social integration and a greater sense of community.

A sense of community can be provided by open spaces of different types for different people and communities. These opportunities include small and large events and both organised and informal gatherings.

1.8

Cultural focus

Should planners, designers and managers assume that people of different cultural backgrounds have different needs and desires with respect to urban open spaces? Is there evidence of cultural differences? Some evidence argues that needs between different cultural and ethnic groups are similar, while other evidence suggests that there are differences. Variations in the manner in which parks are used by different ethnic groups have been identified, although as Hutchison (1987) noted, there is a complex interaction between the factors of ethnicity and social class and it may be difficult to clearly identify which variable is active at a particular time. Black, white and Hispanic groups were studied in thirteen parks in Chicago (Hutchison, 1987). More than half of the black and white groups were observed in mobile activities and more than half of the Hispanic groups in stationary activities. The Hispanic groups were larger than the black groups, which were larger than the white groups. In addition Hispanics were observed as being more in family groups than the other two groups.

In Los Angeles it was identified that people from ethnically and socially diverse backgrounds all used parks because they offered greenery and recreational opportunities for people and their children (Loukaitou-Sideris, 1995). The Hispanic population was the most frequent user group of the public park, usually using the facility in family groups and often defining territory with the use of balloons and streamers while celebrating events such as birthdays. African Americans were observed going to the park more with friends, with half of the groups being of all male composition. The park was used for socialising with friends as well as for organised sports. Caucasians were mainly observed in self-orientated activities, with large numbers visiting the park alone. People from the Chinese community were the smallest ethnic group using the four neighbourhood parks studied, and most of these users were old men who were relaxing, socialising or performing Tai Chi.

At the same time there is growing evidence that parks and open spaces are important for people from different cultures for reasons similar to each other, thus giving credence to the universal importance of open space.

1.8   *A Jewish wedding*
       in Clissold Park, London

In Chicago a study involving 203 Chinese Americans used face-to-face interviews and focus groups to develop an understanding of their leisure activities (Zhang and Gobster, 1998). Basketball, tennis, volleyball and baseball are among the active recreational pursuits identified as being undertaken in parks by these participants. Younger children, aged 6 to 8 years old, reported that they used swings and slides and liked to play games such as 'catch-up', while older children, aged 9 to 12 years old, liked organised games as well as bicycling. Some of these activites were undertaken at school, while others took place within the streets of the local neighbourhood.

People from ethnic minority backgrounds have been identified as under-represented users of urban open spaces in the UK (Greenhalgh and Worpole, 1995; Dunnett *et al.*, 2002). Different approaches to the design and management of urban open spaces have been suggested in order to encourage more people from an ethnic minority background to use these spaces. Some approaches suggested are symbolic reference, experiential reference and facility provision, with the proviso that the approach taken should respond to the local community, the site and the context (Rishbeth, 2001).

Urban open spaces do have the potential to be used as a cultural focus, although this potential is currently not fully understood or realised. This cultural focus will also relate to other social and environmental benefits.

Open spaces as educational resources

The Nature Conservancy Council (Simmons, 1990) accepts that in order to safeguard wildlife in the city the public generally need to be informed about it and involved in measures to preserve it. The Council pays particular regard to the importance of education with respect to children and suggests that every school should be within a five or ten minute walk of an ecological area that can be studied. Another area of education is served by the voluntary sector which may be involved with their local authority, increasingly through wildlife groups, or through organisations such as the Royal Society for the Protection of Birds. It has been suggested that educational approaches could include the provision of facilities within the local neighbourhood, such as nature trails, field study sites and information centres (Teagle, 1974).

'Project Environment', a Schools Council project based at the University of Newcastle upon Tyne, studied the basis of environmental education for 8 to 18 year olds and identified three strands of environmental education. Two of these were traditional approaches of 'education through the environment' and 'education about the environment', when children explore their environment and look for facts about it. The third strand was identified as 'education *for* the environment' and involved children's values and attitudes (Morgan, 1974). A tenet of this project was that it is important to start with the child's world and the things and circumstances around the child; thus developing awareness of the child's urban environnment should be accompanied by linkages to the wider context.

The increasing use of open spaces as an opportunity for education can be seen from many examples. When the project 'Learning through Landscapes' was introduced one of its aims was to extend environmental education to use schools' grounds (Adams, 1989) rather than just relying on nature walks around the park, which many of us experienced as children. Research undertaken in twelve primary schools with 216 pupils identified that the children found the tarmac and concrete to be boring and that children wanted to have trees, grass and opportunities to develop imaginative play (Titman, 1994). A variety of projects affording educational benefits and opportunities have been recorded in research undertaken for the Department of Environment (Department of the Environment, 1996). These include the Ridgeacre Canal Project in the Black Country where a teaching pack, known as GreenIt and related to the National Curriculum, has been developed as part of the project partnership; and Neighbourhood Nature, a programme led by the National Urban Forestry Unit, which has educational projects as one of its outcomes.

The Benefits and Opportunities of Open Spaces

The UK government has acknowledged the importance of external school spaces in its bulletin *The Outdoor Classroom* (Department of Education and Science, 1990) where it suggests that uses for school grounds can include vegetable plots, herb gardens, wild flower meadows, ponds, butterfly gardens, and orchards. Many opportunities exist for linking different subjects of the national curriculum with the design, construction and management of school grounds, thus making subjects come to life by the use of elements that children can see in their daily lives. The authors of the report felt that in order to achieve creative use of school grounds a partnership of educationalists and landscape experts is needed.

More recently work concerned about the use that children with special needs can make of outdoor space has been undertaken by the organisation Learning through Landscapes. This research was a response to the fact that guidance exists for designing interior spaces for children with special needs, but information about what to take into account when designing for external spaces is very scarce. It set out to investigate all types of special needs across the school age range, residential and non-residential schools and mainstream schools where possible. The aim was 'to identify appropriate design and management approaches and collect ideas for projects and practical information of use to those planning and implementing school grounds development' (Stoneham, 1996). Included in this aim was a desire to uncover existing sources of information, advice and publications in order to make such information more easily available to those who might find it useful. Methods used included questionnaires, interviews and site surveys. All special schools and a number of mainstream schools were sent questionnaires and of these 396 were returned. Detailed analysis of the questionnaires was followed by visits to schools that had developed good outdoor projects. The special needs addressed in this work include learning difficulties, autism, visual impairment and blindness, deafness, language impairments and emotional and behavioural disorders. From the responses to the questionnaires it was clear that teachers value outdoor spaces as a resource for the education of children with special needs. The benefits for teachers and pupils identified from the responses, and included in the resultant publication, *Grounds for Sharing*, (Stoneham, 1996) are:

- Improvements in sensory perception, social skills, co-operative skills and work patterns;
- Improvements to children's behaviour, especially enabling emotions to be explored more effectively;
- A reduction in aggressive behaviour;
- Enhanced learning opportunities outdoors;
- A greater variety of patterns of play, both in a physically demanding, adventurous sense and in the provision of quieter, restful opportunities;
- Improvements to the image of the school and to special education in general.

From site visits and interviews a series of suggestions are made in order to help others who wish to transform and use their school playgrounds for educational purposes for children with special needs. Advice on how to manage the change of the grounds is followed by detailed design considerations relating to structuring the landscape, involving the children in the design and management of the grounds, planning for design, management and safety and monitoring the grounds. Details of design considerations and elements that may be required for active, passive and social activities such as accessibility, circulation, signage and sports are discussed. The importance of the use of planting, the opportunities for horticulture and designing for animals are all considered before nine case studies are discussed.

Educational opportunities in urban open spaces are not constrained to school grounds and do in fact abound in many of our urban open spaces. Two other types of urban open spaces, city farms and urban waterways, will be briefly considered with respect to this potential.

The educational opportunity afforded by city farms is acknowledged by the National Federation of City Farms (1998) through a range of means. First, they employ staff relevant to the educational field: this includes a specialist information worker, available to give advice on areas such as funding, animal welfare, youth work and child protection. A youth participation worker supports the volunteers working in different city farms where some 2,000 young people from inner city areas take advantage of the farms. In addition the federation has produced a number of information packs, advisory sheets and a video. A teacher resource centre offers a wide range of relevant educational materials and the federation produces a quarterly newsheet and Teacher Activity Sheets. The educational network provides support for schools with farm units, of which there are 111 (Federation of City Farms and Community Gardens, 1998). Similar opportunities are also available in community gardens, which developed from the 1980s onwards (Federation of City Farms and Community Gardens, 1999).

In America the 'Rivers Curriculum Project' of the 1990s, piloted by eight high schools along the Mississippi and lower Illinois Rivers, grew into an educational programme in twenty-three states. Interdisciplinary teams of teachers in subjects such as science, social studies and English undertook training to learn how to conduct water quality tests, research social and cultural information, facilitate written and graphic work for student-authored publications and how to take action on local river-based problems. The staff were also trained to use the relevant computer software for the ongoing research and monitoring programme. Students then undertook water quality tests and collected insects and other aquatic animals as indicators of river habitats. The outputs from these projects have been as diverse as providing data for the Illinois Environmental Protection Agency report to Congress to the tracking of zebra mussels. Mapping and decision-making opportunities were also included in these processes. In addition to this there were many opportunities for developing writing skills. Poetry, songs, creative writing and artwork were also encouraged through a sub-programme entitled Meanderings (Williams *et al.*, 1994).

Education is an essential component of British Waterways' developing community involvement strategy with the appointment, in recent years, of a National Education Manager who is expected to build on existing local and regional educational initiatives. These have included education packs developed in conjunction with local teachers, floating classrooms with displays and canal artefacts, pond dipping, wildlife spotting and water safety schemes. There has also been a three year theatre-in-education project which has interpreted the history of the waterways and has included in-school workshops, training days for teachers and performances with professional actors. The Canal Adoption Scheme operated by British Waterways, which encourages local communities and particularly children to conserve and protect their local waterway, can also be seen as a contribution to environmental educational (British Waterways, no date).

Summary

In this chapter we have seen that the social benefits of urban open spaces can be many and varied, including opportunities for children's play, passive recreation, active recreation, a focus for the community or a cultural group and educational. Such benefits and opportunities will be available to a different extent in each of the open spaces that one might experience in one's daily, weekly or annual use of such spaces.

The Benefits and Opportunities of Open Spaces

2.1   *Bournville's maypole*

CHAPTER TWO

Health benefits and opportunities

Health is not the mere absence of illness,
but means physical, social and mental wellbeing.
(The World Health Organisation)

Introduction

Open spaces in urban areas have been considered to have benefits for both physical and mental health for many years. This chapter will discuss the contribution that urban open spaces can make to physical and mental health before moving on to discuss the restorative effects of nature, aesthetic benefits and community value that can be afforded in urban open spaces. First though, a reminder of some of the protagonists of health benefits afforded by open spaces in the nineteenth and twentieth centuries.

Olmsted, pioneer of landscape architects (Beveridge and Rocheleau, 1995), was convinced that the reduced levels of plague and pestilence and improved general health and increasing length of life in towns was due to the gradual adoption of laying out of cities with 'much larger spaces open to the sunlight and fresh air'. The garden villages of Port Sunlight and Bournville were developed at the end of the nineteenth century by W. H. Lever and George Cadbury, both of whom had noted the effects of slum housing clearance on industrial productivity and human welfare. These men were advocates of houses in gardens with a sufficiency of open space providing opportunities for outdoor activities from organised recreation to home gardening, probably contributing to the excellent health statistics both companies delighted in. One survey (date unknown) indicated that children at Bournville schools were on average two and a half inches taller at age 12 than their contemporaries at a Birmingham City Council school (Burke, 1971).

In America, at the end of the nineteenth and beginning of the twentieth century, the suburban ideal was developed for and by the 'professional–managerial stratum' of society. This ideal was 'a strategy for positive environmental reform, a non-coercive approach to social improvement in which professional–managerial stratum professionals would redesign the metropolitan residential environment.' (Sies, 1987). Two factors in the development of this ideal are discussed by Sies. The first is the technological advances that facilitated the provision of flush water closets, piped clean water and waste water, hot water heaters, electric generating plants and structures such as well-engineered roads and footpaths and houses. The second factor in the development of the suburban ideal was nature: 'only the exquisite beauty of natural surroundings, it was thought, could inspire the spiritual regeneration and moral uplift that were two of the hoped for influences of the suburban ideal'. Nature was considered important for the fresh air and healthful surroundings that it proffered and the opportunities it provided for gardening, reading, socialising and active and passive recreation such as sports and walking. In addition it was taken for granted, as part of a long-term belief system, that nature had elevating and restorative powers. Such experience with nature was considered to be important from childhood onwards.

Three elements of the relationship with the landscape were taken into account in developing the suburban ideal – and these elements can be understood today as landscape planning and design. First, the choice of site was very important. Consideration was given to the relationship of the site to the city's industry – upwind was preferred – together with the scenic value of the environs. The second consideration was the development of the site. In some instances architects tried to create a large nature park as the setting for houses, carefully locating houses so as not to destroy too many trees or to plant new trees, while building roads along contours. The third important element relating to the land was the provision of parkland or recreational space in order that people could partake of both active and passive recreational activities, considered essential for ongoing mental, spiritual and physical health. Active recreation provision included facilities for tennis, playing fields and ponds for swimming, skating and ice hockey, while passive recreation in the form of the contemplation of nature and observing wildlife was provided for by trails through the park and woodland.

The Benefits and Opportunities of Open Spaces

2.2 *Even babies can benefit
from urban open spaces*

2.2

Contribution to physical health – opportunities for exercise

The health of our nation is currently a matter of concern as an aspect of quality of life. Coupled with this is the increased pressure that an ageing population will put upon the National Health Service and Social Services. Concerns about health begin with the health of the children of the nation.

A study of babies and pre-school children, aged 4, undertaken using data from the Wirral Health Authority, has revealed results that are worrying, especially if this work is indicative of the country as a whole. Data that are normally collected by health visitors – that is height and weight, together with a calculated body mass index (weight divided by height) – were used to study trends over the period of 1989 to 1998. The results can be accepted as valid because 88 per cent of the live birth population was included in the study and the study involved children of comparable ages. In addition, as 97 per cent of the population was of white European origin, variations due to ethnicity were not considered to have affected the study. Over the ten year period there was a highly significant statistical change in the numbers of children who were overweight and obese. Weight and body mass index increased, while height decreased, resulting in increased body mass figures for both boys and girls, with the proportion of overweight boys being greater than that of girls since the early 1990s. The trend also seems to have accelerated during the latter five years of the study. The results clearly indicate that this excessive weight gain occurred between infancy and the age of four. Previous work had indicated that childhood obesity is likely to continue into adult life, resulting in an increased likelihood of morbidity and mortality, with an increased risk of cardiovascular disease. Early intervention in areas such as increased activity and a reduction of high-fat and high-calorific foods in the diet are recommended (Bundred *et al.*, 2001).

Earlier work had identified that unfavourable serum lipid levels were common in children in research based in Exeter.

Blood pressure levels gave no general cause for concern and despite the fact that too many children in the research sample of 707 were overweight, the cardiopulmonary fitness of the children was not a problem. This research concluded that children have a low level of habitual physical activity, with boys being more physically active than girls and girls' levels of activity deteriorating as they move upwards through secondary school. The research suggests that a range of factors could be used to encourage an increase in the activity levels of children. These include a family approach to encouraging physical activity from a young age. The provision of safe, clean play areas, the promotion of physical activity, as well as healthy eating are recommended by health visitors. Walking briskly to and from school on a daily basis and physical education, as required by the National Curriculum, delivered in a fun and enjoyable manner in schools are suggested as ways that can enhance the health of our young people (Armstrong, 1993). These considerations link closely with social and educational benefits as already discussed in chapter one.

Open spaces can, and should, play an important part in providing opportunities for the activities suggested by the above evidence. Children of both pre-school and school ages can benefit from a range of open spaces, such as playgrounds, parks, school playgrounds and playing fields that are designed and maintained in a suitable manner. In addition it would be beneficial to link the use of open spaces in with sports programmes, community programmes and health programmes within each urban area. This does happen in some urban locations and one of the most recently introduced activities is 'health walks' in locations such as Battersea, Chippenham, Oldham and Leeds. In some parts of Sheffield health walks are now being prescribed by doctors.

Nearly a third of 11–16 year olds only participate in physical activity within the context of their secondary school, and it is of considerable concern that secondary schools in England and Wales only allocate two hours a week, on average, for this activity (Fairclough and Stratton, 1997). This is the lowest provision of any of the countries in the European Union (British Heart Foundation, 2000a). Primary schools have more than halved the time spent on physical education during the five years to 2000 (Sport England, 2000b), perhaps as a result of the demands of the National Curriculum, and one-fifth of four year olds are considered to be overweight (Reilly *et al.*, 1999). When these facts are considered alongside the information that a quarter of adults who were involved in sports in their teens remain involved in such activities in adult life, compared to only two in one hundred of those who were not involved in such activities in their teenage years (Sports Council and Health Education Authority, 1992), it can be seen that involvement in sport is to some extent habit forming in the early years of life. The Health Education Authority (HEA) recommends that children should undertake one hour of activity each day (British Heart Foundation, 2000b). Such activity might include walking briskly (perhaps to school), swimming, dancing, active play, cycling, games and sports. In a second recommendation the HEA suggests that 'at least twice a week, some activities should help to enhance and maintain muscular strength and flexibility and bone health' and for primary school age children this could take the form of climbing, skipping, jumping or gymnastics (British Heart Foundation, 2000b). Such activities will benefit children in their early years and later into life, and if habit forming then their early introduction into a weekly routine will encourage continuation into adult life.

With the ongoing increase in the older population of many developed countries, the health of older people is also a significant issue, with poor health making increased demands on both health and social services. Improved health and physical fitness have been shown to be achievable by a range of active recreation pursuits. A series of five components of physical fitness have been identified: cardiovascular endurance, muscular strength, muscular endurance, flexibility and body composition (DiGilio and Howze, 1984; Jacobson and Kulling, 1989). Two of these components, cardiovascular endurance and body composition, can be developed by the activity of walking, which

requires open spaces for its participation. In addition research has shown, and it is now widely accepted, that walking is a good method for preventing the onset of osteoporosis, which is of particular concern to women.

An example of the direct healing possibilities of nature has been recorded by adults involved in visualisation exercises. Over 300 adults, including architects, designers, social workers, psychotherapists, nurses, parents and students, were asked to remember a time when they or someone close to them had been injured or in pain. Participants were also asked to recall the setting of this incident, including the size of the space and elements such as colours and smells associated with the location. Following this the participants were asked to 'envision an environment that would be healing for that wounded person' and then to draw what they had imagined. The responses to this request resulted in more than 75 per cent of the drawings showing healing spaces of outdoor scenes with trees, grass, water, sky, rocks, flowers and birds. The other responses were of interior settings but all contained elements related to nature – the sky, trees, sun, garden or yard through a window or potted plants, flowers or growing things indoors. This work clearly revealed the importance that individuals spontaneously give to nature as a healing agent (Olds, 1989).

The contribution to mental health – restorative effects of nature

Everyday urban life can be very stressful, with elements such as noise, crowding and air pollution even before one begins the daily round of travelling to a job, caring for children or older relatives or coping with the lack of a job or a long-term health problem. Recovery from such stress is important in daily life and has been studied in an increasing number of projects. Other research has confirmed that not only are 'natural' views preferred but they can aid attention and have a restorative effect (see e.g. Ulrich, 1979, 1981).

One such piece of research involved volunteers being shown a short film about the prevention of accidents at work, to induce some level of stress, before being shown a second short film. The second film was one of six types showing either nature vegetation, water, urban heavy traffic, light traffic, urban many pedestrians or few pedestrians. A range of physiological measures were recorded during the experiment in order to identify the levels of stress and recovery experienced by each participant. In addition self-assessment of factors such as fear and anger was undertaken before the first film was shown, between the two films and following the second film, again to determine levels of stress and recovery. Overall both the physiological and self-reporting data indicated that different everyday outdoor environments can have different influences on recovery from stress. Unsurprisingly, recovery from stress was shown to be faster and more complete by exposure to natural rather than urban environments (Ulrich et al., 1991).

Again the beneficial effect of scenes of nature dominated by vegetation over urban landscape was studied with respect to relief of stress. Following an examination, assumed to be a stressful experience, forty-six students at the University of Delaware undertook a test to measure their emotions and levels of anxiety. Half of the students were then exposed to a series of slide photographs of urban scenes, with no vegetation, while the other half were exposed to a series of slide photographs depicting landscape scenes with vegetation. The initial test to measure emotions and anxiety was then repeated with all students. There were clear differences between the two groups of students with respect to their emotional and stress measures, following exposure to the two different types of photographs. Those students who had been exposed to the scenes of nature dominated by vegetation had results that were consistent with a pattern of improvement in a sense of well-being. This included increases in all four measures of positive affect together with a reduction in the negative feelings of fear arousal, strongly suggesting that exposure to the 'nature dominated by vegetation' scenes had had a mitigating impact

on the anxiety level of the participants. In direct contrast to this not only were the responses of participants who had been exposed to urban landscape scenes similar to those when they were tested but some responses had actually deteriorated, with a clear trend towards lower levels of psychological well-being exhibited. This was particularly the case for the emotional measures (Ulrich et al., 1991). A further piece of research, engaging students in Delaware in a variety of research techniques, revealed that park scenes which all contained grass and trees were preferred over views of commercial, university campus and residential locations, which mainly contained little or no grass or trees (Ulrich and Addoms, 1981).

In order to aid recovery from 'directed attention fatigue' four aspects have been identified by Kaplan (1995): being away, fascination, extent and compatibility. Being away can involve experiences such as visiting the seaside, mountains, lakes or forests, but for many people in an urban situation such opportunities are rare or confined to holidays and experiences of green open spaces. Fascination with something such as a small feathered animal is one important aspect of this restorative process. 'Soft' fascination, which is characteristic of some natural settings, can provide the opportunity for reflection. Extent can be the experience of wilderness, desert or forest, or on a smaller scale can be provided by the design of paths winding through an open space or the sense of history connecting the current and previous use or knowledge of a site with its history. Compatibility relates to the fact that there appears to be a special relationship between natural settings and human activities. Thus these four elements that can aid the restoration of directed attention fatigue can be encountered daily when opportunities for experiencing 'near nature' are provided in urban open spaces.

The fact that natural settings can provide opportunity for restoration from fatigue was also confirmed by Herzog and colleagues (Herzog et al., 1997) in a study involving 187 undergraduate students at Grand Valley State University. Students were provided with one of two scenarios. The first involved being at the end of a busy day spent performing dull attention-demanding tasks requiring concentration: having lost concentration their aim was to regain the ability to concentrate. The second, more reflective scenario was set at the beginning of the day with the day ahead set aside for deep thinking about some serious personal problems. Students were shown a series of slides depicting ordinary natural settings, sports or entertainment settings and everyday urban, non-natural, settings. The natural settings consisted of forest or field views, while the sports settings included a range of indoor and outdoor locations and activities such as jet skiing, a bowling alley, a cinema, a night club, a crowded swimming pool, a basketball court, an outdoor music concert and a parade. The urban setting illustrations were ten street scenes with people crossing streets, parking lots filled with cars and a petrol station. All the photographs of the settings were taken in the summer, in fair weather conditions, in order to reduce the possibility of any variance from respondents due to differences in seasons or weather. This research revealed that natural settings were reported as having a uniformly high restorative potential for people with decreased levels of directed attention due to fatigue. Settings with sports or entertainment content had potential for medium levels of restoration, while everyday urban settings had uniformly low levels of restorative potential. The views of natural settings used in this work included trees, forests and fields.

Research undertaken in Japan has shown that negative effects can be brought about by a more urban element in the landscape over a more natural element (Nakamura and Fujii, 1992). The alpha and beta rhythms from the brain were recorded for five different views of a concrete block fence or hedge or combination of the two, when viewed from a sitting position. This work clearly concludes that the view of the concrete block fence induced a sensory stress, while the view of the hedge decreased the level of stress.

The case for the restorative nature of favourite places has been confirmed by the identification that favourite places are most often places with greenery, water and of scenic quality (Korpela and Hartig, 1996). This research, involving seventy-eight students in Finland, required the participants to evaluate seven different settings. These were a square in their own town centre, a favourite and an unpleasant place of their own choosing which participants imagined for the research, together with four locations in or near the campus of the University of California, Irvine, which were represented by colour slides. Many of the favourite places identified by the participants were natural settings, while only just over a quarter identified urban locations as favourite places. Unpleasant places were identified as urban locations by 85 per cent of the respondents, with many of these locations having traffic or crowds in them. Many other studies have shown that adult groups prefer natural landscape views rather than urban ones, with the presence of water and vegetation in such views increasing their value to the onlooker (see e.g. Ulrich, 1981; Herzog et al., 1982; Herzog, 1985; Purcell et al., 1994).

Wildlife – an experience for people of near nature

The importance of contact with nature on a daily basis is obviously not a recently found benefit – perhaps for some it was just lost in the post-industrial latter half of the twentieth century. The introduction of nature into the city had been one of the aims of the early providers of parks in urban areas. But, as Taylor (1994) reports, this was a carefully constructed image of nature; it was not rustic, did not remind people of the agricultural landscapes recently left behind by many new urban dwellers and was not usually wild or awe-inspiring. In fact it was a 'civilised and organised expression of nature' (Taylor, 1994), a nature managed and understood: mankind expressing supremacy over nature, but in a different manner from an agricultural situation.

The word 'nature' can be interpreted to mean different things by different people. Health, peace, loneliness and freedom are some of the words that Nohl (1981) uses to describe nature. In addition to descriptive expressions Nohl identifies three types of meanings that can be associated with nature. First of all there is what he calls the 'vital-utilitarian' meaning of nature that represents food, clothing, shelter, energy and medicines, elements that are obtained either directly or indirectly from nature. Second there is a 'vital-ecological' meaning of nature that relates to mankind's relationship with and treatment of nature; this can be a sensible dominance over nature or exploitation and destruction of nature leading to an environmental detriment to mankind. Third, Nohl discusses the 'symbolic-aesthetic' meaning of nature with respect to the fact that the increasing separation and alienation from nature has resulted in mankind developing an emotional relationship with nature. The expression of these meanings in relation to the potential experience of nature in urban open spaces is suggested in several practical ways. The widespread need and desire to cultivate a garden is seen as an expression of the vital-utilitarian meaning of nature, while physical or intellectual activities of sport or walking and talking are seen as exhibits of vital-ecological meaning. The intrinsic beauty within an open space and the aesthetic image that this can hold are perceived as the symbolic-aesthetic meaning of nature. The experience of open space is primarily an aesthetic one because aesthetic considerations are taking place, both consciously and uncon-sciously, while one is in an open space.

A variety of research has confirmed the importance of near nature – the ability to experience nature at close range – to people's daily experiences in the urban context. Thus wildlife has been accepted as important, giving joy, pleasure and inspiration at a mainly unquantifiable personal level for some time (Halcrow Fox et al., 1987). The Institute of Leisure and Amenity Management (ILAM, 1996) acknowledges the importance that wildlife makes to the urban situation and believes that the creation and protection of wildlife habitats within urban open spaces is an excellent way of encouraging diversity and better quality of life. With respect to designing for an ecological approach the Dutch are considered to have led in this field for some significant time (Ruff, 1979). In the early 1980s

the benefits of ecology and the need to create habitats were introduced into the UK (Baines and Smart, 1984).

The importance of open spaces as a real opportunity for people to make contact with and relate to nature is clearly highlighted by the Greenwich Open Space project (Harrison et al., 1987). Thirty-three people aged 21 to over 65 took part in a six-week series of one-and-a-half hour in-depth discussion groups. The four groups were from different parts of the community in Greenwich and Woolwich and experiences with the natural world and the meanings of these experiences were shared. It was evident that contact with nature in everyday life is of considerable importance to these people. Fascination with animals such as caterpillars, ladybirds and hedgehogs, the opportunity to play on waste land and in woodland together with the lack of variety in the local parks resulted in an analysis that wildlife is fun and that there is a desire for adventure and variety.

Urban parks provide the opportunity for a range of wildlife habitats, the significance of which is discussed in depth by Gilbert (1991). The importance of the presence of urban wildlife in contributing to the quality of life for humans through the opportunity for the sensuous pleasures of touch, sight, smell and sound has also been identified by Gilbert. Such opportunities are available not only in designed spaces but also in informal open spaces such as old industrial sites, disused mills and railway lines which can contribute to the ecology of an area and serve as important sites for natural processes (Hough, 1995).

The actual experience of near nature is one element of the ecological movement that has developed during the last twenty years or so. In particular the opportunity for children to interact with nature has been high on the agenda. One of the common forms of this type of experience has been afforded by the creation of neighbourhood wildlife gardens and ecological parks, where the primary objective has been to provide a variety of naturalistic conditions so that the local community can have contact with the natural world (Goode, 1997). Educational opportunities, as discussed in chapter one, also abound.

Thus the results of a range of studies gives strong support

2.3 *Opportunities for children to interact with nature are important*

2.3

to the fact that nature affords a wide range of both psychological and physical benefits. People feel more satisfied with their homes, jobs and lives when they have sufficient access to nature in the urban environment. People value natural settings for the diverse opportunities they provide – to walk, to see, to think. What value do we as a society give to these open spaces?

Aesthetic appreciation

Aesthetic appreciation relates to the beauty, or ugliness, of the open space. Although the London Planning Advisory Committee (Llewelyn-Davies Planning, 1992) has suggested, rather negatively, that the visual element of the amenity role played by open spaces is difficult both to identify and to separate out from other functions provided by open spaces, we can learn from those who have begun to develop such models.

The Benefits and Opportunities of Open Spaces

The value of an open space lies partially in the knowledge that it exists, can be seen from some angles and is there to be used if required. For some people it is just as important to have a park present as a resource as it is to physically use it (Kaplan, 1980). 'Having it there' provides a level of satisfaction for both users and non-users alike. Others (Bradley and Millward, 1986) identified that the visual amenity of an open space was mentioned frequently by research participants, with words such as 'natural' and 'countryside-like' being used to describe open spaces in a number of urban areas of the UK. The importance of the knowledge that an open space exists was very clearly identified by research in Delaware where non-users of a space stated that 'just knowing the park was there' or 'having it nearby' was important. Further the statement by two respondents that 'I like having it there because I can use it if I have to' reveals the importance of knowing not only that the park is there but that it can be used. This is considered, by the researchers, to allow the non-users a level of control in their lives such that the park could be used if they needed, or wanted, to 'escape' from another situation (Ulrich and Addoms, 1981). Indeed escaping to a park for some private time, away from the public nature of the home with its television, telephone, stereos and family rows has been identified as important for many young people (Worpole, 1999) as well as adults (Dunnett et al., 2002).

A poignant example of the aesthetic importance of urban open spaces is shown in the work of Kuo et al. (1998) in a research project set in Chicago amidst one of America's poorest communities. One of the aims of this work was to suggest that a good quality external environment was a preference of a range of people, not just rich people who can more obviously afford such provisions in their life. This project involved three focus groups – residents, housing administrators and police – to identify attitudes to the possible addition of trees and grass to existing courtyards. The existing layout of the courtyards was dominated by considerable paving with only a few trees and a small area for planting, typical of many small urban spaces within housing areas. The residents were clearly enthusiastic about the possibility of further tree planting within the courtyard and with the possibility of having improved maintenance of the space. However, the administrators were concerned about the increased cost of such treatment. With respect to feelings of safety, the residents felt strongly that tree planting would not decrease their sense of safety, while the administrators and police expressed concerns that criminals might hide behind trees, thus making residents feel less safe.

The possibility of introducing trees to the courtyard, together with different levels of maintenance, was then explored using a series of photographic simulations from four different viewing points allowing the entire courtyard to be seen. The photographs illustrated the courtyard with three different levels of tree planting, formal and informal arrangements of the trees and different levels of grass maintenance. A large majority of the participants expressed that not only did they dislike the existing appearance of the courtyard but that it made them feel unsafe. When shown the illustrations the respondents said that they would like it very much if trees were planted and views improved, while nearly all of the participants stated that it was quite or very important that the space looked more natural. In this particular scenario, the higher the density of tree planting, the more the view was preferred by participants. In addition participants felt safer with the higher levels of tree planting; in other words, the improved aesthetic value outweighed any concerns the residents might have had about safety (Kuo et al., 1998).

Visual preference in urban recreational areas was the focus of a study using one hundred photographs of real locations, of differing characteristics, within seventeen parks in Chicago, Illinois and Atlanta, Georgia (Schroeder and Anderson, 1984). A total of sixty-eight students were involved in the research and they rated the photographs for how safe they would feel in the spaces and the visual quality of the parks. The visual quality was considered to be high for views with undeveloped, dense forests and well-maintained city parks with abundant trees and water. This high scenic quality was evaluated to be adversely affected by the presence of man-made features such as cars, fences, lights or buildings. The presence of graffiti also had a negative impact on preference. Nearby features, not within the boundary of the site, were also shown to have an impact on the participants' ratings of visual elements. This confirms a range of other work that has revealed that people have a preference for natural settings and elements over man-made or urban elements (e.g. Kaplan and Wendt, 1972).

Summary

We have seen in this chapter that there are many health benefits available in urban open spaces. These can be identified primarily as physical and mental health benefits, with the latter including the restorative effects that nature can have and the importance of near nature in daily life. How often the opportunities to improve health by utilising urban open spaces is taken up by any individual or community is something that cannot be measured – it may even be that some people are not aware of the many opportunities for jogging, running, or contemplating nature that exist in our urban open spaces. Yet many people are, even if not consciously, using their urban open spaces for improving and restoring their physical and mental health.

CHAPTER THREE

Environmental benefits and opportunities

Introduction

In siting early settlements across the world mankind knew and understood the character of land, land cover and water surfaces. However, built environments have had an impact on local climates, with such intervention becoming greater with increased urbanisation (Morcos-Asaad, 1978). Urban units that mankind has developed which substitute for the pre-existing landscape of a location, thus changing both physical and chemical properties of the environment, have been discussed at length by a range of authors (e.g. Chandler, 1978).

As well as considering the impact of climate on the city as an entity it is possible to consider the impact of climate on smaller scales of development within the city. Three scales, macro, meso and micro, at which climate can impact on the city have been identified (Dodd, 1988a). The macro-scale is the environment of a town, city or region while, the meso-scale is defined as the environment of a village, parish or close-knit group of buildings such as those within a hospital or university campus. Finally the micro-scale environment is described as relating to an individual building or small group of buildings. There may be an overlap of microclimatic zones where adjoining buildings impact on each other.

It has been claimed that the classical aim of a well-tempered environment has been neglected in the development of twentieth century cities, with many buildings being designed in a 'streamlined' manner reminiscent of cars and aeroplanes, thus increasing rather than decreasing the speed of airflow over some specific surfaces (Dodd, 1988a). As only a few buildings have been designed to suit their immediate landscape appropriately this has led to a failure to use the potential elements of the landscape for improving the micro-climate around and between buildings, thus wasting millions of pounds on energy and heating bills each year in Britain. An understanding of airflow around buildings, ventilation and air movement inside buildings and the effects of landscape and open spaces can provide a successful building solution to a situation, an approach that again is sugges-

ted not only for individual buildings but also for groupings of buildings and evolving built forms within the urban context (Morcos-Asaad, 1978). As well as providing climatic improvements the existence of well-planned, designed and managed landscapes and urban environments provide opportunities for wildlife habitats. Such habitats are important not only for the intrinsic value that they have in providing habitats for living things but also for the opportunities that they provide for people to have daily contact with nature in the urban context, as discussed in chapter two.

The improved environment that can be provided by a well-planned, designed and managed city can be of benefit to many individuals and groups within that conurbation. Yet the process leading to the overall arrangement of buildings and their associated landscapes is not usually undertaken by the people who live or work in a particular place. Those with more impact on the process include the professionals involved in the development, such as architects, landscape architects and planners, while the developer or client, paying for the development, has significant influence due to their financial interest. In addition Rayner and Malone (1998b) are clear in their 'ten suggestions for policy makers' that across the world local government has an impact on people's daily lives by determining, controlling or influencing planning and design issues such as density, mixture and physical layout of developments.

Perhaps one of the most significant facts about the urban climate and the ameliorating impact of green spaces and trees, together with the opportunities for wildlife habitats in cities, is that the benefits are available to everyone. They are available to those who use the spaces and those who do not use the spaces – not just to any one section of society or any one individual or group using an open space. This is the ultimate in social inclusion: the environmental benefits of urban open spaces are there for all, whatever their social class, creed, ethnic background or gender.

Urban climate and environment

A variety of researchers and authors have discussed the environmental factors that can be influenced by urban development and their consequences (see e.g. Frommes and Eng, 1978; Lenihan and Fletcher, 1978; Gregory and Walling, 1981; Gilbert, 1991; Hough, 1995), while others have discussed the ameliorating influence that the landscape can have on these impacts if urban areas are well designed and managed (see e.g. Spirn, 1984; Beer and Higgins, 2000). The changes in both physical and chemical properties of the urbanised environment have also been discussed. Chandler (1978) has identified these environmental changes as airflow, air pollution, radiation and sunshine, temperature, humidity and precipitation. The impact of each of these factors, both individually and in combination, will be different for each individual city but Chandler draws some general conclusions.

Airflow

Airflow is determined by wind speed, wind profile and turbulence. Wind speed is altered when wind flows from the country to an urban area, with the increased surface roughness created by the built form of the city generally lowering the wind speed across the conurbation. For instance in London in autumn, winter and spring, when winds tend to be strong, wind speeds in the centre of the city are reduced by 8, 6 and 8 per cent, respectively. In summer when the winds are lighter there is little or no difference in the mean between urban and rural wind speed. Wind profile is also affected by the change in the landscape brought about by the built form of the city, with localised increases in speed being caused by tall buildings. Turbulence occurs at street level, particularly in the proximity of tall buildings (Chandler, 1978).

Air pollution

Air pollution is produced predominantly in urban areas and similarly affects them, although winds will carry airborne particulates, with no regard for political or economic boundaries. It could be argued that this is not a new threat to the environment of urban areas, but was a developing and changing problem of the twentieth century. Fifty years ago the London smog, the result of industrialisation, killed nearly 4,000 inhabitants (Chandler, 1974). This disaster led to the introduction of the Clean Air Act of 1956 and its strengthened form of 1968. Today the main sources of air pollution are industrial processes and, increasingly, the motor vehicle. These pollutants include metals, oxides of sulphur, carbon monoxide, oxides of nitrogen, hydrocarbons and carbon dioxide. It is not easy to make general assumptions about the concentration of air pollutants within an urban area as these can vary over small distances and within small timescales, often being dependent on climatic factors such as wind and air temperature, together with changes in local activities. Due to the blanket of pollution that covers most urban areas radiation that penetrates to ground level is reduced. Estimates have indicated that in heavily polluted areas this can cause the air temperature to increase by as much as 10° C a day.

Temperature

In general, built-up areas are frequently warmer than the surrounding countryside, particularly at night. This theory of urban environmentalism has become known as the heat island effect of cities and was first described by Lowry (1967). Four factors are described as contributing to this. First, the difference between materials of the city and the country are important. Buildings and streets of the urban area are predominantly rock-like in their nature and this material can conduct heat three times as fast as wet, sometimes sandy soil. Second, the structures within the city have a greater variety in shape and orientation than in the rural landscape. Third, the conurbation generates heat through a variety of sources such as heating and cooking. The fourth factor is the way that the city disposes of water. By the use of drainpipes, gutters and sewers the precipitation is quickly removed from the ground surface. In the country most precipitation remains on or near the surface of the ground with the result that water is available for transpiration and therefore cooling of the atmosphere. In addition, the urban atmosphere also contains gaseous, liquid and solid pollutants, which can slow down the outflow of heat. The night-time difference between urban and rural temperatures has been measured as 5° C but may reach 11° C. This effect is further discussed by Lenihan and Fletcher (1978) and in a more summarised form by authors such as Cotton and Pielke (1995) and Girardet (1996).

Humidity and precipitation

Few comparative studies have been undertaken with respect to humidity in urban and rural areas (Lenihan and Fletcher, 1978). Despite significant areas of many cities being covered in vegetation of some kind there is still an increase, sometimes very significant, of non-porous surfaces in urban situations, compared with rural locations, with surfacing materials such as concrete and tarmac and buildings generally contributing to a lower level of humidity. Despite this increases in precipitation of between 5 and 8 per cent of annual total rainfall have been recorded in many urban areas of the US, with increases of between 17 and 21 per cent being recorded in a number of summer thunderstorms in some locations. It has also been reported that a selection of other cities across the world experience such increases. Due to the higher temperatures and changes in wind patterns an increase in the occurrence of hail has also been shown to occur in some urban locations. Precipitation in cities is considered to have increased due to a range of factors including water vapour from combustion sources, thermal convection due to increased temperatures and mechanical convection due to the greater roughness of a city (see e.g. Peterson, 1969; Rouse, 1981). Overall the hydrology of cities is different from rural situations due to changes in total run-off of precipitation, changes in peak flow characteristics and changes in water quality.

Amelioration of urban climate and environment

Amelioration of airflow

Airflow around buildings, groups of buildings and spaces that people use can be ameliorated by the use of windbreaks – often in the form of fencing or planting. The most effective of these features in the landscape will have a porosity of 50 per cent. The benefits of mixed height, evergreen and deciduous shelter belts together with species selection and dimensions and orientation for shelter belts for different types of locations are discussed at some length by Dodd (1988b). These are discussed for macro-, meso- and micro-scales of development. The effects of shelter planting are summarised as reducing air movement and wind-driven rain, increasing the ambient temperature around buildings and reducing wind speed. Three types of shelter planting are identified as shelter belt planting, usually at the edge of sites, dispersed tree planting, generally found within sites, and deflective techniques of planting (Dodd 1988c). The significance of windbreaks and their importance in ameliorating the impact of wind around buildings and other structures is discussed by others including Morcos-Asaad (1978), who confirms that windbreaks divert air currents upwards with the type of windbreak having an impact upon the area one is seeking to protect. Solid wind barriers or walls create eddies over the top which reduce their effectiveness, while tree belts with greater density and thickness have a larger impact on wind protection. Trees reduce wind speed and in locations adjacent to buildings this can be a positive attribute towards an individual's level of comfort (Federer, 1976).

Reduction of air pollution – carbon dioxide

One function of open spaces is that of helping to improve the quality of the air in a neighbourhood. During this process carbon dioxide is taken up by vegetation and oxygen is released in to the air. Thus open spaces play a vital role in air improvement in the urban environment (Francis et al., 1984). Large tracts of open space can help in the movement and circulation of air and thus

3.1   *The mass of buildings*
       affects micro-climate

3.1

help to enhance the movement of hot and polluted air. Not only do urban parks aid this by exchange of gases, they also benefit the urban situation because they do not have roads and therefore the pollutant combustion engine, cars, in such spaces.

The carbon fixing capacity of trees, and to a lesser extent soil, is well known but some of the facts are worth looking at in closer detail. A range of research has revealed that increased levels of carbon dioxide do indeed result in increased plant growth in species as diverse as soya bean and orange trees (Cotton and Pielke, 1995). They conclude that if such increases are indicative of other crops then it is possible for a substantial amount of carbon dioxide generated by man to be absorbed by biomass. One could suggest that this is the case not only for agricultural crops but for all general plant matter which photosynthesises; thus the presence of any vegetation in an urban area will help to decrease the levels of carbon dioxide in the atmosphere.

It has been calculated that about 1–2 hectares of trees are required to counter the carbon dioxide emissions from the use of one typical new house (Barton *et al.*, 1995). An example of the carbon cost of the operation of a building is discussed with respect to the amount of carbon dioxide produced in generating the electricity and fuel oil consumption for one year. The provision of heating involved the emission of ten times as much carbon as the provision of electricity for lighting and air conditioning (Rowntree and Nowak, 1991). This research goes on to estimate that the amount of carbon produced by these building systems could be stored by a total of 1,000 hardwood or coniferous trees over a period of sixty years, assuming that all the trees survive that long and do not need to be replaced. Furthermore this research indicates that a newborn baby in America needs only forty-five seedlings to be planted and survive in order to counter the impact of their carbon emissions over their lifetime. America has the highest levels of carbon emissions per person in the world, due to a range of factors including its high use of cars accompanied by cheap fuel prices.

Reduction of air pollution – absorption of pollutants

Certain tree and shrub species can act as bio-accumulators in large industrial cities, particularly accumulating elements such as heavy metals without detrimental effects to the plant material (Borhidi, 1988). The toxic elements accumulated in the leaves of deciduous vegetation are thus removed when leaf fall occurs, reducing the concentration of such elements in the atmosphere in vegetated areas. Contamination and accumulation maps made of various districts of Budapest in Hungary indicated that the most unfavourable stress areas were in the industrial, central residential and office districts of the city. Borhidi goes on to suggest that, on a long-term basis, improvement to the air quality of that city will require an increase in green areas by approaches that include the protection of existing forest areas; the introduction of new forest areas; the establishment of new parks, recreation grounds and green sports grounds; the planting of street trees and improved care of parks and gardens.

Others have identified that an individual Douglas Fir tree can absorb 19.5 kilogrammes of sulphur per year without damaging itself (Girardet, 1996). It has also been reported that trees in a parkland setting can filter out up to 85 per cent of suspended particles from the air, with this figure being reduced to 40 per cent in the winter when leaves have fallen from deciduous trees (Johnston and Newton, 1996). Evidence has revealed that trees can reduce dust particles in the air to as little as 10–15 per cent of the dust found in a similar street with no trees (Johnston and Newton, 1996). Further research has revealed that broad-leaved trees can reduce the ambient temperature by up to 17 per cent, over and above grassland, while coniferous plantations can achieve a reduction of 117 per cent (Broadmeadow and Freer-Smith, 1996).

Reduction of air temperature

Trees can provide shelter from precipitation while retaining and evaporating some of it; in summer they can increase humidity when they transpire (Federer, 1976).

A single tree can transpire up to 380 litres of water a day, thus cooling the air in its vicinity (Girardet, 1996). Other research has revealed that individual trees, in small urban areas, do not have much of an impact on air temperature and humidity but that larger groups of trees can ameliorate air temperature at the meso-scale (Heisler, 1977). The size of the urban green space can have a significant impact upon the level of temperature reduction. Thus a space of less than one hectare has no specific cooling effect. The cooling effect of urban green space has been termed the 'park cool island' as opposed to the urban heat island identified by Lowry, although the degree of influence on cooling away from the urban green space requires further research (Spronken-Smith and Oke, 1998). The amount of cooling will also depend upon factors such as the structure of the vegetation – its shape, design and the proportion of vegetation to paved surfaces (Von Stulpnagel *et al.*, 1990).

Amelioration of radiation and sunshine

Perhaps the most obvious benefit of trees is that they absorb and reflect solar radiation, thus providing shade. There is a range of research, mainly from the US, that has studied shade of coniferous and deciduous trees – both in summer with leaves and in the winter without leaves. It has been identified that by absorbing and scattering solar radiation trees can contribute to a reduction in the glare that exists in many cities as a result of the many buildings constructed of glass and light-coloured materials (Federer, 1976). One of these studies was undertaken in Texas in 1980 and evaluated the impact of tree shade from 50 to 60 foot high oak trees upon an established housing area of 15 to 20 years. Analysis of the results revealed that tree shade did in fact reduce energy requirements of air conditioning systems in the climatic context of the study area (Rudie and Dewers, 1984). Such shade provision is seen to be a positive thing in some parts of the world but there is also some concern that tree shading can interfere with solar collectors, both in summer and by bare branches in winter months.

The impact that street trees might have on existing or future solar collectors and the fact that a design policy for street trees, taking the sustainable aspect of solar gain into account, needs to be determined and implemented has been suggested by Thayer and Maeda (1985). This research goes on to demonstrate that trees planted on the south side of properties with solar collectors can reduce solar gain by photovoltaic cells. Using a computer model this situation was studied for five different locations in the US, with varying latitude, altitude, need for winter space heating, need for summer space cooling and available radiation levels. This research provides two sets of factors and conclusions for consideration for designers and house builders with respect to reducing energy costs. First, street trees are not as significant as architectural improvements when considering cost savings with respect to solar gain, although this will vary depending upon factors such as climate and energy rates. Having said this, the researchers are clear in their assertion that the impact of street trees should not be ignored; in fact they claim that the more architecturally energy efficient a house is the more critical is the careful positioning of trees in order to protect solar access. Second, the research confirms that trees can lower the ambient air temperatures in summer and reduce the impact of cold winds in the winter, thus reducing energy costs. Good placing and management of trees can reduce energy consumption but this can depend upon the location of the site, the species of tree used, the position of the tree in relationship to a building and the management of the trees (Heisler, 1986). Because the climate that the UK experiences is different from that of the US, and varies with location and geography, such research would be valuable if carried out in the UK. As reported by Hitchmough and Bonugli (1997), the summer climate is cooler than in US and in some locations the shade that trees cast is seen as a negative factor by some people.

Noise pollution

Although noise has not been discussed in the first part of this chapter it is considered by some to be an element of the urban environment whose impact can be ameliorated by open spaces in the urban situation. Some consider that trees have the capacity to reduce the impact of noise significantly but Heisler (1977) has reviewed results from different research projects and concluded that there are a range of benefits with respect to trees and noise reduction. First, trees cannot reduce a high level of noise unless a wide barrier of trees is used. Second, the rustling of leaves and associated birds, animals and other wildlife can affect human perception of a noise source, reducing it by masking it. Third, trees can act as a psychological barrier: if there is a partial barrier between people and a noise source then the visual impact of the vegetation screen can make people less conscious of the noise source. Altogether the impact of trees with respect to the reduction of noise is a complex issue. It depends on the type of noise and the type of tree being used to try to attenuate the noise because, as indicated, perceptions of noise do not relate directly to actual measured noise.

The Benefits and Opportunities of Open Spaces

Amelioration of urban climate by vegetation and green spaces

Thus it can be seen that at the regional, city-wide and individual building levels, open spaces and elements within those open spaces, particularly trees, can have a beneficial impact on the climate and micro-climate. Such benefits include the accumulation and extraction from the atmosphere of airborne pollutants, the fixing of carbon from the air, cooling of the raised urban temperature, the provision of shade, wind reduction, a decrease in noise and the reduction of energy consumption in buildings. The level to which these benefits may accrue in any one urban conurbation will depend upon the careful and professional planning, design and management of the landscape and the siting of buildings and groups of buildings within that landscape.

Wildlife – opportunities for habitats and human experience

The opportunities afforded for wildlife habitats by the provision of green spaces in the urban context have two themes relating to their importance in city life. The first is the intrinsic benefit of having opportunities for wildlife in the city, thus providing a scientific opportunity for quantifying and qualifying the wildlife of an area. The second is the opportunity for people to experience nature close up and in the urban situation, as discussed in chapter two. It has been acknowledged for some years now (eg. Goode, 1989) that an increasingly important factor with respect to wild-life habitats is the possibility that this provides for people to become involved with wildlife. This may be through involvement in particular projects or by an individual's daily experience of wildlife.

The importance of protecting wildlife has been accepted in some urban situations with significant guidelines and statutory requirements being developed in some locations. A range of policies have been adopted for stucture planning in Berlin which cover a variety of issues relating to open spaces and wildlife habitats (Sukopp and Henke, 1988). These include the prevention of all avoidable disturbance of existing green space,

the establishment of priority areas for nature conservation, consideration of natural development in the city, historical continuity, maintenance of habitat variety, differentiation of use intensities, preservation of large undivided open spaces, the establishment of an open space network, the preservation of the diversity of typical elements in the city landscape and functional integration of buildings into the ecosystem.

A wide variety of animals have been proven to live in urban green spaces. A range of bird life has been identified as living in Amsterdam and London, with heronries flourishing in both these cities (Laurie, 1979). More commonly tits, blackbirds, song thrushes, hedge sparrows and green finches have been revealed as living in the evergreens of old Victorian shrubberies. Buildings in urban situations also provide opportunities for pigeons, starlings, kestrels, gulls, jays and mallards, to name a few. The existence of such birds across the UK has been monitored in recent years by the Breeding Bird Survey that is co-ordinated by the British Trust for Ornithology, Joint Nature Conservation Committee and the Royal Society for the Protection of Birds. Although this survey monitors rural as well as urban areas the trends are useful to look at. One example worth considering is the thrush family, that is the blackbird, song thrush and the mistle thrush. During the 1970s and 1980s these species showed severe decline in their populations, while throughout the 1990s they stabilised with the first two species showing a significant increase in their population (Noble *et al.*, 2000).

Mammals are generally considered to be less adaptable to the urban situation than birds. Grey squirrels, however, are firmly established within the urban fabric and tend to be loved by the public but not so loved by managers of open spaces. Badgers have survived in old setts, often in large private grounds or in wilder suburban open spaces. Hedgehogs and foxes have also attracted publicity in recent years, with the urban fox now being a common sight in many locations. The most popular invertebrates for people in urban locations are butterflies and ladybirds, whilst others such as moths and spiders are often perceived as a nuisance. Some have perceived this increase of wildlife in urban areas to be a response to the use of chemicals and other modern farming techniques in the countryside. An exploration of the environment of the West Midlands in 1975 revealed a wide range of wildlife inhabiting a range of locations in Birmingham. These included kingfishers in the south of the city, kestrels, feral cat colonies and eighty species of moth on the roof of Birmingham Museum (Nicholson-Lord, 1987).

More plant species can be found in urban spaces, particularly at city edges, than on equally large sites in the surrounding landscape (Sukopp and Werner, 1982). Similarly a range of work indicates that urban areas across Europe have significant numbers of bird and animal species. These works emphasise that such a wealth of species does not necessarily relate to ecological wealth, which is determined by the number of rare and endangered species present. Further, the presence of mammals, reptiles, amphibians, birds and invertebrates in European cities, based upon a variety of research, is reported over the years. The squirrel, beech marten, mouse, vole, shrew, rabbit, hedgehog and mole are identified as widely found in urban areas, with the fox acknowledged as increasingly common. The lizard is considered to be the only reptile of significance to urban locations in Europe, with amphibians being represented by toads (Sukopp and Werner, 1982). A range of bird species have been identified as colonising different sectors of a city. In the inner city, often comprised of high buildings, birds originating from cliff landscapes, such as pigeon, swift, redstart, jackdaw and kestrel can be found. Inner city and residential areas provide habitats for prairie species such as the sparrow, while insect eaters and species originating from forest situations, such as the finch and blackbird, can be found in areas of dispersed buildings or larger parks. Habitats for insects are provided by plant communities and individual species together with structures such as buildings, bridges and fences. Typical species include butterflies, earthworms, bees and flies. It is considered that a native oak can support 284 species of insects while a willow will support 266 species and a birch and hawthorn will support 149 and 109 species respectively (Nicholson-Lord, 1987).

The increase in building density from the rural edge to the inner city is reflected in a decline in the number of species of animals and plants, although this is countered by an increase in species in some large open spaces within the city (Harrison et al., 1995). Factors such as the age of the site, continuity of open spaces, disturbance and previous management practices are reported to influence the number and diversity of species on a site. Another significant factor affecting the number of species that can be found on a site is the size of the site and this is considered for sites of 1 hectare, 10 hectares and 100 hectares, with the latter considered as suitable for supporting a full range of wild organisms. Fragmentation, or separation by built form, of green spaces can result in isolated habitat patches, while green corridors and a close mosaic of sites are important for continuity of habitat opportunities (Harrison et al., 1995).

Is there a minimum sized urban site that might sustain wildlife? An area of five hectares has been suggested as the minimum desirable size for wildlife. Benefits of a network of green open spaces and the provision of a green belt around a city are also considered to be important (Ludeman, 1988). The number of birds is reported to vary according to the size, shape and distribution of patches of vegetation (Goldstein et al., 1985). In general the larger the area of woodland vegetation the larger is the number of species present, while the most efficient shape of a patch for territorial defence and foraging is considered to be circular.

The protection of wildlife and nature sites has been promoted under a range of organisations since Charles Rothschild established the Society for the Promotion of Nature Reserves (SPNR) in 1912. This was a network of reserves that involved the co-operation of government, landowners and naturalists. In 1926 the Norfolk Naturalists' Trust was set up and this was succeeded by other trusts in the 1950s. These were added to over the next fifty years with a formalisation of the Urban Wildlife Partnership in 1992 and the name 'Wildlife Trusts' adopted by the different trusts in 1994. The Wildlife Trusts cover both rural and urban locations and consist of a network of forty-six independent wildlife charities and more than 100 urban wildlife groups. The total membership of the trusts is currently more than 325,000 people. In urban areas the wildlife trusts have been involved in the identification and preservation of wildlife (The Wildlife Trusts, 2000). Early projects undertaken by the urban wildlife groups, such as those in Bristol and Birmingham, included the 'wildlife watchdog' scheme, a survey of wildlife within participating cities. Such projects brought professionals and amateurs together, providing different sectors of society, such as children and pensioners, with opportunities to help compile detailed records of metropolitan wildlife habitats. In some instances these records were included in local authority planning files (Nicholson-Lord, 1987). A few of the urban wildlife trusts, such as the Sheffield Wildlife Trust, have taken the concept of protection of wildlife further. Along with the local authority and other partners the Sheffield Wildlife Trust is enabling communities to become involved in issues that are wider than pure wildlife conservation by the regeneration of certain urban open spaces. Some of this work is funded by the Heritage Lottery Fund, Single Regeneration Budget programmes or European funding.

The Nature Conservancy Council (Simmons, 1990) has reported on a framework for action for nature conservation in towns and cities. This framework accepts the underlying tenet that large expanses of green vegetation in urban areas are not necessarily indicative of a varied wildlife habitat because many of these urban areas are covered with 'green deserts' of intensively maintained amenity landscapes – often closely mown grass of little wildlife habitat value. Similarly mass planting of non-native species around buildings holds little habitat value, compared to the diverse communities that can be found in locations such as neglected or abandoned railway land, canal sides or on derelict sites. The framework goes on to provide some 'ecological guidelines for urban development and planning' (Simmons, 1990) which discuss issues such as the avoidance of pollution, maintenance of ground water levels, historical continuity, the value of green corridors and large areas, the maintenance of local variety and diversity and the opportunity of buildings as a resource for wildlife. In addition the framework discusses the importance of the maintenance of existing green spaces for wildlife habitat as well as the creation of new ones.

Summary

The environmental benefits of urban open spaces relate to two elements – climate and environmental amelioration and the opportunities for wildlife habitats. Climate and environmental amelioration are available to everyone who lives within the urban context, whether they use such spaces, or even know that they exist. All the environmental benefits are related to urban green spaces and the quality, quantity and proximity of these spaces to each other will impact upon the value of any one particular environmental benefit at any particular time of year.

CHAPTER FOUR

Economic benefits and opportunities

Introduction

Some quality of life factors have been identified as having an impact on where people choose to live. This has clearly been shown to be the case for leisure and recreational opportunities (Marans and Mohai, 1991). But what of other aspects of life relating to open spaces? Does the existence of open spaces in urban locations affect people's choice of where to live? Does the existence of open spaces in urban areas have an impact on the value of properties in a location? Does the existence of open spaces in a location have any other impacts on the economy – such as on job creation, regeneration or tourism?

There appears to be no significant research and little written proof in the UK, although there is some from the US, that the existence of open spaces has an impact on the economy of a city. The National Urban Forestry Unit has undertaken research into the methodologies that might be appropriate for them to use in research investigating property prices and their relationship with proximity of properties to trees. Their feasibility study indicated, from interviews with developers and purchasers, that the landscape of the area can have an impact on the value people put on a property (Somper, 2001). Despite a lack of empirical research in the UK, there does seem to be a presumption that proximity to a park or open space increases the value of property. The Department of the Environment (1996) takes the fact that greening the cities increases property value as an accepted tenet. In London telephone questions undertaken with estate agents have indicated that larger open spaces have an influence on property prices (Llewelyn-Davies Planning, 1992). In cities such as Birmingham, Bristol and Sheffield there is anecdotal evidence, sometimes from newspapers or professionals who are involved in regeneration projects that involve open spaces, that in many instances an improved external environment has had, or is having, an upward impact on property values and/or aspects of the economy. But there is no comprehensive evidence that open spaces in urban areas have an impact on a range of economic issues in the urban context.

This chapter has identified some evidence that is worth considering, but the lack of evidence indicates that much future research is required in these areas. First the chapter discusses some research relating to property values – predominantly housing – with respect to proximity to trees and open spaces. Most of this evidence is from the US but there is limited research from Europe. Then the chapter moves on to discuss issues relating to the opportunities for employment that exist in different types of open spaces. Job opportunities exist for people with a range of skills, experiences and expectations in life. Crop production is discussed, despite the fact that it is not a major contribution to the economy in the UK and is often more a tool for community building. Tourism is mentioned briefly as being used by some who manage key open spaces in urban areas. Perhaps more should be done to promote our urban open spaces to people from other urban areas, counties or countries for the many benefits that they afford.

The impact on property values

Writings about early urban park developments in several countries indicate that the value of land and or property adjacent to park developments was higher than land or property further away from the park. It has even been claimed that Birkenhead Park, constructed in Liverpool in 1847, was primarily constructed to raise land values in the area (Hoyles, 1994), while it was recorded that the value of leasehold land around the park rose from one shilling to eleven shillings per square yard within two years. It has also been reported that Prince's Park in Liverpool was central to a speculative housing development (Taylor, 1994). In Chicago the value of land in the vicinity of the proposed site of the West Chicago Park increased before the park was constructed (Danzer, 1987). After the park was laid out housing plots next to the park were twice as expensive as the plots slightly further away. The second annual report of the West Chicago Park Commissioners reports that land plots immediately adjacent to the new parks increased in value by between three and five times and the president of the Commissioners cited the experience of other cities with respect to the value of land near parks increasing (Danzer, 1987).

Frederick Law Olmsted, who created over 3,000 landscapes in North America following his success with Central Park in New York, was able to convince local and national politicians that parks and open spaces were important both socially and economically to urban populations (Barber, 1994). Olmsted knew that New York City would be concerned about the costs of land acquisition and construction of Central Park. He followed the value of properties in three wards surrounding the park between 1856 and 1873. By the end of 1873 the park had cost the city $5 million for land acquisition and $8.9 million for improvements, a total of $13.9 million. Olmsted assumed that without the park the surrounding property prices would have increased by the same rate, 100 per cent, as property in other city wards during the 18 year period. He showed most clearly that the actual value of properties in the three surrounding wards during this 18 year period actually increased by nearly 900 per cent (Crompton, 1999).

There is, however, some more recent evidence to indicate that property prices can increase with proximity to open space, although some claim that the methods used need refining further (More et al., 1988). This work, in particular, reminds us that using techniques to investigate property prices adjacent to open spaces does not take into account the value that people who live in the rented sector put on open space. In addition the economic value of open space may not lie only in the value of property but also in the unquantified value that individual users place on the experience of using the open space. Most internal leisure facilities and activities have to be paid for, while the experience of a public open space in a city does not usually involve payment; thus how can we place an economic value on the use of open space? For some the experience provided may be priceless. Having said that, let us consider some of the research undertaken during the last thirty years that has tried to understand the relationship between proximity to open

space and the economic value of property.

The presence of trees on a site has been shown to affect residential property values. Two methods have been used for this purpose: hypothetical sales data and actual sales data. Hypothetical values were used when a landscape architect's model of undeveloped land was used to ask people what they thought the value of parcels of land should be. Using different degrees of tree cover the research identified that trees added approximately 30 per cent to the perceived value of undeveloped land (Payne and Strom, 1975). It was thought that once the land had been developed the difference in homes with trees and without might be nearer 2 per cent. House builders in Georgia, US, have reported that homes on wooded plots of land sell for an average of 7 per cent more than equivalent homes on un-wooded plots of land (Seila and Anderson, 1982).

Again hypothetical house prices were used to identify that houses similar in appearance in Amherst, Massachusetts, had a difference on average of 7 per cent between those with less or more tree planting. Actual sales data were used to examine house prices in Manchester, Connecticut. Here properties with tree cover, with other variables constant, indicated a 6 per cent increase over properties without tree cover (Morales et al., 1976).

Other research has shown that the number of trees on a plot can have an impact on the actual selling price of houses. In this work the number of trees in the front garden also related to the size of the house, the number of amenities and the number of bathrooms. An increase of 3.5 to 4.5 per cent was identified in prices for properties having trees over those without trees. Hardwood trees were identified as adding slightly more value to a property than softwood trees, while intermediate and large sized trees (size was not defined any more than this) were identified as adding more to the price than small trees. This latter work does discuss the fact that most of the studies about trees and property prices have been undertaken in the eastern region of America and suggests that further research is required to look at these factors in other parts of the US (Anderson and Cordell, 1988).

4.1　*The proximity of a
property to a tree can
increase its value*

4.1

It has been reported that the value of subdivided land adjacent to a park or other open space is higher than land further from such amenities. The Federal Housing Administration has reported that such price increases can be as much as 15 to 20 per cent (Gold, 1973). In addition a positive relationship was found between the actual selling price of individual family houses and their proximity to the green belt in Boulder Colorado (Correll *et*

al., 1978). This study identified that for each foot a property was from the green belt the price reduced by $4.20, taking into account the possible variables of plot size, floor space and age of each house and the number of rooms each property had.

In the City of Worcester, Massachusetts, prices of properties within 4,000 feet of four different parks were monitored over a five year period, using hedonic pricing methods (More *et al.*, 1988). This work identified that house prices, on average, increased with proximity to a park. Properties only 20 feet from a park were, on average, $2,765 more expensive than similar properties that were 200 feet away from the park. This increase in price disappeared for properties more than 2,000 feet from a park entrance. This work also found differences in such price increases that were apparently dependent upon the type of open space that a property is adjacent to. Properties close to open space-type parks were deemed to have a higher economic value than those close to spaces with developed sports facilities, although the authors clearly suggest that the careful design of edges of open spaces with developed sports facilities might overcome this negative impact.

In the UK preference for hilly locations with views, especially over commons and open spaces, has been identified (Young and Wilmott, 1973). Some have argued that the approach of planting in advance of the development of the built form, as at Warrington New Town in the 1980s, could increase land values for private developers (Tregay and Gustavsson, 1983). They asserted that developers are image conscious and that selling houses surrounded by an established and attractive landscape is easier than persuading people to live on the demolished bomb factory that was the particular development site under discussion in Warrington.

Powe *et al.*, (1995) studied house prices in the Tyne and Wear area of the north-east of England between 1990 and 1992 using the hedonic pricing method. The amenity benefits of being within 500 metres of a deciduous tree and 500 metres of a large open space were identified as increasing property values by 8 and 5 per cent respectively. These results may be affected by the fact that the areas with these amenity benefits tend to be inhabited by middle-class and professional people. The areas with less amenity benefits, including proximity to deciduous trees and large open spaces, correlated with lower socio-economic classes. Thus the two aspects of amenity and social class appear to have some sort of relationship. It could be argued that this relationship could be transformed and that if the lower socio-economic areas were provided with more deciduous trees and large open spaces then the value of prop-erty in these areas might increase.

The compatibility of parks with respect to residential land use has been shown to have a positive effect on property prices in Dallas (Waddell et al., 1993). In Durham, North Carolina, property prices in the proximity of the Eno River Corridor have been examined. This river corridor comprises some 1,327 acres and includes the Eno River State Park, West Point on the Eno, Old Farm and River Forest city parks, and provides opportunities for a range of active and passive recreational pursuits. The prices of 195 homes sold between 1988 and 1992 and located within 3,000 feet of the river corridor were monitored. As well as considering individual house features, neighbourhood character-istics such as the distance to the nearest shopping mall and park entrance were taken into account. The results of this work clearly show that proximity to the Eno River Corridor is desirable and adds approximately $16,000 to the value of an average home, relative to the home's distance from the park. Proximity to the park gate was identified as being desirable with $5.91 being added to the sale price of a house for each foot distance (Parks and Jenkins, unpublished).

Perhaps more significant, due to the size of the sample involved, is research that has been undertaken in the Nether-lands. A pilot study carried out in Apledoorn, a medium sized town in the east of the country, analysed the prices of 106 houses built around a park. Properties within 400 metres of the park attracted prices of 60 per cent more than houses further from the park. On top of this a house with a view of the park appeared to attract a premium of 800 per cent. A more detailed study built upon this initial pilot one involved 3,000 house transactions in three locations, Emmen, Apledoorn and Leiden. Differing responses were found between factors such as a view to a green strip, park, canal or lake, the presence of woods, a lake or different landscape types and some of these being in the vicinity of houses. In Emmen the lake was a significant factor with respect to house prices. Properties within 1,000 metres of the lake were 7 per cent higher in price than those not so close. A view to water increased the price by 10 per cent and a property with a garden bordering on water resulted in an increase in price of 11 per cent. In Apledoorn 6 per cent was added on to house prices for properties within 400 metres of the park. A view of the park added an extra 8 per cent on to the price, while a view of a multi-storey building could decrease the house price by 7 per cent. In Leiden the estimated premium for a view of 'attractive landscape with water ... over less attractive settings' was 7 per cent. Traffic noise had a negative impact on prices, reducing them by 5 per cent, while a pleasant view of water was shown to add 8 per cent and a pleasant view of open space was shown to add 9 per cent to the price (Luttik, 2000).

Employment opportunities

Green spaces in urban areas can provide opportunities for community involvement that can in turn help to develop a sense of self-esteem and enable individuals and communities to develop skills new to themselves. In addition all open spaces in urban areas, whether green – that is, dominated by soft landscape – or grey – dominated by hard landscape – provide opportunities for a variety of employment types.

Gardeners and park rangers are perhaps the two types of employment opportunities that immediately come to mind when considering open spaces such as parks. The significance of both of these, and particularly the latter, is important not just for the fact that they provide jobs for people but for the functions that the particular employment opportunities undertake.

A park ranger service was established in Warrington New Town in 1979 with a role of aftercare, protecting and maximising the benefit of the initial investment. The service had three primary objectives (Tregay and Gustavsson, 1983):

1 To protect the investment made by the Development Corporation in the new landscape structure and park system;
2 To maximise the use of the parks and open spaces for recreation, education and other beneficial functions;
3 To develop greater awareness of the environment and environmental issues, locally, nationally and world-wide.

The rangers developed contacts with schools and encouraged use of the open spaces for a variety of educational purposes, and facilitated a range of events, such as carnivals, firework displays, civil war battles and family sports events, along with smaller activities such as tree planting and outdoor theatrical events. Organising the use of outdoor sports grounds, the provision of interpretive events and material, patrolling the open spaces and marketing were also within the remit of the rangers. Similar activities are still undertaken. The Park Ranger Service of Warrington Borough Council had a programme from January to June of 2001 that included organised walks, wildlife mosaics, an egg painting session for Easter, a treasure trail and rambles, instructive composting sessions, a dawn patrol, an arts festival, pond life sessions, nest box making times and a photography competition (Warrington Borough Council, 2001).

From the late 1970s onwards thousands of staff in public sector jobs, including park keepers, were removed from their positions, partly due to the increased use of technology and partly due to budget restrictions, in what Worpole and Greenhalgh (1996) describe as 'missing people' in our cities. Towards the end of the 1990s the beginnings of a change could be seen, with park rangers being reintroduced in some urban locations. This happened in Sheffield in 1995 and there are now about twenty-four rangers there. They are funded by a variety of sources: Sheffield City Council, the Single Regeneration Budget, the Heritage Lottery Fund, the European Regional Development Fund, Health Action Zone, Sheffield Wildlife Trust or the New Deal and some by a combination of some of these sources. The rangers undertake educational activities by visiting schools, arranging events in parks and supporting events organised by local communities. They arrange safe walks for women and health walks and activities for children in school holidays. Security is not one of the roles of the rangers, but they add to the feeling of safety by their presence, visibility and approachability.

Many other urban locations now have ranger services with a similar range of activities building on the benefits of education, relaxation and walking for health, to name a few, that can be afforded in parks and other urban open spaces. More than 450 ranger services now exist across the country, many in urban areas and providing a wide range of activities encouraging positive use of urban parks and open spaces.

The employment of people in the area of urban open spaces is, however, limited within the UK. As a comparison one only has to look at Central Park in New York, where 250 people are employed on a full-time basis as well as additional staff at seasonal times. These full-time staff include 11 landscape architects who are involved in restoration projects, large teams of 'zone gardeners' who undertake the maintenance and rangers who arrange and facilitate activities. A private body, the Central Park Conservancy, funds most of these positions, while the City of New York provides the funding for the base-line maintenance.

Other employment opportunities in the UK cover a wide range of skills and levels of formal education. Grounds maintenance staff and their managers are very important to the perception of people's day-to-day experience of open spaces. If a park is well maintained or a city centre square is litter free then users are happy; but if the opposite is the case and such spaces appear to be uncared for the public's perception is a negative one and the unkempt feel of an area may lead to fear of crime and thus

Sheffield Urban & Countryside Ranger Service

Easter Egg Fun Day

Wednesday 18th April - 1.00 till...

Meet the rangers down at the bottom field off Upperthorpe entrance for some Easter Egg activities.

Spring Clean

Tuesday 24th April - 1.00 till 3.00...

Come and help us clear your green open space of litter and support the Tidy Britain Group's campaign 'Just Bin It'. Meet the rangers by the Upperthorpe Road entrance.

Environmental Fun Day

Wednesday 16th May - 1...

Come and take part in environmental games and activities during *Environment Weeks*. Meet the rangers in the middle field next to the mini football pitch

Wildflower and Orchard Guided Tour

Tuesday 5th June - 6.30 till 7.30pm

Come and find out about wildflowers and fruit trees residing on your green open space. Meet us at the Oxford Road entrance.

History Walk

Saturday 16th June - 6.45 till 9...

Come and join the rangers on this informative guided walk taking you back in time through the Ponderosa, Crookes Valley and Weston Parks. Meet us at the Crookes Valley car park.

Good Greeny Me!

This is organised in conjunction with the Family Support Feedback Conference taking place at the Crookesmoor Training Centre.

Saturday 30th June - 11.00 till 4.00pm

Come and take part in more environmental fun games and activities and you'll be amazed at just how green you can get! Meet us in the middle field next to the mini football pitch. Free food and drinks available from the Crookesmoor Training Centre.

SHEFFIELD

For further information ring Saul...

0773 0202 ...

4.2 *Some ranger activities advertised*

disuse. In some parks and sports areas sports development officers, usually employed by local authorities, make use of the facilities by involving communities, often young people, in sporting and coaching activities such as football and tennis.

Employment that is directly linked to the provision of open spaces in urban areas and yet is perhaps more hidden in its nature is that of Chartered Landscape Architects. They work to provide and maintain good quality spaces for people in a variety of locations within the urban situation. Increasingly Chartered Landscape Architects are working with the communities that they plan, design and manage for, rather than dealing solely with a traditional client.

Many of these employment opportunities have traditionally been provided by local authorities, but during the last twenty years private consultancies, groundwork trusts, wildlife trusts and development trusts have increasingly moved into this field. In addition emplyment is also available at city farms in support and advisory roles for the Federation of City Farms and Community Gardens (Federation of City Farms and Community Gardens, 1999).

Other long-standing forms of employment opportunities in urban areas include highway engineers, lighting engineers, mechanical and electrical engineers, road sweepers, bin emptiers and litter pickers. Some of these, traditionally local authority jobs, are now being supported by partnerships such as town centre management schemes, where local authorities and businesses are working together to improve the external public realm. All of these types of jobs are supported by a variety of support staff and services that might be clerical, technical and administrative across the range of possible employment sectors.

The number of people employed in the different jobs associated with open spaces is not available but must surely contribute significantly to the economy of the UK.

As well as providing opportunities for these employment types, some urban open spaces have afforded economic benefits by opportunities for community commitment as an integral part of successful neighbourhood regeneration schemes (Dunnett *et al.*, 2002). These successful regeneration schemes involve partnerships of local authorities with local communities, often in the form of friends groups. In some situations additional outside agencies are also involved. Specifically some of these projects have realised that young people are important potential users of urban green spaces now and in the future, and have targeted resources towards provision for young people as well as involving them in some of the regeneration processes of the green open spaces. In other situations not only has a local park been developed but there have been additional regeneration benefits in the form of the creation of jobs and the initiation of various youth and community development programmes. In addition new businesses have been set up in the vicinity of the park and training and education programmes have been initiated (Dunnett *et al.*, 2002).

Crop production

The opportunity for growing crops for consumption in open spaces can easily be overlooked in the urban situation because so many city dwellers believe that agriculture is for the countryside. But production of fruit and crops in an urban situation can contribute to the economy of a city. Across the world some open spaces in urban areas are used for growing food. In Chipata, formerly Fort Jameson, in Zambia, a large proportion of the urban population is of local origin and through a dual desire to sustain tradition and survive in the urban situation many people cultivate their own crops on vacant land (Chidumayo, 1988). Urban production of maize was reported as being up to 30 per cent of the city's total consumption in 1980. Other authors have acknowledged that urban land used for food production does not give high economic yields but should have a long-term value attributed to it (Ganapathy, 1988). In cities such as Delhi large areas of land are devoted to highly cultivated lawns, using significant resources such as water, when such land could be devoted to urban agriculture which would benefit

4.3   *Crop production in a
community garden*

4.3

many, particularly the poor of the city. Addis Ababa, Lae, Shanghai, Hong Kong and Lusaka are reported as having a viable urban agriculture, mainly due to the support provided by the state (Ganapathy, 1988). Such urban agriculture is emphasised by Girardet (1996), who confirms that fourteen of China's fifteen largest cities have their own farm belts around them that were largely self-sufficient until recently. Major cities including Beijing, Shanghai, Tianjin, Shenyang and Wuhan still produce large quantities of the food required by their inhabitants. However, the continued use of such land for agriculture is increasingly under threat because of the demand for land for the development of roads and housing. In the Western world gardens, allotments, community gardens and orchards and city farms, actually within the framework of the built environment rather than on the fringes of the city, are the typical type of open spaces that can offer opportunities for food production.

The growing of food in urban areas in the UK has traditionally taken place on allotments and in gardens. There is a long history of food production in the city and farming in the city has a range of issues associated with it, including the opportunity for community development, biodiversity, tackling waste and the pleasure of growing one's own food. Parks and the regeneration of housing areas can both benefit from this approach (Paxton, 1997). While growing food in urban areas has several benefits, both for individuals and for the community, it has also been described as 'a way of involving people in an activity which can make a visible difference to the quality of city life' (Paxton, 1997). Such projects can offer the opportunity for community empowerment, attachment to the local community and a sense of ownership and can lead to action to 'defend and improve local communities'.

The growing of fruit in urban orchards has been developed from traditions such as apple bobbing. Such orchards primarily exist for fruit production, not for direct economic benefit, and also offer a range of community benefits. This approach is supported and encouraged by organisations such as Common Ground, Learning through Landscapes and the National Urban Forestry Unit. Urban orchards can provide opportunities for communities to share knowledge and skills, enhance a range of urban locations such as hospital grounds and housing areas and provide opportunities to link in with the National Curriculum where orchards are provided in school locations. The health benefit of having fruit readily available is also a consideration (National Urban Forestry Unit, 1999a).

Tourism

Some urban open spaces not only provide opportunities for local people and their daily life but can also be used as regional or national attractions for tourists. Instead of constantly using open space in rural areas for recreation and other benefits, and putting additional stress on the rural landscape, many city dwellers use their urban open spaces for the wide range of benefits and opportunities discussed in this section of the book. This was particularly highlighted during 2001 when many regions of the UK were paralysed by the foot-and-mouth epidemic and people were excluded from vast tracts of the rural landscape for most of the year. Normal leisure activities in the countryside, such as walking and visiting stately homes, were denied to urban dwellers. Increased numbers of people used their urban open spaces during this time.

Some open spaces can provide opportunities to attract tourists from outside the home urban location. Such tourist attractions can include botanical gardens, and civic spaces associated with well known attractions such as museums and exhibition halls. Some open spaces in urban areas overtly advertise themselves as tourist destinations – and perhaps more should do this. Kew Gardens in London is perhaps one of the most obvious and famous of these. Interestingly some cemeteries also play a role in the tourism industry including Highgate Cemetery in London (Rugg, 2000). This tourism benefit of urban open spaces is not as widely acknowledged as it might be. Despite this it was mentioned to a limited extent in some of the focus group discussions for the research for the Department of Transport, Local Government and the Regions (DTLR), indicating that some people do consider it to be a benefit (Dunnett et al., 2002). Only a few local authorities within the UK give the urban green environment a high profile as a means of attracting inward investment and as a means of attracting tourists. Some have used the Britain in Bloom scheme as a tool for attracting tourists, but there are few towns renowned for innovation and creativity in attracting tourists to public landscapes compared to some German cities (Dunnett et al., 2002).

Summary

Although the economic benefits and opportunities of urban open spaces are less well understood and recorded than other benefits, this does not belittle their importance where they are understood and valued. The issues of property prices, land values, employment opportunities, crop production and tourism all have some sort of role to play in the economy, but warrant further research in order that a deeper understanding of the processes and mechanisms that influence and affect these issues with respect to urban open spaces can be understood.

Urban Open Spaces – Spaces for All

Intoduction: open space typologies

As we have seen in the first section of this book there are many reasons – social, health, environmental and economic – why open spaces are important to daily urban life. But what types of open space are important? The grouping of urban open spaces into types or categories has been undertaken from time to time as a planning tool. Such groupings have usually resulted in either a typology or a hierarchy of urban open spaces.

Lynch (1981) developed a typology for open space that identified regional parks, squares, plazas, linear parks, adventure playgrounds, wastelands, playgrounds and playing fields. This typology perhaps focuses more on spaces that are dominated by hard landscape, rather than later typologies that have included or focused on green open spaces. Other research about open spaces, undertaken for the London Planning Advisory Committee, defined a hierarchy to include small local park, local park, district park, metropolitan park, regional park and linear open space (Llewelyn-Davies Planning, 1992). The Institute of Leisure and Amenity Management has discussed a typology for open spaces that is based upon land use, covers urban and rural spaces but which also includes cultural and visual value (ILAM, 1996). In practice some local authorities have developed their own typologies or hierarchies of urban open spaces. Both typologies and hierarchies of urban open spaces have tended to focus on land use and developed groupings accordingly.

Some have argued that a hierarchical approach to the provision of urban open space fails to recognise the potential that smaller open spaces provide for the experiences of different users and that people want to use open spaces close to their homes (Morgan, 1991). However, open spaces can also be discussed and classified in terms of their functions. A range of positive functions of open spaces, including provision for relaxation and recreation, conservation of wildlife, natural and agricultural resources, scenery and the shaping and control of urbanisation, have been suggested by Eckbo (1969). More recently work undertaken for the London Planning Advisory Committee (Llewelyn-Davies Planning, 1992) suggests that parks have seven functions – recreational, structural, amenity, ecological, social, cultural and educational – and that the benefits of parks and recreation are personal, social, economic and environmental.

An urban open and green space typology has recently been proposed (Department of Transport, Local Government and the Regions, 2002) by the Green Spaces Taskforce that defines two major types of urban open spaces as green spaces and civic spaces. The first of these categories is further divided into parks and gardens, provision for children and teenagers, amenity green space, outdoor sports facilities, allotments, community gardens and urban farms, and natural and semi-natural urban green spaces – including woodland and urban forestry and green spaces. The purpose of this typology is to provide a nationwide basis for planning purposes and the development of open spaces strategies and it is accompanied by a more detailed classification for open space audits and academic research.

Such typologies and hierarchies do not, in the main, describe the quality of the space, the experience of the space for the user or the value that an individual might give to a particular space. Thus most traditional typologies have been determined from the point of view of the planner, designer or manager – sometimes as a tool for the distribution of resources or to help prioritise urban open spaces for development or regeneration. Such classifications may be helpful, but I would like us to consider the situation with respect to daily urban living and to discuss a typology that has the user as the focus of attention.

Spaces for all

Different types of urban open spaces can be used at different stages of a person's journey through life – childhood, adolescence, early and late adult life and finally the later years of life. These different urban open spaces are not used at one discreet time of life; many are used at different times of life and some are never used at all by some people. For instance, a hospital may be where someone is born, but a person may also be a patient in youth for an accident or tonsillectomy, while an adult may need treatment for cancer or an elderly patient may need special treatment for other reasons. On the other hand some may never see the inside of a hospital – not even as a visitor. Similarly a park may be somewhere that a baby is walked though in the pram, where children play and ride bikes, where adults jog for health reasons and where an elderly person might go for a walk and to visit the café.

A typology has thus been suggested from the user's point of view which consists of three groupings of urban open spaces – domestic, neighbourhood and civic – based upon the concept of home range. There are two reasons that this tripartite grouping might be helpful. The first is a physical one and relates to the physical distance the spaces are from home. The second measure is social and relates to the people one might spend time with, meet or just see in these different spaces. The experiences of the three groupings of urban open spaces suggest three social levels of familiarity, sociability and anonymity. Although any of these three social experiences might take place in any of the three types of urban open space, in general there is likely to be a transition of experiences between them.

Thus domestic urban open spaces are physically associated most closely with the home and socially are likely to be used mainly by the family, friends and neighbours. Neighbourhood urban open spaces are physically not directly related to the home but to the neighbourhood and community within which one lives. Socially, these spaces will be used not only by family, friends and neighbours but also, predominantly, by others within the community who are likely to live within the vicinity of the space. Civic urban open spaces, then, are those that are set within the urban context but which are, usually, physically farthest from the home or are places at strategic or specific locations. Such spaces are more of a social mix where one is most likely to meet people from different walks of life and from a different physical part of the conurbation. With the transition between these three groups of urban open spaces – from domestic to neighbour-hood to civic – there is an increasing likelihood that users will know a smaller percentage of the other users.

Early in life most of people's experiences of urban open spaces are likely to be within the domestic spaces, but the neighbour-hood spaces will soon also become important. The civic urban open spaces usually begin to impact on life's experiences in the pre-teenage years and may dominate into adult life. Some of these civic spaces are still important in the later years of life, but this may depend upon a person's physical and mental ability to cope as well as a person's needs or desires in later life. Thus some people in their later years may return to using the neighbourhood and domestic urban open spaces, while others only use the latter. Of course this apparent circle of life is not this simple, because some of the civic spaces (perhaps particularly the hospital) may be experienced earlier in life. No doubt some people will disagree with this overall approach. However, this home range concept of urban, neighbourhood and civic urban open spaces does seek to address the typology of urban open spaces from the point of view of the user and not the planner, designer or manager.

CHAPTER FIVE

Domestic urban open spaces

Introduction

Domestic urban open spaces are those open spaces in the urban context that are physically closest to home – they may also be the open spaces that are valued most at different times of life. In this chapter urban open spaces associated with housing will be discussed. These include spaces that are integral within a housing area, private gardens, community gardens and allotments. The first two are those most closely linked with the home because they are the physical setting within which the home is placed. Community gardens may be associated with a small group of family houses, a small block of flats for professional people or perhaps a group of bungalows for the elderly. Community gardens are thus shared physically but the use of them may not be a shared experience – it may be that one might be the only user at a particular time. On the other hand community gardens also provide opportunities for getting together with a small group of people – whether children for play or adults for a cup of coffee and a chat. Allotments could be considered to be an extension or, for some, a replacement of the garden. This is where an individual or a family can grow vegetables, fruit and flowers, for some with the aim of a degree of being self-sustaining. There may be a physical distance between the home and the allotment but a practical and emotional tie to this space. Children can learn how to cultivate ground and grow plants in the allotment in the same way that they can in a private garden. Due to the shared physical space of community gardens and the physical separation of allotments from home some may be reluctant to accept these as domestic urban open spaces; yet I consider that they are, because the predominant use is domestic in scale, but I accept that they are verging towards the neighbourhood group. Indeed there is potential for allotments and their users to develop into an alternative neighbourhood community, with all the alliances and friendships, norms and rivalries that any urban anthropologist would describe in any built neighbourhood.

As mentioned in the introduction to this section of the book, domestic urban open spaces are probably used throughout a person's lifetime. They may be of particular importance in the early years for play and in the later years when one might be less confident about going further afield. This does not deny the fact that for many adults and people in their middle years domestic open spaces provide opportunities for relaxation, environmental appreciation – such as birdwatching – recreation – perhaps in the form of gardening – and socialising with family and friends. The benefits thus afforded in domestic urban open spaces clearly relate to some of the social benefits of chapter one: children's play, passive recreation and active recreation through gardening and children's active games. Health benefits, as discussed in chapter two, may be physical – again the experience of gardening – and psychological in the opportunities for relaxation and the experience of near nature. Environmental benefits of climate amelioration are by definition present, to a greater or lesser extent, in any urban green space, while the opportunities for wildlife habitat are also determined by the quantity and quality of vegetation to support wildlife. The economic benefits of domestic urban open spaces may be somewhat more hidden, although there are surely many people who will pay more for a house with a good-sized garden than for a similar property that does not have a garden.

Thus across the different domestic urban open spaces some of the benefits and opportunities outlined in section one of this book can be found – particularly social, health and environmental benefits. With respect to the people one is likely to find in these spaces it is anticipated that they will predominantly be family, friends and close neighbours – with occasional invitations to less well-known people. Thus in domestic urban open spaces there is likely to be a high level of familiarity amongst the users. One user is likely to know all the users by face and by name and to have known them for a considerable period of time, sometimes years.

5.1   *Bournville village green*
5.2   *Housing dominated*
       by a green external
       environment
5.3   *A communal gathering*
       amidst housing

5.1

Housing

Our homes are perhaps the place where we spend most of our time and for many are the favoured places in life. Some people's homes are set within a network of green spaces and so these may be experienced while living in this location – from childhood through youth, adult life and into old age. But not everyone is lucky enough to live close to or within a complex of green spaces.

Throughout the twentieth century the incorporation of open spaces into areas of housing has been of concern and a matter for deliberation. The industrial villages of Port Sunlight and Bournville, built towards the end of the nineteenth century, were the precursors of the garden city movement and clearly incorporated opportunities for passive, active and recreational activities within a sequence of open spaces. Such open spaces were also perceived as adding to the quality of life for the factories' employees. At this time cities had overcrowded housing and poor physical environments and Howard, who launched the concept of the garden city, understood that the countryside offered fields and fresh air, but did not have the employment or social opportunities (Hall and Ward, 1998). Combining the benefits of both rural and city locations became the aim of the garden city, suggested as having a fixed upper population number and mixed use of medium density. The centre of such proposed develop-ments would be a public garden surrounded by public buildings, which would overlook a larger central park. The Garden City Association (GCA) initiated the first garden city at Letchworth, which was finally completed following the end of the Second World War. Later the GCA became the Garden Cities and Town Planning Association and diversified its interests to include the promotion of garden suburbs and garden villages as well as garden cities. Abercrombie developed a plan of expansion for London, among other cities, to incorporate new towns and planned town expansions outside the green belt. This approach was criticised by the GCTPA, now the Town and Country Planning Association, who also opposed the high-rise, high-density solutions then being suggested by modernist architects (Hall and Ward, 1998). Garden cities were 're-badged' as New Towns (Hall and Ward, 1998) and the 1946 New Towns Act for England resulted in two waves of new towns; Stevenage was the first of twenty-eight. These new towns varied in population size and geography but were built on the sustainable principles of jobs and services being within easy reach of people's homes. Once again open space networks were important as part of the contribution to the quality of life for the residents of the different groups of new town developments.

Open spaces associated with our homes can be in one of several forms including gardens, community gardens, courtyards, public open space and playgrounds. This can be more fully understood as part of Newman's theory of defensible space where he discusses a hierarchy of spaces, which can be reinforced by opportunities for surveillance (Newman, 1972). These levels of space are described as public, semi-public, semi-private and private, and the work suggests that physical design can have an impact on the levels of crime.

5.2

5.3

In Warrington New Town, in the north-west of England, one of the aims of the development was to provide areas of housing, together with industry, within an overall landscape framework so that the experience of nature was readily available to people on a daily basis. The wildflowers and areas of shrubs and woodland provide daily opportunities for such experiences as well as for play (Nicholson-Lord, 1987).

The arrangement of the built form of houses and their physical relationship with open space should be considered carefully in the design of new housing. A study in Istanbul investigated the use, levels of satisfaction, environmental consciousness and effect of plan layout and design characteristics of three housing areas with different relationships of the built form to the open space (Ozsoy et al., 1996). Information was gathered, using questionnaires, from users of the open spaces, owners of flats surrounding the open spaces and the people who manage the flats. The open spaces were identified as being used for a range of reasons, from sporting activities to a 'resting place'. Some used them for meetings and others for childcaring activities. The spaces were predominantly used in the evenings, a fact that may be a response to the climate or the employment situation of respondents. It is clear that the open spaces were used frequently, with a quarter to nearly two-thirds using them daily, sometimes three times a day, and with nearly everyone admitting that they use the spaces sometimes. Social interaction is facilitated in two of the housing areas by the layouts providing for different functions such as sports, playing areas and gardens, while the third area has flexibly designed green courtyards, separated from parking and sports areas, thus providing a safe place for children to play. This work concludes that user satisfaction can be maximised by providing:

• Different activity areas – that is by providing variety;
• The creation of spaces with different levels of privacy;
• A layout that takes human comfort into account;
• Management of the space under the control of a management organisation of that housing group.

Contemporary society is faced with the issue of how to approach the provision of the 4.1 million houses that are required by the government. This issue is of the utmost importance as we move towards this massive house building programme. This is not the place to enter into a full discussion about the issue of density of housing in cities, but any consideration of the issue of housing density must also address the importance of open space to people's daily lives. In addition, how this vast number of houses are designed and built will have an impact on a range of social issues that should not be ignored. The proposal to use underused and derelict land or brown field sites for housing in cities is to be welcomed, especially if colonised areas of such sites are retained as a basis for a green structure, but this should not be at the expense of the provision of the many benefits and opportunities that open spaces provide in urban areas. Increased densities of housing are being suggested by many people and to some extent this is a good thing for community building in an urban area, but as we have seen in section one urban open spaces are also good at helping to develop a sense of ownership and community.

What would increasing densities mean for open space provision? Would it mean no gardens, no natural green spaces, no squares or parks? There is no desire to return to the tower blocks, of the 1960s, with grass and trees – many of these types of housing developments, such as Park Hill and Kelvin Flats in Sheffield and Hulme in Manchester, have been demolished and redeveloped. But the provision of open space in housing areas will increase the quality of life for people by providing for the benefits and opportunities outlined in section one of this book. One of the important elements around this issue is that of the quality of, and resources provided for, the design and management of the open spaces that are provided. Bland spaces are not what people want and will not provide a good quality of life, while well-planned, designed, built and maintained spaces, with community involvement, where appropriate, will add to the quality of life.

Private gardens

For those who have private gardens these can often be the first experience of open spaces in life. As a child these can be very important places for individual and group play with memories that are carried into adult life. In adult life the garden can play a different role – relaxation, gardening, games and passive recreation.

Since the beginning of earliest civilisations gardens have been an important part of human environments, providing both active and passive opportunities for recreation (Parsons *et al.*, 1994). In Britain gardening is such a popular activity that claims are often made that the British are 'a nation of gardeners'. It has been suggested that 85 per cent of UK households have gardens, with people spending an average of six or seven hours a week looking after them (Hoyles, 1994). The readership numbers of a range of gardening magazines have increased significantly during the last decade. *Gardener's World*, the BBC gardening magazine, holds about 55 per cent of the market share with a circulation of over 370,000 a month. The explosion of garden and gardening programmes on television over recent years is another expression of the increasing significance of domestic gardens to many people's everyday lives. The very popular television programme *Groundforce*, where people's gardens are made over in three days, has attracted over nine million viewers and more than a third of the television audience share (Warren, 2000). However, some have expressed concern that such 'quick-fix' television programmes are not good in the long term for gardening because they are not taking horticulture seriously enough. Tim Smit, originator of the Eden Project in Cornwall, has claimed that 'horticulture is not seen as an important profession. *Groundforce* shows people doing something useful, but in a false way – it is all speed and no regard for the seasons'. This is disputed by the executive producer of the programme who claims that the programme 'encourages more people to take an interest in gardening ... we are promoting active involvement, not the opposite' (Milmo, 2001).

Private gardens allow for a range of activities – both private and sociable. Children's parties, barbecues and community activities have been known to take place in gardens. In addition the opportunity to tend one's own piece of land is appreciated by a wide range of age groups and goes beyond the most immediately obvious groups such as individual home owners to include hospital patients, disabled people and others. Detailed research has identified that gardens afford satisfaction in a range of ways which have been categorised as peacefulness and quiet; nature fascination; tangible benefits; sensory benefits; novelty; 'in my control'; share knowledge; tidy and neat (Kaplan and Kaplan, 1989). Other benefits identified from the experience of having access to gardens include having easy opportunities for contact with nature, both for adults and children (Francis, 1995). With respect to children such opportunities can help to develop 'ideas and attitudes towards the natural and built world' (Francis, 1995). These attitudes and memories are then carried into adult life and have an impact on the development of adult attitudes.

A more detailed understanding of the use, benefits and meanings of gardens to ordinary people has been revealed by a larger study, involving 376 people in the City of Sheffield (Dunnett and Qasim, 2000). Responses to questionnaires revealed interesting information about time spent in the garden each week. To some extent the results reported in this research contradict the figures reported earlier by Hoyles (1994), that on average people spend six or seven hours each week in the garden. This more recent and larger, random, sample in Sheffield revealed that time spent in the garden is very much age dependent. Adults under the age of 35 reported only spending up to one hour each week gardening, while 35–45 year olds reported spending two to four hours and over 55 year olds reported typically spending five hours a week in the garden. One could suggest that the older adults might not only choose to spend more time in the garden but be able to due to less restrictions on available time as they are less likely to have young children or paid employment. The enjoyment of gardens in different ways was also identified as having a relationship with age, in that creativity and personal expression were favoured more by those aged 35 to 54 while fresh air and exercise were appreciated more by respondents older than 55. The benefit of being close to nature was most appreciated by those aged 45 to 54 while those over 65 years old ranked gardening first as a leisure pursuit, more than other age groups. This research clearly identified that personal satisfaction and relaxation, even undertaking gardening, not just being in the garden, are important in everyday life. The opportunities that being in the garden provide for creative expression, health and restoration, contact with nature and the production of fruit and vegetables are discussed. In addition, for some the opportunity to meet or talk with neighbours was considered to be a significant benefit (Dunnett and Qasim, 2000).

An example of the opportunity that gardens provide for wildlife habitat has been recorded in a garden in Leicester during the 1970s and 1980s. Over a period of years the garden's owner, an ecologist, recorded the existence of moths, toadstools, wasps, hoverflies and butterflies in abundance. The garden, which produces food as well as flowers, avoids pure monocultures and instead provides an ever-changing ecological diversity (Nicholson-Lord, 1987). Since the 1970s wildlife gardens have become more popular, and the British Trust for Conservation Volunteers built such a garden at the 1985 Chelsea Flower Show (Nicholson-Lord, 1987). Such gardens might include not only ecological planting but also bird or bat boxes, ponds for frogs and newts and wood for hedgehogs, toads, spiders and fungi.

Gardens are an important asset for children as we seek to decide how to best use our country's land in order to provide for the projected 4.1 million houses that are required. The discussion about dense living in cities might also address the benefits of gardens to children. Gardening is considered by some to be the best way of teaching children about nature, but this should be balanced by the fact that the experience of gardening is not only enjoyable and potentially leisurely but also hard work and sometimes frustrating (Wolschke-Bulmahn and Groning, 1994) – perhaps a reflection of life itself. Others are concerned that children are spending increasing amounts of time in virtual

activities such as watching television and playing computer games and as a result are losing contact with the natural world in their daily lives (Moore, 1995). Opportunities for children to experience gardening in a San Francisco school were undertaken, as part of a larger regenerative design process. The largely asphalt school yard was transformed into a hive of educational activities. Initially donated seeds and topsoil were used to grow seedlings in containers such as milk and yoghurt cartons until they were large enough to be planted out. Protection from balls was provided by enclosure of the planting areas and the development of composting, at one time in association with university students, was another stage in the educational process. Moore discusses how this project, which was undertaken in the 1970s and 1980s, provided opportunities for a wide range of educational opportunities. These included the growing of flowers and vegetables, biological investigations, mathematical enquiry, discussions about 'pests' and pest control, visits to off-site locations such as the university's experimental garden and the buying and preparation of food. All these provide a context of sustainable issues for young people through the experience of gardening that hopefully will impact upon their adult life (Wolschke-Bulmahn and Groning, 1994).

Even the dissemination of aspects of gardening through the message of children's comics has been identified as a useful tool that uses language and graphics that can be easily understood by children (Wolschke-Bulmahn and Groning, 1994). Comics cover a wide range of life experiences including sport, art, science, leisure and gardening, the latter being portrayed as human interactions with plants and gardens. Topics such as topiary, lawn maintenance, ecological and biodynamic gardening and Japanese gardens were identified as being covered in a small selection of the British comic the Beano, the German comic Fix und Foxi and Walt Disney's Donald Duck. Such comics can be a secondary means of raising awareness and providing educational opportunities about gardens and the environment.

One small example of the importance of an individual garden, but most significant to those involved in it, was the

5.4   *Culpepper community
          gardens, Islington*

5.4

renovation of a garden to a Georgian house in Lancaster (Wilson, 1997). The author, a teacher and student counsellor, worked with one colleague and three students with special needs. Together with other volunteers the group set about their task and by the end the shy pupils were mixing, through tasks required to be undertaken, and working together, physically exerting themselves on the manual side of the garden restoration. Sometimes fun, sometimes argumentative, the project provided an opportunity to talk through difficult feelings and for the personal development of these young people.

Community gardens

Community gardens should also be mentioned at this point. These may be of importance in childhood but perhaps have more importance to adult life and the development of a sense of community.

Community gardens have become a common sight in many urban areas of America. In the Lower East Side of New York there are more than seventy-five community gardens (Schmelzkopf, 1995). Most of these gardens have both vegetables and flowers, providing an opportunity for home-grown produce and ornamentation. A limited number have flowers only, providing a park-like appearance throughout the year and reducing the risk of soil contamination through eating vegetables grown on the site. Most of the sites were originally housing sites that were demolished following reductions in public funding in New York during the 1970s. Four types of community gardens have been identified in the area: family orientated gardens which are primarily run by women, casita-based gardens which are primarily run by men, large high-profile gardens operated by gardeners from ethnically diverse backgrounds and a small number of gardens operated by schools. Most of the residents of this part of the city are poor, with nearly one-third of the population living below the poverty level. For these people these gardens provide opportunity to escape from the physical constraints of their poverty, often one- or two-roomed apartments. General benefits of these gardens were acknowledged as being able to grow food, an estimated value of $1 million across the city, and having a safe outdoor place. The last factor is particularly significant because this is a neighbourhood with drug dealers and the banning of drugs from the gardens provides a haven as well as discouraging the gardeners from using drugs. Women and girls in particular expressed pleasure at being able to feel safe outside with other people, with many of them being 'restricted by their lack of money, the dangers in the street and responsibilities for children' (Schmelzkopf, 1995). The opportunity to look after children, undertake household chores and grow food are seen as benefits by these women. On the other hand men enjoy relaxing, some of them recreating a lifestyle similar to that of their native Puerto Rico, and having the opportunity of not having 'to answer to any one else' (Schmelzkopf, 1995). An overriding benefit has been the development of a sense of community by those involved with these gardens.

Inspired by this community garden movement in America some community groups in the UK decided to develop community gardens on derelict sites within their neighbour-hoods. Such gardens are run by local communities and produce food; unlike city farms they do not have animals. By the turn of the century it was estimated that there were more than 520 community gardens in the UK, with the smallest one being only ten square metres (http://www.cityfarm.org.uk/, last accessed 19 April 2002). The benefits of community gardens are focused around economic and social issues of food production and community involvement in this country and in the US, and perhaps reflect an earlier agricultural way of life but also point the way forward as part of a more sustainable approach to urban living.

It is also worth mentioning that in reality it may be for some people that a community garden is understood to be a communal garden – that is a semi-private space that is shared between a small number of dwellings. Such a space may be maintained as part of an overall management package, by a warden or by individuals living within the dwellings. These spaces offer similar benefits to those of traditional gardens, with perhaps the most obvious factor being that they provide clear opportunities for meeting the people who live in the other dwellings. Such communal gardens are sometimes appropriate for groups of dwellings for the elderly or for young professional people. Where families share such spaces the children automatically have friends to play with on a daily basis.

Allotments

For some people allotments provide an alternative to gardens, while for others an allotment will supplement their garden. The contemporary use of allotments is usually for growing fruit and vegetables, although some people use these spaces for growing flowers. The use of allotments over the years has varied with changes being influenced by national land use requirements, legislation and personal choice.

Maps and records reveal that allotments have existed within the urban framework of Birmingham, England, since at least 1731 (Thorpe et al., 1976). The rent on such plots, usually owned by well-known local families, was often as much as one guinea, giving rise to the more popular name of 'guinea garden' rather than allotment. The guinea gardens provided an opportunity for the cultivation of both ornamental and edible produce by middle-class citizens living nearby. The history of allotments in Birmingham, as recorded by Thorpe et al., could well be used as an indicator of the history of allotments across the UK. The peak of the guinea gardens, considered as highly desirable, was between 1820 and 1830, before much private land was sold off for development associated with the urban growth of the time. For many urban dwellers who had recently moved from the country, urban allotments provided the opportunity to supplement their low wages with fruit and vegetables. There was no statutory requirement for allotments until the introduction of the Allotments Acts of 1887 and 1890 and the Local Government Act of 1894. Such legislation did, however, have a 'get out' clause, stating that allotment provision was only obligatory where an authority was satisfied that allotments could not reasonably be provided by private treaty. Thus private landowners continued to be mainly responsible for the provision of allotments during the remainder of the nineteenth century. The major provision of allotments by local authorities developed from the introduction of the 1907 and 1908 Small Holdings and Allotments Acts, although the provision by private land owners continued to dominate distribution patterns. For example, in Birmingham in 1913, 177 allotment sites existed within the city boundary, covering about 296 hectares, 173 hectares of which were held by the local authority.

The number of allotments in existence in the UK rose dramatically from half a million in 1913 to one and a half million by the end of the First World War. The introduction of the Defence of the Realm Act in December 1916 empowered local authorities to secure as much land as possible for cultivation, as part of the war effort. In Birmingham, and across England, hundreds of hectares of land were converted, with plot sizes often reducing from 418 square metres to 215 square metres, the more general size in use today (Thorpe et al., 1976). After the war pressure for the release of land for redevelopment of the urban fabric became a conflict with those tenants who wanted to retain their plots for economic reasons. The 1922 Allotments Act reflected this dichotomy by trying to secure better conditions for plot holders. In the interwar period some former, temporary, wartime allotments were retained while others were developed in association with contemporary housing schemes. The Allotments Act of 1925 required that sites should be included in town planning schemes and established statutory allotment land where the freehold was invested in the local authority.

The wartime peak in numbers of allotments in 1918 was followed by a similar increase in numbers in the Second World War, brought about by the 'Dig for Victory' campaign. Again figures from Birmingham will serve as an example: at the outbreak of the Second World War the City Council controlled 11,716 plots, with a peak provision of 20,417 plots being reached in 1944 (Thorpe et al., 1976), and one and a half million nationally Hoyles (1994). The return to peace and relative prosperity resulted in a decrease in allotments, with much land again being taken over for housing and other reconstruction work. By 1949 one-third of Birmingham's 18,000 statutory plots were uncultivated and another third only partly cultivated. The Allotments Act of 1950, the result of the deliberations of the Government's Allotments Advisory Committee, identified that some of the decline in the popularity of allotments had been brought about due to concerns about issues such as security of tenure and compensation for disturbance. In 1965, at a time when one-fifth of all allotment land in Great Britain lay vacant, a Government Inquiry into Allotments was set up to review the contemporary situation with respect to allotments and to recommend any legislative and associated changes thought necessary. The outcome of this was the Thorpe Report (1969), which included a range of recommendations for legislative, administrative matters, design and planning issues, related to the role of local and national government and the National Allotments and Gardens Society. It also identified that the majority of allotment users were utilising the facility as a recreational, rather than as an economic, tool. As a result of this report attempts were made to create leisure gardens in some parts of the country. These were upgraded and redesigned sites which could include the provision of toilets, piped water, storage, car parking and secure fencing and or gates.

Allotments are good for the production of food and flowers and for recreation, but despite this research has found that allotments are in fact of little importance to wildlife habitat creation in the urban context (Elkin *et al.*, 1991).

The future of allotments has been the subject of the Environment, Transport and Regional Affairs Committee which reported in 1998, making a variety of suggestions relating to legislation, policy and practice that affects allotments. The government's response to this paper was supportive in some areas but acknowledged that any legislative changes would not be high up on their current agenda. The response acknowledged and confirmed not only the importance of allotments for the production of fruit, flowers and vegetables but also the positive social contribution that allotments can make: 'allotments will often form a component part of healthy neighbourhoods' (Government's Response, 1998).

CHAPTER SIX

Neighbourhood urban open spaces

Introduction

Neighbourhood urban open spaces are those that are part of the neighbourhood in two ways. First of all they are physically further from home, except on rare occasions, than domestic urban open spaces. This means that to use neighbourhood urban open spaces one has to make a very specific decision to do so. This may be different from some domestic urban open spaces which one can almost treat as an extension of the home. The decision to use any particular neighbourhood urban open space thus requires a journey of some sort – whether it is 200 yards or further. In some communities such journeys will be – or should be – made on foot, the walk to the park or school being a good example. Unfortunately many such journeys are in fact made by car, some by choice on bicycle and some by necessity are made by public transport. It is anticipated that in general the distances travelled to neighbourhood urban open spaces will be of a limited length, although there are some who travel outside their own physical neighbourhoods and communities to others for services such as schooling and thus use open spaces in other people's neighbourhoods. Travel and accessibility to neighbourhood urban open spaces thus begin to raise issues of cost and perceived safety for one's self and one's children.

The second way in which neighbourhood urban open spaces are part of the neighbourhood relates not to a physical issue but to the social context. The people that one might meet in the range of neighbourhood urban open spaces are likely to be the people who live and possibly work in the area. This could involve different networks of people such as residential neighbours, workmates, parents, carers and staff from nursery or school as well as people from other activities in life such as clubs, organisations and religious and cultural groupings.

Those spaces considered as neighbourhood urban open spaces are parks, playgrounds, playing fields and sports grounds, school playgrounds, streets, city farms and incidental spaces. Parks can be considered to be the most democratic of urban open spaces because they are available to all – in theory anyway.

Sometimes babies are taken to them for the fresh air, while children love the opportunities for play – on formal play equipment and informally in a creative way. Walking a dog, jogging, and meeting friends and family members are all activities that are daily undertaken in parks – as the evidence that follows shows. Playgrounds – in many situations despite their imperfections – are often a favourite with children from an early age. Playgrounds are often located within a park but may also be independent of such a location. Sports grounds may be situated within a park, although many secondary schools also have these facilities. Such spaces are used by those participating in a specific sport such as football, hockey or cricket at a particular time. But these spaces are peculiar in that when they are not being used for the one specific activity, they are, in the main, left unusable by others. School playgrounds are again spaces that are only used for limited periods of time – school playtimes and lunchtimes in school terms. The concept of dual use of such spaces has been around for many years but has not been fully achieved in many communities. Streets are places in the neighbourhood where people travel to other spaces and may be spaces for lingering with neighbours and friends to pass the time of day, but such activity will depend upon the design and management of any individual street. It is unlikely that there will be more than one city farm in any urban conurbation, and some might see such a facility as a civic urban open space, but I believe, by definition of the type of facility that a city farm is, that it should be described as a neighbourhood urban open space. City farms are often initiated by a community on a particular piece of land with the intention of providing opportunities for the immediate neighbourhood. Incidental urban open spaces may be planned and designed or they may just happen. They may be designed as a small play area or sitting area, perhaps near to the shops, or they may be a piece of land that has been 'claimed' by a particular group of users.

When considering the benefits discussed in section one of this book it can be seen that opportunities for children's play and both passive and active recreation abound in neighbourhood urban open spaces – whether that be a park, a playground, a playing field or a school playground. In addition such spaces – perhaps especially parks – provide opportunities for community and cultural activities, allowing groups within a neighbourhood to have a focus for some of their activities. Educational opportunities in neighbourhood urban open spaces are also many, being specifically available in parks, school playgrounds and city farms. Opportunities for improving physical health are provided by both organised and informal use of neighbourhood urban open spaces such as football, hockey and tennis, jogging and walking. The restorative effects of nature and thus benefits for mental health are available and appreciated in city farms and particularly parks, with much evidence showing that people go to parks for peace and quiet or to get away from family members, noise and the everyday stress of life. The contribution that neighbourhood urban open spaces make to the environmental benefits of a conurbation are possibly immeasurable – especially when the neighbourhood urban open spaces across an entire town or city are considered. The environmental benefits of the different spaces do not act in isolation from each other – together they contribute to the amelioration of the urban climate and environment, as discussed in chapter three. In addition the opportunities for wildlife habitats are potentially greater in neighbourhood than domestic urban open spaces. Many neighbourhood urban open spaces are predominantly green with different layers of vegetation and are in close enough proximity to each other to allow migration of some species from one space to another. When considering neighbourhood urban open spaces with respect to possible economic benefits and opportunities any impact on property values is not proven in this country, as discussed in chapter four, but there are many employment opportunities in parks, playgrounds, playing fields, school playgrounds and city farms. Crop production is possible in both city farms and school grounds. It is unlikely that tourism will be much of an issue for neighbourhood urban open spaces, although some parks may provide opportunities for this benefit, by widening their remit to a regional context.

However, it can be seen that the range of benefits and opportunities available in neighbourhood urban open spaces is in fact greater than in domestic urban open spaces. This applies across the social, health, environmental and economic benefits and opportunities. In addition the range of people one might encounter is also greater, perhaps moving from a level of familiarity to a level of sociability. In neighbourhood urban open spaces one might not only meet family, friends and close neighbours or invited people but also acquaintances or other regular users – who may be known by sight but not name – such as a fellow dog walker or other parents or carers.

Parks

Parks may be experienced very early in life – very often the playground used by young children is in their local park. But parks are also used at different times of life and perhaps early use of a park in childhood encourages adult use.

As a response to growing concern about the rapid and unplanned proliferation of urban centres throughout the UK a Select Committee on Public Walks addressed the issues of ill-health, lack of morals and morale in 1833 (Taylor, 1994). The reasons for addressing these issues included a desire to achieve the 'greatest happiness for the greatest number' and a fear of the threat of 'barbaric behaviour' believed to be inherent in an uneducated, newly urban working-class generation. The outcome of the deliberations of this select committee, in 1840, was the recommendation that publicly owned parks should be provided, a suggestion first made in 1804 by Loudon (Nicholson-Lord, 1987). In 1848 the Public Health Act empowered Local Boards of Health to provide, maintain and improve land for municipal parks. It also enabled local authorities to contribute towards land provided by others for such purposes (Barber, 1994). This link between health and parks has been all but forgotten for over a century, but, as discussed in chapter two, the link has now been picked up in some parts of the country with issues such as

Urban Open Spaces – Spaces for All

6.1 *A family enjoys its
      local park*

6.1

organised health walks being introduced. Historically parks were initiated for a range of reasons in urban situations. In Edingburgh recreation in a park was thought to cure drunkenness, while in Macclesfield a decrease in crime and the death rate were attributed to the existence of parks (Hoyles, 1994). In Liverpool the average life expectancy in the 1840s was only thirty-two, and like many other expanding industrial cities most of the land was covered with tightly-packed housing and there were few opportunities for relaxation apart from the pub and the gin house.

In London the first public park was Victoria Park where it is estimated that 118,000 people visited on one June Sunday afternoon, shortly after it opened. It was also recorded that 25,000 bathers took to the open-air lakes before 8 o'clock one morning. These vast numbers of people using such parks led to authorities restricting activities such as games and contact with areas of grass, installing railings to control access and use and employing park police to break up the large numbers of people (Nicholson-Lord, 1987). The first public park outside London

6.2 *Dogs walking their people*

6.2

was Derby Arboretum which aimed 'to give people of Derby an opportunity to learn botany, enjoy the pure air of the park as an alternative to the debasing pursuits and brutalising pleasure of drinking and cockfighting' (Taylor, 1994). But this park was well used by people from outside Derby, especially on Sundays, when people would travel 60 or more miles, and arrive by third-class rail carriages from other conurbations such as Nottingham, Sheffield, Birmingham and Leeds. The Derby Arboretum was followed by Princes' Park in Liverpool, in 1842, Phillip's Park and Queen's Park in Manchester in 1846 and Birkenhead Park in 1847, which soon became known as the 'People's Park'. Other cities, such as Bristol and Sheffield, then developed a large number of public parks, some with land purchased by the authorities and others with land given by large land owners, such as the Duke of Norfolk and Alderman Graves in Sheffield. Birkenhead Park had a significant impact on Frederick Law Olmsted when he visited this country in the 1850s and inspired him to create many urban parks in America, including Central Park in New York (Taylor, 1994), the economic impact of which was discussed in chapter four.

During the latter part of the twentieth century urban parks in the UK went into decline due to low political priority and the 'withering of local government' (Holden, 1988). The financial costs of provision and upkeep of parks, although the responsibility of local authorities, has increasingly had to compete with other provisions that local authorities have to make. Government money given to local authorities under the Standard Spending Assessment does not include parks as a compulsory element, resulting in funding for parks being at the discretion of individual local authorities under the category of 'other' facilities. In addition funding for the upkeep of parks in many cities has been adversely affected by other commitments, thus supporting the perception that parks are not important.

It has been suggested that in the nineteenth century urban parks were an opportunity to encounter the countryside in the city. Rather than the wild and unkempt character that some identify with the countryside, this experience has been in a tamed and tidied form with manicured grassland and brightly coloured floral arrangements, and is considered by some to be a sad end for the public parks movement (Nicholson-Lord, 1987). Others would claim that this was not the end of the public park and that a new trend of developing such parks has been evolving as we move further into the twenty-first century.

Later research has clearly shown that parks are important socially to contemporary society: they are probably the most used and best-known open spaces in the urban environment. Discussion groups with park users in London revealed that parks are places for all the family and for all types of people (Harrison and Burgess, 1989). A range of passive uses were clearly identified as being important to different groups within the community.

Concern about the need for the regeneration of urban parks, including the need to diversify provision to cater for a wide range of public, such as toddlers, teenagers, adults and pensioners, and cultural groups has been expressed (Turner, 1996b). Turner also discusses how parks should reflect a variety of political stances, ethnic groups and religions and the range of outdoor leisure activities currently enjoyed. Comedia's work identified that as many as 40 per cent of the people they interviewed used their parks daily, spending about 30 minutes on each visit. The main reason given for using the parks was bringing children to the parks – so as long as people in this country go on having children we shall need parks! Other reasons were strolling and walking the dog – a total of 1 dog for every 8 people using the parks was recorded (Greenhalgh and Worpole, 1995).

Urban parks are appreciated globally. Parks, particularly neighbourhood parks, are valued, as revealed by research studying the use of parks by 516 people in Singapore (Yuen, 1996). Face-to-face structured interviews were used and when English was not the first language of a participant the responses were translated into English. About 50 per cent of these respondents reported that they use neighbourhood parks, with 60 per cent of the users claiming to use the parks at least once a week and another 20 per cent claiming to use the parks once or more a month. Nearly 90 per cent of these users were identified as being families with children who go to the neighbourhood park for a stroll, to jog, to socialise or for the children to use the playground. Four themes emerged as being important with respect to the neighbourhood spaces of those who were involved in this study. First, there was a clear expression of attitudes towards the neighbourhood park. These responses related to how good or bad people considered the environment to be, with variables including, clean–dirty, relaxed–tense and pleasant–unpleasant. Second, the actual physical setting of the neighbourhood park was appreciated with respect to opportunity for activities. Third, the opportunity to experience nature was repeatedly seen as a benefit by the participants. This is expressed beautifully by one of the respondents who described how they like to look at plants and animals and enjoy the quiet scenery and be part of a place 'where people can touch the earth and relax'. In fact many of the respondents spoke of the 'feeling of relaxation that natural elements seem to give', thus reflecting the theory of restoration from mental fatigue and stress supported by the work of researchers such as the Kaplans and Ulrich, and discussed in chapter two. Fourth, the proximity and accessibility of the neighbourhood parks were attributes that were highly favoured, echoing the findings and deliberations of others (Harrison *et al.*, 1987; Greenhalgh and Worpole, 1995) and expressed by Greenhalgh and Worpole thus: 'People need green open places to go to; when they are close they use them'.

More recently, a piece of research initiated by the Institute of Leisure and Amenity Management and completed by the Urban Parks Forum has revealed some thought-provoking facts about urban parks. This research was funded by the Department of Transport, Local Government and the Regions, the Heritage Lottery Fund (HLF), the Countryside Agency and English Heritage (Urban Parks Forum, 2001). The aim of the study was to establish need in relation to all public parks and to help inform decision-making on grants made to local authorities by HLF under the Urban Parks Programme. In order to achieve this the research set about developing a database of all local authority-owned parks and open spaces by establishing:

- The number, size, condition and trend of condition for each council's stock;
- The policies that local authorities have for their parks;
- Identification of all parks considered to be of local or national historical importance;
- An inventory of features and facilities lost to each historic park;
- An assessment of the condition of soft and hard landscape features;
- A schedule of designations relating to each park – both historic and scientific designations and of entire parks and elements within parks;
- Visitor numbers for parks;
- Trends in capital and revenue spending on parks.

In order to elicit the information required a questionnaire was distributed to 475 local authorities in the UK; after much telephoning to specific individuals a final response rate of 85 per cent (405 local authorities) was achieved. The research revealed that there are 27,000 urban parks, covering 143,000 hectares, in the UK and that £630 million is spent on the upkeep of these parks each year. However, it is clear that during the last twenty years there have been dramatic reductions in revenue expenditure, resulting in a cumulative cut of £1.3 billion over that time period. This work estimates that over 1.5 billion visits are made to all parks and open spaces each year, by all sectors of society. Only 18 per cent of local authorities consider that their parks and open spaces are in a 'good' condition, while 69 per cent report that they are in 'fair' condition and 13 per cent are described as being in 'poor' condition. About one-third of the parks and open spaces stock is considered to be improving, one-third is stable, and one-third is in decline. What is also significant is that 60 per cent of the stock considered to be in good condition is improving, while 86 per cent of the stock in poor condition is considered to be in decline. Thus it is clear from this research that parks and open spaces are used by large numbers of people within our communities. But it is also

6.3

apparent that the importance that such places obviously provide to urban living is not reflected in an increase in capital or revenue expenditure over a period of twenty years. Indeed the massive reduction in expenditure on this facility, across the UK, indicates that politicians and funding bodies do not give the same importance to parks and open spaces that ordinary citizens do. The trends with respect to the condition of parks give cause for concern, especially where those considered to be in a poor condition are getting worse (Urban Parks Forum, 2001).

Further evidence of the large numbers of people who enjoy their urban parks comes from one specific urban conurbation. Sheffield is the fourth largest city in England and for many years boasted of its large quantities of green space and woodland. During the last ten years this wonderful asset has been less used as a marketing tool, despite the fact that the residents of Sheffield greatly value the benefits of their urban green spaces and woodlands. A calculation of the number of visitors to open spaces has been undertaken by Sheffield City Council (Sheffield City Council, 2001). Using responses from the Citizens' Panel,

and relating this to the population of the city, it has been estimated that the number of visitors to parks and woodlands in the City of Sheffield is more than 25 million a year. This figure does not include children or visitors to the city who would add more millions to the figure. It is of some interest to note that the target number of visits to sports facilities for the year 1999/2000 was only 2.3 million (Sheffield City Council, 2000). These high figures for use of urban parks and woodlands reconfirm the national situation identified by the above research – urban parks are highly used and appreciated facilities.

The high level of users indicated by both the Urban Parks Forum work and the Sheffield survey have been reinforced by the most recent research to investigate users and non-users of urban green spaces across England which was undertaken for the Office of the Deputy Prime Minister (formerly the Department of Transport, Local Government and the Regions). This has revealed that across ten case study locations 184 million visits are made each year to urban green spaces, let alone those urban spaces that are not dominantly green (Dunnett *et al.*,

2002). In most of these locations between 50 and 60 per cent of people stated that they use urban green spaces more than once a week, with many using them daily or more than once a day. This research also reveals that, assuming the urban population of England to be 37.8 million, as per the Urban White Paper (Department of the Environment, Transport and the Regions, 2000), then 33 million people in urban areas make more than 2.5 billion visits a year to urban green spaces.

The House of Commons Environment, Transport and Regional Sub-Committee investigating Town and Country Parks (House of Commons, 1999) received evidence from nearly seventy contributors, explaining their individual or groups' experience, concerns and suggestions for the future of urban parks. The committee suggested, among other things, joint funding of projects by the Heritage Lottery Fund and the New Opportunities Fund. It also suggested a framework for an Urban Parks and Green Spaces Agency. The Urban White Paper (Department of the Environment, Transport and the Regions, 2000) did not confirm this latter suggestion but did state that the government would work in partnership with the Urban Parks Forum to develop a programme for identifying and spreading good practice on the maintenance and care of urban parks to parks staff, professionals and user groups. One of the practical outcomes of the Urban White Paper has been the contribution of significant funding to the Urban Parks Forum for a period of three years. Another outcome has been the setting up of an advisory committee or Taskforce on Urban Green Spaces and the commissioning of the research project called Improving Urban Parks Play Areas and Green Spaces and undertaken by the Department of Landscape at the University of Sheffield (see Dunnett *et al.*, 2002).

Playgrounds

> A playground should not be 'an island'
> isolated from the rest of the neighbourhood,
> but one of the places that children have access to in the neighbourhood
> (Noschis, 1992).

Playgrounds, one assumes, are predomin-antly provided for children – even if they are not designed in the ideal way a child might like. But it must also be acknowledged that playgrounds provide opportunities for some parents and carers to meet and discuss issues of school, health, community and life in general.

Some people assume that play only takes place in playgrounds that have been especially designed, by adults for children. Two issues can be challenged in such assumptions. The first is that children should be excluded from the design of specific play locations. Often older children are seen as an 'outsider' group who are not involved in the provision of the facilities for them (Matthews, 1994). The second issue that needs to be challenged is the fundamental one that children will only play in specially designed playgrounds. Anyone with children will know that children will, and do, play anywhere, whether it be in a playground, the bedroom, the garden, the hall or even at the breakfast table. Play is experiencing life and happens constantly for children. There is a vast amount of evidence indicating that children make creative use of a range of different types of spaces – that where places are not even designed for play children identify opportunities for play (see Ward, 1978; Hart, 1979; Moore, 1995).

Historically playgrounds were considered to be a means of isolating children from the dangerous city. A greater variety of experience and opportunities for skills' development is available to children who are not restricted to using only playgrounds. The street, when safe enough, places in front of houses and a range of other spaces in the neighbourhood are all invaluable for play opportunities. Many authors have written about the importance

6.4   *A conventional playground*

6.4

of the 'city as playground' (Ward, 1978; Abercrombie, 1981; Dreyfuss, 1981), accepting that traditional playgrounds do not and cannot provide the entire play opportunity that children require. However, for many children the opportunity to develop skills through play comes, at least in part, in the form of a playground, often in the local park. Such playgrounds are usually provided and maintained by local authorities and because of this we will now consider playgrounds.

A conventional playground contains moving equipment such as a roundabout and swings and fixed equipment such as slides and climbing frames, with tarmac or in some situations a rubber-based surface in order to reduce the impact of any falls from equipment. But these playgrounds have not tended to include the opportunities for manipulating the environment identified in some of the evidence reported in chapter one as being important for children and what they like to play with (Hart, 1979).

Increasing industrialisation in developing urban areas, coupled with changes in farming techniques during the eighteenth and nineteenth centuries, led to increased pressure on land in the UK, resulting in specialisation and eventually the concept of land use planning, zoning all land for a speciific use. This resulted in many areas where children used to play no longer being available for this purpose. The Recreation Grounds Act of 1859 provides the first reference on the statute book to children and play and recommends that identifiable areas for such activities should be set aside in urban areas. The first equipped children's playground in England was opened in 1877 at Burberry Street Recreation Ground in Birmingham (Heseltine and Holborn, 1987), while the first American playground, a sand garden for 5 to 10 year olds, was opened in Boston in 1897 (Oberlander and Nadel, 1978). In some locations, such as London, Guilds of Play organised games in the city parks. In Manchester recreation grounds were organised in 1911 by voluntary groups and later adopted by the Parks Committee of the local authority. Development of primary school playgrounds expressed an increasing acceptance that play was important for children. Between the First and Second World Wars the number of children's playgrounds increased in parks and

recreation grounds, although these were dominated by heavy fixed equipment, tarmac surfacing and an occasional sandpit (Holme and Massie, 1970).

The Physical Training and Recreation Act of 1937 enabled local authorities and voluntary organisations to provide playgrounds and playing fields and was an early result of the National Playing Fields Association's activities (Heseltine and Holborn, 1987). The Street Playgrounds Act of 1938 allowed for the possibility of play streets: home zones, currently being researched and supported by the Department for Transport, can be seen as a modern version of this facility.

Spaces that had previously been available for children to play on began to decline after the Second World War; some of the sites used for play had been bombed and were redeveloped, others were streets that could no longer support play as an activity (Miller, 1972; Bengtsson, 1974). Other spaces were left over after planned space. Throughout the period since the Second World War playgrounds have been created in parks, recreation grounds and housing developments. Many of these have been of the type that have fixed play equipment, such as swings, slides, roundabouts and climbing frames, and are surfaced with tarmac. Alongside these has been the construction of playgrounds believed to have been inspired by the one on the roof of Le Corbusier's flats in Marseilles. These tended to be 'architectural in design, dominated by bricks and concrete and without consideration to climate, culture or child' (Heseltine and Holborn, 1987).

Such formally designed playgrounds with moving and fixed play equipment, often in parks, were installed on the very plausible assumption that they would be the most needed facilities; but usage studies and ethnographic studies of what children do all day indicate otherwise. Thus some consider that such playgrounds have minimal value as far as child development is concerned (Hughes, 1994). Hughes contends that for play provision to have a meaningful future its relevance, safety and security must be considered. The relevance should relate to the development of the child and provide for mental and physical

6.5

6.6

flexibility, being stimulating, novel and containing elements that will provoke a desire to return again and again to the experience. Safety relates to the need for well-designed play sites to be well maintained, being kept free from litter, glass, dog faeces and hypodermic needles, which unfortunately are sometimes found in playgrounds, as reported in the press. Safety also depends upon the motivation and training of play workers, together with the financing of workers and sites. Security relates to real and perceived concerns whether from humans or dogs. Solutions to these issues may relate to fencing, lighting, the location of facilities or the involvement of communities in the development of schemes.

Junk or adventure playgrounds, on the other hand, provide more creative opportunities for play than many of the playgrounds of the types described above. Adventure playgrounds were first proposed by a Danish landscape architect, Sorensen, in 1932, with the first being built in 1943 in Copenhagen. The first play leader was a former teacher who 'saw the playground as a place where children could have opportunities for constructive play bearing upon the activities of the outside world where they can play and spontaneously learn by playing' (Benjamen, 1974), thus reflecting some of the evidence of research about child development reported in chapter one. The concept of adventure playgrounds was translated to England by Lady Allen of Hurtwood, and the first of its kind in England was built in 1948 in Camberwell (Holme and Massie, 1970, Benjamen, 1974). Other locations in England, such as Grimsby, Birmingham, Richmond, Barnes and Lancaster, and locations in other European countries, such as Switzerland (1955) and Western Germany (1967), also developed adventure playgrounds (Bengtsson, 1974; Lambert, 1974). In such playgrounds it is the children who are considered as sovereign, not the adults (Benjamen, 1974).

Over the years some local authorities have developed a hierarchy of play spaces with suggestions for the provision of play for different aged children at different distances from home. In some instances the provision by developers of play areas under such guidelines has been required under planning gain legislation. Such hierarchies provide for toddlers close to home,

primary school children at a further distance and secondary school children at a further distance again. Often teenagers are not specifically included as a category in such hierarchies. Such hierarchies should, however, take issues other than just distance into account – for instance roads and the related traffic may cut off children's access to a playground (Hurtwood, 1968).

The National Playing Fields Association has made suggestions for different types of play areas, with an acknowledgement that the walking distance to a play space for a child may be impeded by obstacles such as railway lines, busy roads, canals and isolated areas. Three different types of play areas are suggested. A local area for play (LAP) is an unsupervised open space for young children for play close to where they live. A local equipped area for play (LEAP) is an unsupervised play area, with equipment, for children of early school age. A neighbourhood equipped area for play (NEAP) is a site for a mainly housing area. It will have play equipment for older children and may have play opportunities for younger children as well (National Playing Fields Association, 1992).

Playgrounds, both traditional and adventure style, can have a role to play in providing opportunities for children to play in urban areas. But it is also clear that playgrounds are not the only places that provide opportunities for play stimulation – many different spaces and places in the urban environment can provide these opportunities. It is therefore important that people who plan, design and manage the urban environment keep the knowledge of the importance of play in mind and create and maintain an environment with play opportunities that are not just confined to playgrounds; involving children and young people where it is practicable.

Playing fields and sports grounds

Playing fields and sports grounds are the open spaces within the urban framework that most directly provide opportunities for active activities, and thereby for improving physical health, as

6.5 *An adventure playground*

6.6 *A kick-about area*

6.7 *Football pitches provide for limited recreation and ecology and have high maintenance cost*

6.7

discussed in chapters one and two. In this way playing fields become a part of life, and the regular weekly routine, for some people within our communities – but not for everyone. Such facilities are not just football – or soccer – pitches, but also include other sports such as hockey, netball and rounders.

The National Playing Fields Association (NPFA) was established in 1925, under the influence of King George V, with aims to:

- Secure playing fields for the present and future needs of all sections of the community;
- Secure proper playing fields for children;
- Save the few open spaces that still exist in and around our increasingly congested cities and towns.
  (Heseltine and Holborn, 1987)

As long ago as 1938 the NPFA was urging the development of a minimum standard for play and recreational space. This recommendation of six acres per 1,000 population has traditionally been known as the NPFA six acre (2.4 hectares) standard and still exists today. It is suggested that this standard be broken into two elements of outdoor sport – 1.6 to 1.8 hectares – and children's playing space – 0.6 to 0.8 hectares. A review of this standard undertaken in 1989 suggested specific levels of provision for youth and adult use, and children's playing space. The types of spaces and pitches suggested as suitable for inclusion in the standard include private pitches, local authority pitches and educational pitches that are 'available for public use on a regular and sustained basis'. The standard also considers that it is important to protect playing fields from development (National Playing Fields Association, 1992). Some consider that it is not reasonable to have a national standard for playing fields due to differences in the dispersal of the population in different parts of the UK.

The importance of playing fields was confirmed by the Scott Committee of 1942 (Great Britain, Committee on Land Utilisation in Rural Areas, 1942) which concluded that playing fields were so important that 'not only towns but every village should have adequate playing fields, together with a social centre'. In

concluding that 'the playing field is vital to community life' it sug-gested that such playing fields should have provision for cricket, football and other games, with a separate field being provided for children. To some extent the suggestion that playing fields should exist in these locations was another expression of concern for the physical health of people, as discussed in chapter two.

The provision of playing fields, whether on educational sites or elsewhere, is very important for both sport and health, but some have, quite rightly, questioned their overall role in the urban landscape. In many towns and cities local community football teams use football pitches for games on Saturday or Sunday. Despite these uses the amount of space given specifically to sports pitches in the UK has begun to be questioned because such pitches tend to be under-used, bleak and offer no ecological or aesthetic benefits. It is also considered that such pitches are mainly used by a small proportion of the male population and that the amount of space and money they require is disproportionate to the benefits derived from them (Greenhalgh and Worpole, 1995). Indeed it has been estimated that only 6 per cent of the users of urban parks go for organised sports, while facilities for these sports take up 25 per cent of the space and over 50 per cent of the maintenance budget (Holden *et al.*, 1992).

Clearly the role that sports pitches play in the urban fabric can be considered in the wider context of a range of issues, relating to the benefits discussed in the first section of this book and taking a broader social remit into account. Such a re-evaluation of sports pitches could address questions such as:

- Can pitches be used for more than one sport?
- Can the use of pitches be spread over the week and not concentrated into three or four hours out of 168 hours in a total week?
- Is there a need for women to have greater access to sports pitches? If so, what type of pitches?
- Is there a need for young people to have greater access to sports pitches?

6.8   *School playgrounds
        are for play*
6.9   *A space for chatting,
        or a lesson*

- Is there a need for ethnic minority groups to have greater access to sports pitches? If so, what type of pitches?
- Is there a need for increased provision or improved accessibility for people who are disabled by the external environment? If so, what form should that provision or improved access take? (see e.g. Woolley, 2002).
- What methods are there to reduce the maintenance costs of pitches?
- Is it possible to reduce the areas adjacent to pitches that have little ecological value?
- Can schools, institutions and communities share pitches more than they do at present?

To some these questions may appear provocative, but if we are trying to provide active and passive facilities for different members of our urban communities, to optimise the benefits available to all, then they could help in a review of the current provision of costly sports pitches for a minority of the population.

School playgrounds

School playgrounds are experienced by everyone because everyone attends school; thus the impact that school play-grounds have on childhood is very important and very often overlooked in life. An imaginatively designed and well-maintained school playground can have a positive impact on early life, while a poorly designed and maintained school playground can result in a range of social and educational problems.

An increase in school gardening at the end of the nineteenth century has been reported by Hoyles (1994) who has identified that a variety of county councils, such as Kent, Middlesex, Northamptonshire and Surrey appointed horticultural super-intendents to establish school gardens. Often playgrounds were dug up to create these gardens and horticulture was included in the curriculum. In 1909, in Manchester, a Children's Flower Guild was initiated with the aim of organising gardening for

children and of encouraging the growing of plants and flowers. This guild arranged school flower shows, gave advice and provided a range of prizes for successful efforts. Children's flower shows were often held annually in locations such as Sheffield and the East End of London. Such activities may still exist, to a lesser extent, in some parts of the UK, but now there are very few links to schools (Hoyles, 1994).

In 1976 a pilot project was undertaken in South Yorkshire to introduce nature reserves into school grounds. By 1980 nearly ninety schools in Sheffield and Barnsley had taken up this theme of producing a 'green patch' and a 'wild pile' of logs and rubble. In 1983 the British Trust for Conservation Volunteers worked with 20,000 children in more then 500 schools. This was followed by the initiation of the Learning through Landscapes Trust. One of the early participants in this movement reminded people that even twenty years previously concern had been expressed about the sterile state of school playing grounds (Denton-Thompson, 1989). As is well documented, and was discussed earlier, childhood memories are important to later life; if the school playground provides a negative experience, in some cases to the extent of bullying, then this is not a situation that we as a civilised society should be content with. On the positive side, many have argued that early experiences of caring for the natural world (including its wildlife) can have lasting, positive effects on an individual.

The charity Learning though Landscapes was initiated in 1985 as a research team, bringing together Berkshire, Hampshire and Surrey County Councils, the Department of Education and Science and the South East Region of the Countryside Commission. The two main aims were to understand how educational opportunities could be extended and how the environmental quality in school grounds could be improved (Adams, 1989). The early work highlighted four areas of particular importance: educational uses, design considerations and development and management of school grounds. Over the years the charity has pioneered work with respect to school playgrounds and continues to be dedicated to helping schools

6.9

6.8

improve their grounds for the benefit of children. Specific acknowledgements of the value of well-designed school grounds are provided by Butler (1989) and Humphries and Rowe (1989) who discuss some of the ways in which the redesigned school grounds have provided opportunities for educational experiences in subjects such as science and English. In addition, by allowing the children to be creators and active participants they are having an educational experience and the opportunity to develop and satisfy emotional, aesthetic and spiritual needs.

Some assert that school grounds across the country are undervalued as a learning experience, and it is clear that they can have a profound influence on pupil's attitude and behaviour. In fact it has been suggested that school playgrounds should become a theatre, a garden and a drawing board for the arts (Lucas, 1995). Lucas and Russell (1997) discuss the concerns about school grounds and buildings that were raised following the killing of children in Dunblane, Scotland, and headteacher Philip Lawrence in London. Such events, relating to intruders from outside the school are indeed very rare. In fact other problems such as trespass, bullying, theft, vandalism, accidents and

arson are more common. Solutions such as tall and aggressive fencing, keep out signs and CCTV, all negative elements in the landscape, are not considered to be the best way forward. Even after these events Learning through Landscapes, and others, remain committed to the conviction that schools that involve the whole community and the local neighbourhood in the process of assessing and developing the school grounds discover that a range of benefits occur: behaviour improves, accidents are less frequent and vandalism decreases. The sense of ownership instilled by such involvement has a beneficial impact on the attitudes and behaviour of pupils and is of significant benefit to the community as a whole.

In addition to the educational opportunities that school playgrounds afford for children and staff, the playground can also support what has been considered to be a community. Focus groups with parents in Edinburgh have revealed that 'the school playground was seen as a focus point, where people from all sorts of backgrounds and with different interests are thrown together under the common purpose of delivering and collecting their children' (Kelly, unpublished). The level of interaction at which parents choose to engage in this location may vary depending upon their other commitments on the day, social or religious concerns or the extent to which they are prepared to become involved in the playground community. Even within the playground community there can be sub-communities. Different groups of people were identified as regularly using different parts of the playground. The 'railing community' was identified as the smokers' corner, while dog owners were considered to be another of the sub-communities. Interestingly women were identified as being more involved in the playground community than men. If you are a parent with a child at school perhaps you might like to consider which playground community you belong to.

Schools can very obviously provide for the educational benefits outlined in chapter one but also afford opportunities for play and other benefits discussed in chapter one such as active and passive recreation.

6.10

Streets

Streets are experienced by all from a young age, but the quality of that experience is vastly different. If a street has a lot of traffic then the experience will be dominated by vehicles and the concept that the street is only for travelling along as fast as is possible. When a street has a lower level of traffic it may be more person-friendly and in some instances may allow for play, in a way that many streets did in the past.

Originally streets developed as a means of carrying people, animals and then goods between places. As the Roman civilisation marched across Europe roads were first developed as a hierarchical system. Paved roads or streets, taking heavier loads, were accompanied by ways, unpaved routes across the country.

6.10   *Streets are used for religious*
          processions
6.11   *Streets are used for markets*

6.11

Following the decline of the Roman invasion of Britain, through traffic for military purposes decreased, and streets and roads were needed primarily for local travel and transport. During Saxon times the responsibility for the maintenance of these routes, and associated bridges, fell upon the relevant landowner. By the middle of the seventeenth century roads in Britain were in a poor state of repair. The principle of road hierarchies was re-introduced with fifty-eight of the main routes being identified as first-class roads and their maintenance being funded by a national charge. Thus the foundation for the current structure, whereby local authorities are responsible for local routes, while motorways are a national responsibility, was laid (Whyatt, 1923).

The introduction of toll-gate roads was opposed by many but was intended to make those who used specific routes pay for the wear and tear they put upon the facility. Turnpike road charges acknowledged the change from animal to mechanised travel and were meant to contribute not only to the maintenance of the roads but also to their improvement. Streets had been built by the removal of soft material to a hard base and then boulders, rocks and stones were randomly placed in the resulting trench, with drainage not being considered. John Loudon Macadam introduced the concept of 'artificial flooring' for roads and streets, with the strength being such that even the heaviest of vehicles would not damage the surface. Stone was broken up into small pieces and three layers, bound by mud or water, were placed where the road was required. Thomas Telford was also involved in the development of layered road surfacing with the use of stones broken into specified sizes. Modern road structures developed from these systems, with the use of local materials being overtaken as the movement of stone became easier due to the roads being built. The advent of the car resulted in an increased problem of dust and a remedy being required for this nuisance. Tar was used to bind the materials with painting of the substance being followed by the mixing of the tar with the 'macadamised' stone; thus the materials from which most roads and streets are made in the developed countries (Whyatt, 1923). As the twentieth century progressed

other materials were devised, in particular a variety of forms of concrete, stone and wood are currently used for both vehicular and pedestrian routes. The use of streets has changed over the centuries and for much of that time these changes have influenced the type of surfacing used for protecting the ground from loads.

Currently it is estimated that 80 per cent of public open space within urban areas is in the form of streets. Yet the fact that streets impinge upon urban life as routes, locations for services, frontages to both residential and business properties and often are the boundary between public and private life is often ignored by professionals, politicians and decision makers (Institute of Civil Engineers, 2000). Towards the end of the twentieth century the amount of vehicular traffic increased beyond expectations of the early days of the century to such an extent that most streets became and continue to be dominated by the car. In many locations there are few people using streets as a pedestrian resource, with the resultant loss of the 'eyes of the street' as described by Jacobs (1961).

Although transportation of people, animals and goods were the original reasons for the development of streets, over the years they have also been used for many other activities. In ancient days the street played the part of our public parks and gardens – the scene for social activities and civic and religious gatherings (Mumford, 1966). Public parades, coronations, religious events, cultural events and political demonstrations have all taken place in streets around the world over the years and continue to do so. The Mardi Gras, Notting Hill Festival and the Via Dolorosa are all examples of such street celebrations.

Acclaimed work investigating the 'livability and quality of the street environment' was undertaken thirty years ago (Appleyard and Lintell, 1972). Factors investigated included the absence of noise, stress, pollution, levels of social interaction, territorial extent, environmental awareness and safety in relation to three levels of traffic – heavy, medium and light – on streets in San Francisco. The research revealed that all of these aspects had an inverse correlation with traffic intensity. Despite this being a small

6.12 *Slower speeds mean less accidents*

study it has been acclaimed by many as a significant piece of work, including the government's Urban Task Force (1999). The study concluded that the intensive levels of traffic on 'heavy' streets led to stress and withdrawal, and some families with children had moved elsewhere to avoid the situation. The people who did live on this street only used it when they needed to in order to visit friends and acquaintances and predominantly lived in the back of their houses. Those who lived on the street with light traffic saw it as their own territory, had many friends and acquaintances on the street and were aware of details of the street environment. The people who lived on the street with moderate traffic had satisfaction levels between the residents of the other two streets. Three hypotheses were suggested for future study. The first was that heavy traffic is associated with more residents renting rather than buying their properties and fewer families with children. Second, heavy traffic was associated with less social activity, while light traffic is associated with 'a rich social climate and a strong sense of community' (Appleyard and Lintell, 1972). Third, it is suggested that heavy traffic is associated with a withdrawal from the physical environment, while residents on the street with light traffic expressed 'an acute, critical, and appreciative awareness of and care for the physical environment' (Appleyard and Lintell, 1972). The hypotheses suggested in this research have in some instances been accepted as truth – the use of culs-de-sac in many housing areas and the current move towards home zones are two of the expressions of the theory of lower levels of traffic resulting in increased social activity, including children's play (Appleyard and Lintell, 1972).

Opportunities for play in the street have been recorded by a variety of different authors. In America the lack of access to parks for poor children, even to New York's Central Park – to the displeasure of its designers Olmsted and Vaux – at the end of the nineteenth and the beginning of the twentieth century led to many children playing on the street – and these children were not restrained from doing so by parents. Streets were, though, still considered to be primarily for commercial use, but by 1920 sixty streets in New York were closed for children's play during certain hours (Gaster, 1992).

More recently discussions with parents in Edinburgh have revealed that traffic on streets is a disincentive to the development of community relationships (Kelly, unpublished). Where roads are large and busy they are perceived as a physical barrier and restrict the development of relationships. Someone from a discussion group suggested that the development of the playground community – briefly discussed earlier in this chapter – may be as a result of the reduction of the use of streets for social interaction by adults and play by children.

In America there is now something of a trend towards reclaiming the streets for pedestrians (Abrams and Ozdil, 2000). To some extent this has come about as part of the redevelopment of main street and the 'Main Streets' programme to revitalise downtown areas.

One of the developments relating to the concern about the increase in cars on the street is the report 'Designing Streets for People', produced by the Institute of Civil Engineers on behalf of the Urban Design Alliance (Institute of Civil Engineers, 2000). Following a discussion about the importance of the street to daily lives and a selection of views from relevant professionals about the current and future status of the street, suggestions and recommendations are made. First it is important to state that this work has defined a difference between roads and streets. Roads are recognised as primarily being for motor vehicles, but with dual purposes, while streets are defined as being primarily for people. From this premise the importance of streets, as part of the current debate and action as an aspect of urban regeneration, is acknowledged. A Street Excellence Model (SEM) is suggested as an opportunity of dealing in a comprehensive manner with the many complex issues of the street and the range of individuals and organisations that might have an interest in the street. The overall aim of such processes would be to improve the management of the street and to empower communities to be involved in these improvement processes, thus realising streets designed for people (Institute of Civil Engineers, 2000).

6.13 *Watering plants at a
city farm*

6.14 *Children enjoy a visit
to a city farm*

6.15 *Incidental spaces are
important*

6.13

6.14

The public realm of the city is where children can meet other people, imitate them and learn from them. Within this public realm the street and associated spaces especially can offer such social opportunities. Traditionally such spaces were where communities celebrated events and maintained rituals and ceremonies. This provided a sense of belonging and trust and was a good thing. The increasing dominance of the car in many cities, accompanied by the neglect of public spaces and the loss of residents from the centre of cities, has resulted in physical and social decline in many city centres. In some European cities there has been a deliberate attempt to reverse this situation by improving the social, physical and economic fabric of the city centre. Many of these have thus improved opportunities for children's social interaction with adults (Lennard and Lennard, 1992).

The second exhibition of concern about the dominance of cars on streets in England is the acknowledgement that Home Zones should be considered. Home Zones are a concept that has been developed in the Netherlands and Germany over a period of years and has been campaigned for in England for some time by groups such as Transport 2000 and the Children's Play Council. 'A home zone is a street or groups of streets designed primarily to meet the interests of pedestrians and cyclists rather than motorists, opening up the street for social use' (Hanson-Kahn, 2000). Nine pilot projects were set up in England and Wales in 1999 and are being monitored for criteria such as volume of vehicles, speed of vehicles, numbers of accidents, parking provision and activity and pedestrian flows and activity. In early 2002 £30 million was distributed to a further 61 Home Zone schemes, as a response to the interest shown in many local authority Local Transport Plans, and as an assertion of the value and benefit that Home Zones are to the local communities.

Many people in the urban situation live in fear and urban policies should be developed in order to instil a sense of trust in the city (Worpole, 1999). This need for a sense of trust has been taken further as far as children are concerned. It has been suggested that in order for children to feel that they can freely use the streets they need to have trust in the city in the form

of trust in the street, trust in peers, trust in parents and trust in strangers (Woolley *et al.*, 2001). Home Zones may be one way of engendering this trust by returning some streets to being more of a social than a vehicular experience.

City farms

City farms are available in some urban locations. They give an opportunity for experience with farm animals together with other forms of nature and are considered important as an educational resource for children and as a community resource for adults.

During the last thirty years many city farms have developed across the UK. The first to be initiated in England was the Kentish Town City Farm, in 1972, which developed from a squat in disused stables (Nicholson-Lord, 1987). There are now more than twenty in the London area alone. Others have sprung up in locations such as Cardiff, Newcastle and Middlesborough. In Sheffield the Heeley City Farm has the benefits of a café/community centre, a herb garden and a plant nursery, while in Bristol at Windmill Hill there is a farmshop, a café and opportunities for those more isolated in society to participate in crafts and other activities. During the late 1970s and early 1980s there was an exponential growth in the number of city farms across the country, but with the subsequent increase in land values local authorities became reluctant to release suitable land for other farm developments. The National Federation of City Farms was launched in 1980 with thirty-three members (Nicholson-Lord, 1987). The Federation of City Farms (1998) estimates that one new farm is opening up each year. There are now 64 city farms in the UK ranging in size from 0.1 hectare to 37 hectares. Such farms have to meet all animal welfare requirements and the Federation provides support and advice in a range of areas.

Such schemes have provided an educational link for predominantly deprived areas with rural occupations and connections. They also return derelict land to a positive use, have

6.15

lower running costs than traditional parks and are not usually serious targets for vandalism because of the sense of ownership developed by the community (Hough, 1995).

Incidental spaces and natural green space

In addition to the formally designed open spaces available to the public it is important to acknowledge that incidental spaces can be used as they provide a range of opportunities for people in the city, including play for children. This has clearly been the case with community gardens, discussed earlier, where such facilities have often sprung up on plots of land following the demolition of other buildings.

When temporary sites with wildlife that have been accessible to the public are developed, they are often missed. The loss felt by the community is a result of the amenity value that such a space provides together with the shared public value that has been attributed to such sites (Box and Harrison, 1993). Such sites have been identified as being rich with wildlife habitats and geological features. The term 'natural green space' has been suggested for such spaces that are awaiting redevelopment but which have been 'colonised by spontaneous assemblages of plants and animals' (Box and Harrison, 1993). In areas lacking in open space these natural green spaces can contribute to the recreational facilities of an area, being valued and used by both children and adults. Although these spaces are valued by individuals and communities, this is often not reflected in the statutory system of planning. Despite this, in some parts of the country, such as the West Midlands, Greater London, the Black Country and Bristol, strategies have been developed that acknowledge the importance of natural green spaces and the need for their proximity to people. In some locations such spaces have been designated as Local Nature Reserves and it is suggested that this could increasingly happen as a method of supporting local communities and acknowledging the value that they place on such incidental but important spaces (Box and Harrison, 1993).

In addition to these natural green spaces there are incidental spaces that are designed and /or managed. Such spaces might include small areas by a road junction or some local shops or even a bus stop. The smallest of these may include only one seat and a tree.

CHAPTER SEVEN

Civic urban open spaces

Introduction

The largest number of urban open spaces discussed in this section of the book fall into the third category of civic urban open spaces. This does not necessarily mean that because this section has the largest number of types of spaces these are the most important or valued by either individuals or communities. It may well be that domestic and neighbourhood urban open spaces are more valued than civic ones, but this is a question that research has not yet sought to answer. The open spaces within this group naturally fall into the separate groupings of commercial, health and education, transport and recreational, so this chapter is divided up to discuss the spaces in this order.

Commercial urban open spaces include squares, plazas, water features and office grounds. Squares, plazas and spaces associated with offices have an obvious commercial link, while water features – not necessarily a space within their own right but often an element within a space – may not, and some might argue that these should have been included with health or recreational open spaces or even within the neighbourhood category. Of course water features of different types can exist in any type of urban open space, but they have been included with civic commercial spaces because they are often to be found within the setting of a square or office grounds. With the evidence of the preference that people have for water – some of which is mentioned in chapter two – it is perhaps surprising that water features are not included more, in other types of urban open spaces, than they are.

Hospital grounds and university campuses seem to form a sub-grouping and although courtyards and roof gardens could be, and sometimes are, associated with spaces such as offices, they are included here because there is a tradition of these types of spaces being associated with these two major types of buildings. Some, of course, would argue that roof gardens should be in the domestic category because of the many opportunities that there are for green roofs, of one type or another, within housing areas, but for the purposes of this book roof gardens will be discussed within the civic health and education section.

Urban open spaces relating to the transport system of a conurbation can easily be overlooked, or even completely forgotten about. Some of these spaces are no longer used for their original purpose – such as some ports and docks – while transport and waterway corridors such as rivers, canals, railways and roads are still primarily used as part of the transport network and in the case of the last are constantly increasing in volume.

The final group within this civic category is that of recreational urban open spaces. It can be argued that to some extent all urban open spaces are recreational because both passive and active recreation can take place in all of them, but in this book civic recreational urban open spaces are those which hold specific importance for a conurbation, not just a neighbourhood, and where the primary use by people – rather than the desire of the creator of the spaces – is for recreation. Cemeteries could, in one way, be taken as a classification by themselves. But they are definitely civic in nature and after the short time spent at a graveside for a funeral the most time spent in such a space is for emotional recreation, or even play for some children; thus cemeteries have been included as part of the civic recreational grouping of urban open spaces.

The physical and social differences between civic and both neighbourhood and domestic urban open spaces are significant. Physically civic urban open spaces, unless one happens to live within the central business district of a conurbation or on the doorstep of, say, a golf course or hospital, tend to be physically further from home than either domestic or neighbourhood urban open spaces. Thus for most users there has to be a very specific decision to visit civic spaces or the buildings associated with them. This decision might be part of the daily routine of going to work at an office, a cyclical decision such as visiting a university each term, though different parts of the campus on a daily basis, or of visiting a golf course on a weekly basis. There might also be spaces that are visited on an occasional basis, for a day out at a regenerated dockside or a funeral at a cemetery.

It can be assumed, perhaps incorrectly, that most of the visits to civic urban open spaces will be by choice, although some of the visits might be out of necessity, as defined by Gehl (1987) and discussed in the introduction to this book. In this case though, necessary visits might include going for a hospital appointment or a meeting in an office. In addition there will be some instances when the visit to the civic urban space will not be a specific decision but a result of a different activity. This might particularly be the case for squares where one might be shopping in town and end up in the square for a breath of fresh air, away from the commercial pressure of the retail environment.

Another key factor about the physical nature of civic urban open spaces is the way in which people get to them. Due to the distance of civic urban open spaces from most people's homes most people are not likely to walk to these spaces. The methods of transport may be public, trains or more likely buses, or private in the form of bicycles or more likely cars. These forms of transport create their own spatial issues within the urban context with the requirements for bus stops, stations, car parks and secure cycle storage areas. In the way that the decision to visit any particular civic urban open space may be voluntary, necessary or accidental, the form of transport used to reach the space may also be voluntary, necessary or accidental. Again, perhaps more than with neighbourhood urban open spaces, cost, travel and accessibility, together with concerns and even fear about the safety of visiting civic urban open spaces, may be an issue for some.

Socially, civic urban open spaces provide the greatest opportunity, over and above domestic and neighbourhood urban open spaces, for meeting a huge variety of people – or none – in the urban context. So in civic spaces one might not only meet family, friends, neighbours and acquaintances – or unnamed faces – but a whole range of people from other neighbourhoods within the conurbation who are completely unknown, that is strangers. Having said this, many people go to civic urban open spaces with family or friends, but while there the likelihood is that the percentage of people that they will know will be less than in either domestic or neighbourhood spaces, although, of course, this is likely to vary from space to space and even from visit to visit. More than domestic or neighbourhood urban open spaces then, civic urban open spaces allow for the opportunity of anonymity for a period of time. Such anonymity can be a welcome break from the daily or weekly round of tasks, but of course the social and familiar aspects that may predominate in domestic and neighbourhood urban open spaces are also available to experience in civic urban open spaces.

So what of the benefits of civic urban open spaces? The different benefits of urban open spaces, discussed in chapters one to four of this book, will be available to some extent or another in civic urban open spaces, although it is likely that different benefits may predominate in different spaces. Thus social benefits might be more dominant in recreational civic urban open spaces than commercial spaces, where opportunities for active and passive recreation abound. In addition these recreational spaces can provide opportunities for improving physical and mental health. Opportunities for health benefits, as discussed in chapter two, are available not only in recreational spaces but also in health and educational spaces as well as office grounds. Indeed mental health benefits are available, to some extent, in all of the civic urban open spaces. The environmental benefits of civic urban open spaces will depend upon the design of each individual space and the proportion of hard materials to soft. Often commercial spaces are dominated by hard surfacing with limited vegetation and thus afford less opportunities for environmental benefits, while health, education, transport and particularly recreational civic urban open spaces tend to support more vegetation and thus contribute in a greater way to the amelioration of the urban climate and offer opportunities for wildlife, as discussed in chapter three. As for economic benefits, these may be more relevant to the commercial than to the other types of civic urban open spaces and yet spaces that, for instance, are the result of regenerated docksides might well contribute to the local

7.1   *St Mark's Square, Venice*

6.1

7.1

economy by attracting tourists from the local or a distant conurbation. Of course all of these spaces require maintenance and management, and thus jobs may be created in these sectors of the economy.

Many of the benefits and opportunities outlined in section one of this book can be found across the different civic urban open spaces, with some of the benefits and opportunities being more available in some of the spaces than others. With respect to the people one is likely to encounter in civic urban open spaces, there will be a higher percentage of unknown people and perhaps greater opportunities for anonymous moments.

Commercial

Squares

Is it a square or is it a plaza? Does the definition of these titles reflect the age, location, use, or size of the space?

'Without the square there is no city...
There is no substitute for the spontaneous social conflux whose atoms unite, precisely as citizens of the city'
P and P Goodman
(Communitas, 1960)

Squares are one of the oldest types of open space within a city and thus usually exist in the older parts of cities. Market squares were initially part of the temple precincts and therefore not accessible to all – increased access developed in later years. The separation of the marketplace from the temple precinct took place in Mesopotamia and Greece. The market was a by-product of the 'coming together of consumers who had many other reasons for assembling than merely doing business' (Mumford, 1966). Thus the marketplace became the place where people met or gathered and where news was exchanged. This social function of the marketplace has continued to develop in a range of urban open spaces. Many mediaeval European towns had a square around which were major public buildings – a church, customs house, hospital, town hall. In many instances when Europeans from these cities voyaged across the oceans and landed in America they built new towns and cities with the market square at the heart of the development (Loukaitou-Sideris and Banerjee, 1998).

Most squares are clearly defined by the built form that surrounds them, and are in fact contained by the walls of such buildings. In most instances the city square is linked to the street pattern of the city centre. In America the square may be the result of the omission of buildings within a square of the grid system of the city. In a European city the square may be purposely designed into the city fabric or may just be the widening of a road as it diverges around a landmark such as a fountain, a memorial or a statue (Heckscher, 1977). In some cities, such as Florence, extensions to squares were the result of the demolition of buildings in order to make way for grander schemes. Some of these squares were purely devoted to markets and had residential properties for the different types of traders associated with them – and workshops, arcades and shops. Meanwhile some cities developed the civic square in order to segregate the retailing functions from the civic activities (Girouard, 1985). The use of squares may have been for more than just markets. Fairs and events also took place in these urban spaces and on holidays and festivals activites such as bullfighting, fire-eating, acrobats and fireworks were not unknown. In addition many squares, in different parts of the world, were and are still used as part of a religious ceremony or procession, taking a route through the city. Some of the civic squares would be used as gathering places for the nobility.

We must not forget that some of the styles of design and activities that take place in squares may differ according to custom, culture and religion in different parts of the world. In fact squares, as other public spaces, can symbolise the community and larger society or culture of which it is a part (Carr *et al.*, 1992). One example of such differences is the long-standing tradition that in Paris squares were for public experiences and

7.2 *Plazas can be well used –*
the Broadgate Centre,
London

would therefore not work well as part of a housing layout, whereas in London a square acting as a semi-private garden was perfectly acceptable (Girouard, 1985).

In some instances squares have been used for political activities or when there is social unrest. Such activity continued into the twentieth century with the squares across Germany being used by Hitler for parades and Red Square in Moscow holding the annual May Day parade of the forces for many years. In Paris squares were the setting for student riots in the 1960s and Tiananmen Square in Beijing was the venue for democracy demonstrations in 1989 and celebrations after Beijing was awarded the Olympic games in 2001.

Squares eventually became an important part of some housing developments, and London is perhaps the city where this is most frequently expressed. London's first formal Renaissance square owed its existence to three people. Charles I was happy to grant permission for the expansion of London, despite Elizabethan restrictions on expansion still being in force. The Earl of Bedford wanted to develop fields behind his own house in the Strand with town houses, for letting. And Inigo Jones, having been greatly influenced by Italian architecture and form, was to design the piazza in Covent Garden. Lincoln's Inn Fields, Leicester Square, Blooms-bury Square, Soho, Red Lion, Saint James's, Grosvenor and Berkeley squares all followed before 1700. Such squares were built by speculators who included aristocrats, merchants, lawyers and builders (Burke, 1971). Some of these have survived the test of time and some have not. In Covent Garden the open space became a market and the housing went into decline. In locations where the open space was in the form of an enclosed garden the housing was more successful (Girouard, 1985).

The success of a contemporary square, though, is not just related to how it was formed, what contains it or what it contains, but also what happens within it. Is it a lively square that holds markets and is of retail significance to the city? Is it a quiet contemplative space for chatting with friends and catching up with the local news or putting the world right? Is it a place for political and social debate? Or might it be a place where all of these activities can happen at different times of the day, or week or year?

Plazas

Plazas are larger urban spaces than squares, not small, confined areas but significant spaces in size. They may be designed for one purpose but used for others. This has particularly been the experience in many American cities over the last forty years. Since 1961 New York City has given bonuses to builders who provide plazas. Ten square feet of commercial space, over and above the amount usually allowed for by zoning, was built for each square foot of plaza. Thus by 1972 20 acres of the world's most expensive space had been developed from the plazas provided with new office space (Whyte, 1980). Some of these plazas, studied as part of the Street Life Project, were identified as attracting many people, especially at lunchtime. But many of the plazas were not used for much except walking across. Plazas have been identified as under-used spaces that tend to be large, ceremonial and monumental by other researchers (Carr et al., 1992). Others have described plazas as 'high-speed footpaths' and as 'an architectural device rather than a social device' (Jensen, 1981). Why are many of these spaces perceived as so under-used?

For three years the Street Life Project studied 16 plazas, although most of the major conclusions had been reached after six months of study. Unsurprisingly, office workers were the dominant user group of these city centre spaces. The most used plazas were ones where social activity was to the fore: lovers met, people were in groups, and friends met to catch up on the latest news. These well-used spaces not only afforded opportunities for social activity but also attracted more individuals than the less well used spaces did. More women than men were observed in these well-used spaces, reflecting a consideration that they have probably chosen to use the space because it is a well-designed one, and because they felt relatively safe. Throughout the day the cycle of life is represented by the numbers of people using the space and is reflected in the main

7.2

peak of use between the hours of noon and two o'clock in the afternoon. During this peak time the numbers of users varied according to the weather and season. Sitting, standing and movement patterns were all studied in this research. Factors such as sun, aesthetics, events at eye level, sense of enclosure, shape and amount of space were among the many elements of design that were studied. The most important factor identified for users was that of 'sitability' and yet it was identified that many of the plazas studied lacked basic amenities such as seating opportunities, food concessions, shade, water elements and general landscape (Whyte, 1980).

Further research identified that the design of the plaza is important with respect to its use and the context and location of the plaza are significant. Thus five plazas in Minneapolis were investigated. Again these showed that there was a peak in use during a somewhat longer lunchtime period from 11 am to 2 pm. Plazas with more restaurants, bars, offices and car parking were used more than those with a lower level of such provisions. In addition plazas associated with housing and department stores had lower levels of use, while those associated with banks had the lowest level of use. It was concluded that the land use surrounding the plaza had an impact on the use of the plaza itself (Chidister, 1986).

A study of three plazas in downtown Los Angeles has confirmed the often sterile nature of such places. The first plaza is designed as an artificial 'hole in the ground', sweeping people away from the street, and is associated with retail use. The second is designed as a formal garden and is associated with corporate use. The third plaza is more of a ceremonial space and is associated with cultural uses. In all three plazas it was clear that design features such as enclosing walls, blank façades and major entrances through car parking had resulted in inward-looking plazas and provided a defensive style of design. In addition the spaces are rigid, which does not allow for the changing needs of users (Loukaitou-Sideris and Banerjee, 1998).

Water features

Water is an essential component of human bodies, carrying minerals and composing about 60 per cent of an average person's body weight. It also provides for other desires and senses. Water features often appear in squares or plazas, places that one might consider to be part of adult – business and retail – life. But water features also attract children and should be provided for their enjoyment and enhancement of their life as well.

Initially water in urban areas was there for functional reasons such as drinking and as part of drainage systems. The first

7.3 *Water provides sensual experiences*

7.3

fountains in Rome were utilitarian and it was not until the second half of the sixteenth century that ornamental fountains, some very elaborate, were purpose built (Girouard, 1985). The increase in the use of fountains at this time was made possible by new supplies of water and new fountains that were not of the classical design. In Rome many garden fountains were developed in this period, bringing together art and nature. Some of these fountains appeared to be naturalistic – but often, ironically, incorporated the river within the fountain in an unnatural manner (MacDougall, 1994). A survey taken in 312–315 revealed that Rome had some 700 public pools or basins and 500 fountains from 130 collecting heads or reservoirs (Mumford, 1966) – a considerable number of water features for a city of nearly five acres.

Although Great Britain is an island country, with many historical relationships with the sea, the water that surrounds us, we as a nation have generally exploited water only for its life support, waste disposal, industrial and power generation properties and potential (Winter, 1992). Apart from a few wealthy families, such as the Devonshires at Chatsworth House, the majority of the population has not utilised water for play or recreation apart from within swimming pools. In fact many of our communities fear water and a preponderance of railings and danger notices has prevailed. A healthy attitude to being able to deal with open water in urban areas has been replaced by an over-cautious approach. This is despite the fact that much research has revealed that water in the environment is a desirable element for many people (see Ulrich, 1981; Purcell et al., 1994).

Preference between different types of water bodies has clearly been identified in a project undertaken with 259 psychology students in North Carolina. Mountain lakes and rivers were highly valued, whereas swampy and stagnant areas were not. The clarity and freshness of the preferred elements can be applied in the urban situation by the creation of water sculptures and symbols of 'rushing water'. The research revealed that the waterscapes that were most preferred made sense –

that is the scene 'hangs together' and provides complexity and mystery – a scene containing a lot of elements with promise of further interest. In addition spaciousness was identified as a preference. Thus water that provides a long view, or can be seen at the end of a view, is preferable (Herzog, 1985). In addition the importance of water features in the town centre for young people has been identified by research in the UK. In particular young people felt most aggrieved when in one location the water features were taken out and replaced by planters. 'There used to be a little fountain ... now they've given up on it and concreted it over' (Woolley et al., 1999).

Water in an urban situation can provide three sensual opportunities – sight, sound and touch – although designs and management of water features do not always allow for these experiences. Should water in public places be for ornamental use only? Or should people be allowed to experience the water more than just by looking at it? Often safety is given as the reason for keeping people away from water, but careful design and management can provide water features that can be experienced more than just visually and audially. The case study of the Peace Gardens in Sheffield is a good example of an urban open space, in the city centre, where people can experience water through all the senses.

Office grounds

Offices are definitely an adult experience – but are not experienced by all adults – only those who work in such locations. The development of business parks in the 1980s is surely a reflection of the importance of the external environment to the employer and the workforce.

For those who are in work, the environment in which they work is significant because of the amount of time spent in it. If one is working a thirty-seven hour week over forty-six weeks each year this is a total of over 1,700 hours a year. Perhaps we do not give enough significance to the importance of that working environment – particularly the physical environment and the impact it can have on one's mental and physical well-being and ability to undertake one's work, as discussed in chapter two.

Among the psychological issues that can affect performance at work are motivation, job satisfaction and well-being. There may be some overlapping of these issues, but surely it is clear that employers should attend to these in order to support the best response or best value from their employees. One element of well-being relates to the environment in which people work and research has addressed this issue. Windows and the view from them play an important role in this environmental consideration. Not only do windows provide light, sunshine, information about the weather and the opportunity to see what is happening in the outside world, they may also provide the opportunity for a restorative view. If nature is present in that view, even if only in the form of a small number of trees, then there appears to be a difference in job satisfaction and challenge together with overall health (Kaplan, 1993). Participants rated job challenge, frustration, task enthusiasm, patience, life satisfaction and general health higher when they had a natural rather than a built view from their office window.

More recently employees of a wine-producing organisation in Southern Europe were studied with respect to their responses to access to a view and different types of views from a window (Leather et al, 1998). One hundred employees completed questionnaires that monitored levels of job strain, illumination, sunlight penetration, view from the window, job satisfaction, intention to quit and sense of well-being. The responses revealed that a wide range of environmental situations were being experienced by the workforce, ranging from dim to very bright levels of light and no view of rural elements from a window to a full view of rural elements from a window. Several positive benefits were identified for those employees experiencing a view from a window and particularly a view with rural elements. (I suggest that the term 'rural elements' in this research is more or less synonymous with the term 'natural' in other research reported in this book.) The existence of a view was positively correlated with job satisfaction

as well as relating to decreased levels of symptoms of impaired well-being. It was also clear that having a greater view of rural elements helped to buffer the negative impact of job strain or the intention to quit the job. Thus as well as a view of rural elements being preferred by respondents, this research revealed that it had other beneficial impacts in increasing job satisfaction and sense of well-being and reducing the intention to leave a job.

In Scotland, the Scottish Enterprise Network, together with its twelve local enterprise companies has been developing economic regeneration through the delivery of innovative, good quality projects. One of the requirements of projects funded in this way is that the landscape design must be related to clear economic objectives. A range of science parks have been constructed, where the landscape structure has been developed before the infrastucture and built form. In some instances it is clear that the private sector has accepted that there are benefits of good landscape design being carried out before the development (White, 1999). The Edinburgh Park case study in section three is an example of this approach.

Health and education

Hospital grounds

Hospitals have been important as places of healing for thousands of years and the potential therapeutic benefits afforded by the grounds of a hospital have been acknowledged since ancient civilisations. Around 500 BC Greek *asklepieia* were built with a long axis oriented east to west, from a northern wall, in order that patients could enjoy the sunshine from the southerly direction and dream – at that time believed to be a cure for illness. Roman military hospitals, *valetudinarium*, were designed to aid recovery of injured soldiers. Some of these structures consisted of a series of concentric rectangular wards with a courtyard as a central feature. Such a courtyard could offer opportunities for 'fresh air and ambulation' (Westphal, 2000), considered to be important in recovery. Other cultures and civilisations also contributed to the concept and development of the healing landscape. Nature has been relied upon as a healing tool since at least 2500 BC in China, where the philosophy is built upon the five elements of the universe: wood, fire, metal, earth and water. The key to health is believed to be the keeping of these elements in balance, since each element represents emotion and temperament. In India a relationship between health and nature was acknowledged as long ago as 2500 BC. Ayurveda, meaning the science of life, was in fact a bringing together of herbal traditional influences from the cultures of the Persians, the Greeks and the Moguls (Burnett, 1997).

The term 'hospital' evolved from the word 'hospice' in the Middle Ages. Hospices were built, from as early as 300 AD, for pilgrims who wished to seek repentance and thus be spiritually and physically healed. The pilgrims would receive hospitality from monasteries or convents with facilities such as herb gardens, and in return would work the vineyards or gardens. With the onset of the Renaissance, hospitals were less dominated by religion and public hospitals of two or three storeys and with courtyards became more familiar (Westphal, 2000). The concept of physic gardens was also developed at this time, when universities first emerged (Burnett, 1997). By the end of the nineteenth century the importance of courtyards, gardens and open spaces associated with hospitals had been all but lost. With the onset of the industrial revolution and modern building materials and techniques, twentieth century architecture has also tended to ignore the beneficial effects of external spaces, although there was increasing concern about this issue towards the end of the century (Westphal, 2000). Advances in medical treatment may also have had an impact on the external environment, with money not being made available for the latter because of its forgotten importance. It has been argued that 'medicines and machines have been given top priority over views and one's connection to the healing qualities of nature' (Burnett, 1997).

More recently than the observations about health and well-being of Olmsted, Lever and Cadbury, and more specifically than the benefits to health that are afforded by the provision of open space in urban areas in general, it is possible to consider the situation with respect to the setting of hospitals. Some hospitals have benefited from being built upon sites with parkland-type settings, while others have had gardens and estates that were planted with 'imagination and skill' (Hosking and Haggard, 1999). Yet it has been argued that modern hospitals, those which are not purely confined to being a built form upon a small urban site, do not use their land as well as they might do. Reasons for this less than perfect management of land include the fact that estates staff often are responsible for buildings, and give priority to these. Thus traditional layouts and formal gardens have been lost, and a low value is given to the aesthetic benefits grounds can provide. Money, being constrained, is not considered to be well spent on the external environment (Hosking and Haggard, 1999). It has been suggested that allotments could be provided within hospital grounds, helping to cater for the increased interest in this facility, while orchards should be planted only on sites that are established as having a long-term future. Herb and wildlife gardens within hospital grounds can provide the opportunity for sensual experiences and direct contact with nature in the form of ducks and plants. In some, perhaps less frequent circumstances, hospital grounds have cemeteries, specifically for the burial of small babies. All of these options are available to those who design and manage hospital grounds.

Patients who undergo surgery are considered to be particularly at risk of anxiety and stress. Research has been carried out in order to study differences between the recovery of surgical patients in rooms with a view of 'nature' and a view of the brown brick wall of a building (Ulrich, 1984). Pairs of patients undergoing the same operation who were as close to each other as possible in variables such as age, gender, weight, tobacco consumption and previous hospitalisation were selected for inclusion in the study. One of each pair was allocated to the rooms with different types of views and their recovery from the operation was monitored. The patients who were in rooms with a view of nature appeared to benefit in two different ways.

First, their stay in hospital was shorter than that of the patients who were in a room with a view of the brick wall. Second, the former group tended to have a lower incidence of minor post-surgical complications, including receiving weaker painkillers than the latter group. Ulrich concludes that 'these findings strongly suggest that the view of the trees had comparatively therapeutic influences on the patients' (Ulrich, 1984).

The quality of the view from a window has also been shown to be a significant factor in the recovery of patients in physical medicine and rehabilitation wards in hospitals (Verderber, 1986). One hundred and twenty-five staff and one hundred and twenty-five patients, of three months or more, were shown a series of sixty-four photographs varying from windowless to a high level of windows. In addition respondents were asked to respond to ten written questions 'concerning preference, self-ratings of one's general satisfaction with window's in one's unit and the extent to which patients and staff engaged in behaviour judged to be associated with "windowness"' (Verderber, 1986). The photographs revealed that views of trees and lawns, the surrounding neighbourhood, people outside, and near and distant views were the most desired views from therapy rooms. Views that provided opportunities for activities outside were particularly important. This preference for external views with landscape and people in them should be taken into account when siting and designing hospitals.

A most moving example of the benefits of a view from a hospital window was recorded following the death of a research student in Colorado (Baird and Bell, 1995). Some of Carol Baird's experiences of treatment in an oncology unit and in an isolation unit, following her diagnosis of leukaemia, were recorded as part of her dissertation. Her observations were recorded by her family, friends and mentors during this difficult time. Carol clearly expressed a preference for a room with a window with a view of the hospital grounds and distant mountains, ironically with a cemetery in the middle ground, over a room with little view, each time she was admitted to the oncology unit. In addition when in the isolation unit, which was depressing, Carol

was pleased to be moved to a room with a more natural view – a move which was associated with an improved affective state and change of being from despair to optimism.

More recently a study of preferences for different types of activity was undertaken at a psychiatric hospital in Guelph, Ontario (Barnhart et al., 1998). A series of photographs of the hospital grounds were taken with different degrees of 'naturalness' and enclosure. The images were sorted into categories – natural, mixed or built and open, mixed or enclosed. Images were arranged to cover the different combinations of the categories and shown upon a computer. Both patients and staff were then invited to give first, second and third preferences, from nine images, for a range of active, mixed active and passive activities that they might undertake in the settings. Active activities included walking, talking or standing with friends, having a smoke or being by oneself, while mixed active activities included talking, visiting and eating lunch and passive activities included a variety of sitting experiences. It was clear from the results and analysis of these that both staff and patients preferred natural settings for both active and passive activities. In addition they indicated a preference for open settings for passive activities and enclosed settings for active activities.

The impact that the surroundings can have on patients is well understood by Hosking and Haggard (1999), who identify four aesthetics – psychological, spiritual, physical and intellectual – which can to a greater or lesser extent be 'stimulated, encouraged, maintained or extinguished' (Hosking and Haggard, 1999) by one's surroundings. In relating this to the hospital environment they discuss ways in which architecture, landscape, art, the health profession and the complexities of the British National Health Service can impact upon patients. The importance of the external physical environment is emphasised by their discussion about gardens, allotments, orchards, herb and healing gardens, wildlife gardens, cemeteries, play opportunities for children, accommodation of animals and the provision of 'secret gardens', all within the context of hospital grounds. The poor state in which some grounds are maintained was considered by Hosking and Haggard (1999) to be detrimental to patients' experiences, and it is suggested that all hospitals should have a professional team that includes a good architect, an interior designer, an arts co-ordinator and a landscape architect in order to facilitate an ongoing programme relating to the built environment and its surroundings.

Outpatients, women in labour and visitors to hospitals are also a significant consideration, for as Churchman and Fieldhouse (1990) state such people are often in a stressed and sometimes confused state when they arrive at a hospital. Thus the relationship of car parking, access to and from public transport and access points into the buildings themselves need to be clear and easy to understand. This should be an important consideration in the master planning of a hospital site. In addition access for services, not only ambulances but deliveries of goods and food, need to be taken into account in the planning, design and management processes.

A hospital site must surely be one of the busiest places in an urban centre. People do not just fall ill or need medical attention and care between the hours of nine and five. In order to cover nursing provision for twenty-four hours in the day nursing, medical and support staff, working shifts, arrive and leave a hospital at different times of the day. Their security during these times is of utmost importance and the design of the external layout of hospital grounds can have an impact on their actual and perceived safety. The layout and design of paths from buildings to bus stops and car parks, together with the use of vegetation in planting schemes and levels and types of lighting, must all be considered with respect to the movement of people within and to the facilities.

Despite the fact that many babies are born in hospital in the UK these days, such babies are not likely to experience the hospital grounds – if such grounds exist. With increasing pressure for mothers to return home as soon as possible after the birth they hardly have time to appreciate their surroundings. As we travel through life we may be unfortunate enough to require the services of a hospital – perhaps for an appendectomy or tonsill-ectomy as a child, perhaps to set a broken limb as a teenager or to treat some illness or accident later in life. With the increasingly ageing population the hospital environment will become even more important for larger numbers of older people. Perhaps we might consider how much importance we give to the stimulation of the senses – sight, sound, texture, smell and taste – when people are recovering from illness or operations. We give flowers to stimulate sight and smell, we give fruit or chocolate to stimulate taste and smell. Why then do we not insist that these senses are stimulated by the environment of the hospital grounds themselves? There is much potential for the provision of good quality and well designed and managed hospital grounds to provide for the benefits discussed in section one and in particular for the mental health benefits of chapter two to be realised.

University campuses

The Oxbridge and red-brick universities tend to have been developed on a series of sites, with many colleges within the former having access to privileged courtyards and waterside spaces, while the latter generally have a range of small open spaces associated with them. Some of the white-tiled universities of the 1970s, such as Sussex, East Anglia, York, Essex and Stirling, were developed within the setting of existing estates of large country houses or even castles (Epstein, 1978). These campus universities are characterised by their surrounding and inter-building landscape that is considered a valuable asset to the property and the learning experience, as can be seen in the case study of Heriot-Watt University in section three.

However, with increasing competition for students between higher and further educational establishments some institutes have begun to address the quality of their environment and landscape (Penning-Rowsell, 1999). Citing the redesign of a car park into a temporary landscaped area at the old Working Men's College in Stratford, London and the design of a hierarchy of spaces and subspaces at the new Shoreditch site of the Hackney Community College, she comments that, 'a campus that looks good, with bright new designs, can pull in the numbers [of students] that make all the difference' (Penning-Rowsell, 1999). Technology in the form of websites now increasingly include a virtual tour of the campus, and research on student choice of universities indicates how important image and impression are on such choices.

In chapter two, we saw that following an examination students restorative capacity was increased with views of nature. Other research with students has included a study to identify whether natural views as opposed to urban views have an impact on the restoration of the attention of students. Students involved in the research all inhabited rooms, in university-owned and managed accommodation, with a view, ranging from being all natural, through mostly natural and mostly built to all built. A series of measures were administered to identify ability to direct attention, while other possible variables had been eliminated during selection of the sample. Generally it was found that students who had a natural view from their window were more able to direct their attention than those with less natural views (Tennessen and Crimprich, 1995). In order to successfully master the different demands placed upon students in the university situation the provision of a view of nature from the window in their room would be a benefit, helping their directed attention or concentration.

With the government seeking to increase the number of students studying at universities across the UK, the experience of the university campus will have an impact on the daily lives of an increasing proportion of our population. Even if changes to funding for students forces more to study at their local university they will still experience the internal and external environment of their educational establishment regularly. Thus open spaces associated with universities will become important to increasing numbers of people who will have the opportunity to benefit from familial, social and anonymous moments as they choose.

Courtyards

From ancient times, across the world, courtyards have been part of the urban and civic fabric. Such courtyards have usually been part of the structure of buildings with a specific purpose: religious, official, military or domestic. In pre-Hispanic America temples of stepped pyramids with courtyards and large esplanades were built between 1300 and 1200 BC, while temples of the Middle East and Egypt also had courtyards in them (Portland House, 1988). Many Greek towns had an acropolis, initially a fortress containing the king's palace and later a religious centre with the courtyard filled with temples to gods and goddesses (Corbishley, 1995). Chinese palaces of the first century AD had imperial courtyards, while their temples of the seventh century constituted a series of buildings placed around a courtyard and linked by galleries. Buddhist monasteries in Japan, built between the late sixth century and the mid-eighth century had buildings whose location within the courtyard varied, depending upon the time of construction. By the seventeenth century Korea too had temples with individual buildings within courtyards with connecting galleries. In Italy, Spain and Portugal palaces of the fifteenth and sixteenth centuries had courtyards within them. Islamic architecture too has made good use of courtyards, some influenced by the architecture of Eastern Asia, with courtyards often being surrounded by arcades, within a mosque (Portland House, 1988).

Courtyards as part of a defence mechanism, and therefore having a military purpose, have been used by many different cultures. One could even argue that cities and entire countries could be considered to be a form of courtyard when they are surrounded by a significant wall. Thus Jericho, built some 10,000 years ago and believed to be the earliest city built, and Catal Huyuk in Turkey, almost as old, were defended by their city walls (Wood, 1994). The people of Mycenae and Judah, together with those of many other ancient civilisations, built walls to defend themselves. Study of Iron Age forts, such as that on the site of Maiden Castle, in southern England, reveal complex defence systems of earthworks and structures such as ramparts with smaller enclosures, providing domestic-scale courtyards within the major enclosure. Roman forts, Norman forts and Planta-genet castles all included courtyards that were used for military

7.4

purposes as well as daily living. Japanese castles of the fourteenth century onwards, together with French and European castles of the sixteenth century, all included courtyards as an essential component (Day, 1995).

Domestic courtyards have been identified from the first and second centuries BC from models of farm buildings in China. These show buildings symmetrically arranged around a courtyard, supposedly with animals and humans both using the courtyard (Portland House, 1988). Homes of Ancient Greeks would often be built around a courtyard and this would frequently incorporate an altar within it (Freeman, 1996). Many hospitals have traditionally included a courtyard on a domestic scale for the use of patients. The Greek *asklepieia* or hospital included a south-facing courtyard to facilitate the experience of

sunshine and fresh air (Westphal, 2000). Many Middle-Eastern houses would be built around a courtyard structure and in many situations they are still built in this way today.

So what use are courtyards put to in contemporary life in the Western world? I would suggest that modern uses of courtyards are not religious, official or military, but mainly domestic or commercial. Domestic courtyards may be built into the houses of those who can afford them or into housing complexes for the elderly, where they can enjoy each other's company in the fine weather. Courtyards can still be found in hospital complexes – particularly those built since the 1960s, even if some have been neglected. Otherwise the contemporary use of courtyards tends to be restricted to commercial locations such as offices and banks, although there is much potential for

7.4   *An extensive green roof*

including them within housing develop-ments. It has been claimed that many spaces that could be courtyards are neglected and not developed as such (Johnston and Newton, 1996).

Roof gardens

Despite the fact that it is generally accepted that there are two types of green roofs – intensive and extensive – for most people a roof garden is usually the former. Intensive roof gardens generally require intensive management (Johnston and Newton, 1996), although this depends upon their design and management aims. Intensive roof gardens will typically have paving, growing medium for vegetation, a drainage system, irrigation and vegetation. Such a garden is likely to be accessible by people, even if only a limited number of people from a specific building. The type of planting chosen may depend upon the location, the micro-climate of the roof and the desired effect. Technically one of the major issues that has to be taken into account at the design stage is that of the weight loading of the roof. Growing medium, vegetation, features, water and other elements all have to be considered with respect to the extra weight that they will bring to the structure and engineers must be involved in early discussions about these issues. Intensive roof gardens then tend to be available for use by people.

Extensive green roofs will be briefly mentioned, because although they are less likely to be used by people, they make a visual contribution to the urban skyline and can enhance the progress towards sustainability in a town or city, by their contribution to the amelioration of the urban climate discussed in chapter three. Extensive green roofs are generally developed for their ecological and aesthetic value (Johnston and Newton, 1996). The growing medium is often significantly thinner and the system is designed to be more self-sustaining, with low inputs of water, fertiliser, and plants chosen for their suitability to such conditions. There are few examples of extensive green roofs in the UK but there are many on the continent.

The development of all types of roof gardens in the UK is behind that of continental countries. Despite this as long ago as 1978 roof gardens at the Royal Northern College of Music, the Scottish Widows Office Building in Edinburgh and Gateway House in Basingstoke were reported in the landscape press (Whalley, 1978). More recent examples of roof gardens include the Kensington High Street site, the Ready Mixed Concrete Headquarters in Thorpe, Surrey, and the garden above Cannon Street railway station in London (Johnston and Newton, 1996). The roof garden in the case study, in section three, is somewhat unusual for this country because it is an extensive roof garden above a dual carriageway that has been 'adopted' by a charity. It clearly supports both social and environmental benefits as discussed in chapters one and three.

Somehow the concept of roof gardens, whether extensive or intensive, is not a normal part of the development of new or re-generated areas, despite the fact that they provide opportunities for benefits, especially the environmental benefits discussed in chapter three. Perhaps their use will increase in the future.

Transport

Ports and docks

Ports and docks are generally experienced by fewer numbers of people than they were when they were part of the heart of cities. Today they may be experienced when travelling abroad for holidays or on a day visit to such locations. They are now less a place of employment and more a place of recreation.

At one time ports, originally developed due to their geographic location close to the sea and their physical characteristics of being able to service ships, were a hive of activity. The waterfront associated with a port 'was the most important public arena for the distribution and barter, the giving and taking and making of objects and services that made up the material life of any great port city' (Wakeman, 1996). Goods were landed, sold and distributed and sailors would come and go, making the port a bustle of activity. The port was the economic heart of the city, providing many opportunities for social interaction: the port was both viable and vital. In America in 1920 the ten largest cities were developed as ports and have remained as significant economic centres. Many medieaeval ports, docks or quays were adorned with cranes that facilitated the movements of goods on and off the ships, and which dominated the skyline (Girouard, 1985).

The life and activity of many such ports changed in most Western countries during the 1960s and 1970s, due to a series of technological developments (Wakeman, 1996). The first of these changes was the decline of the fishing industry, brought about by new fishing methods that led to the closing or contraction of some established fishing ports. The second change was due to the way many people travel – instead of going by ship many passengers now travel by air. The third change relates to economies of scale and the introduction of containerisation, developments which had significant physical and ecological impacts. Cargo ships increased significantly in size, with the result that many ports had to be dredged to accommodate the vehicles with a deeper draught. In some locations original ports were all but abandoned for the creation of container terminals on nearby pieces of land, sometimes estuaries with expanses of open land. The development of such areas into 'technological link[s] in a vast transportation network, rather than a distinctive and lengthy terminal point involving complex commercial processes' (Wakeman, 1996) has resulted in losses for the urban fabric. These costs are both social and physical and are expressed as the loss of employment and the physical cost of separation of the port from the city in what has been called a 'retreat from the waterfront' (Wakeman, 1996).

During the 1990s a number of ports around the world were redeveloped, not primarily for traditional commercial purposes but for combinations of commercial, residential, retailing and leisure purposes. Much of this development has no association with the maritime culture or functions originally associated with such ports and does not seek to reconnect the city and the port (Wakeman, 1996). Such redevelopments include ports and docks in Bristol, Liverpool and London. Some of these redevelopments have been successful for economic reasons, but others have been criticised for their lack of involvement of the local community in their redevelopment. The case study, in section three, of Chatham Maritime is one example of regeneration that must surely enhance the local economy through tourism.

Transport and waterway corridors

Transport and waterway corridors can be considered together because in the main they have a commonality of form – linear – as well as use – travel. Such features may be used in daily life, both for working, perhaps driving along a road or travelling on a train, and for relaxation, perhaps on a river boat or narrow boat canal holiday. The speed at which one travels will affect the visual impact these areas might have on an individual. At the same time it must be remembered that these linear urban open spaces can be significant supporters of habitat (Spellerberg and Gaywood, 1993) – although of course that does depend upon the design. Others provide the opportunity for amenity recreation.

Water has been used for carrying goods and people since primitive times; the first canal is thought to have been built around the cataract at Aswan, Egypt, in about 2300 BC. In Britain navigations such as the Fossdyke were created by the Romans, while the Exeter Canal was first cut in 1566. The Sankey Brook (St Helen's Canal) of 1757 was followed by the Bridgewater Canal of 1761 which was built by the Duke of Bridgewater 'to carry coal from his mines at Worsley to the markets of Manchester' (British Waterways, no date). The benefit of canals as a method of transporting goods – one canal boat could carry far more than pack animals on poor roads – was rapidly accepted and the 'Canal Age' followed, with both rich and poor people investing in the development of canals. This had a significant impact on the landscape of eighteenth-century Britain. At the height of the canal network there were some '4,250 miles of inland waterways carrying 30 million tons of goods and raw materials' across Britain (British Waterways, no date). The country's mainly agrarian society was rapidly transformed as many industries that had previously relied upon local materials were able to import a range of supplies, with the result that many small villages grew into towns. Most of today's towns and cities had canals at this time.

The advent of the railway is considered by some to have had a detrimental impact upon the canal system, but freight was still carried on the narrow canals until after the Second World War. The onset of the new motorways, a better quality of road than the packhorse had experienced, had the most significant impact on freight travel on the canals. Some consider that the bad winter of 1962/63 also contributed to the downturn in freight use of the canal system. Waterway enthusiasts Tom Rolt and Robert Aickman founded the Inland Waterways Association in 1946 and as a result of their and other's efforts the priceless national treasure of our waterways has been saved. During the 1960s many canals were abandoned or filled in, sometimes because of the cost of repairing a few bridges. The British Waterways Board was created under the auspices of the Transport Act of 1962 and it is this body that, forty years on, continues to be the steward of the 2,000 miles of British inland waterways. Associated with the waterways is a wealth of heritage artefacts of 2,800 listed buildings and structures; locks; pumping houses; 397 aqueducts; 4,763 bridges; warehouses; toll offices; cottages and sixty tunnels.

Today the use of the canals is more varied. More than 3.5 million tonnes of freight are still transported by the waterways each year, which is the equivalent of 200,000 lorry journeys. Such freight is mainly carried on the wider navigations of the north of England and Scotland and includes timber (British Waterways, 2000a). Leisure and recreation activities have increasingly become associated with the canal network during the last forty years. British Waterways report that 160 million visits are made each year to waterways in Britain. The research section of British Waterways determined that 10 million people made at least one recreational visit to canals and navigable rivers. Angling is one of the most popular activities of the waterside with 100,000 anglers regularly using the waterways, while 7 million cyclist visits a year are made to the waterside. Boating is also a recreational activity enjoyed by many, with 25,000 powered craft privately owned and 1,500 powered boats available for hire across the network (British Waterways, 2000b). In addition there are 150 trip, restaurant and hotel boats available for a range of activities and celebrations. None of these figures include the numbers of people who have free access for walking on the 1,500 miles of towpaths associated with the waterways (British Waterways, no date).

In urban areas many of the activities associated with waterways are readily accessible to the entire population. Angling, walking, boating, sitting and photography are all easily undertaken in association with urban canals. It has been estimated that 50 million journeys a day go directly past, over or on a canal (British Waterways, 2000b), highlighting the fact that these waterways form part of the urban core and fabric of many of our cities.

The importance of waterside regeneration as an asset in the urban environment has been identified, along with the acceptance that headway in such schemes is being made in the UK (Cary-Elwes, 1996). In Birmingham, which boasts of having more canals than Venice, a major partnership programme facilitated the rejuvenation of the area in the city centre around Gas Street Basin. This area alone now attracts over two million visitors a year and has been transformed from a legacy of the Industrial Revolution into a thriving location with pubs, restaurants, hotels, galleries and the International Convention Centre. Trip boats and a floating patisserie and coffee boat add to the many different ways in which one can experience this regenerated waterside.

At this stage rivers could be discussed at length, but many of the benefits they afford are similar to those of canals, so we will give them limited consideration. The passive recreational opportunities of rivers in urban conurbations are considerable, with many people enjoying a walk or watching wildlife or boats

7.5 *Woodland along a*
       highway route

7.5

and associated events. Some of these rivers attract tourists from other locations and thus aid the local economy, whether it is for half a day out or a fortnight's holiday. Yet there are many urban locations where the possible benefits – especially environmental and social – are sadly missed because such rivers are culverted – often under concrete – through the urban framework. There are, no doubt, many missed opportunities for the opening up of such river courses that would add greatly to the quality of life if they were appropriately designed and managed.

The land associated with railway lines was originally designed to cater for steam trains and the associated risk of fire; thus vegetation was planned as low grassland, because the provision of shrubs and trees could significantly increase the risk of fire. The design and management of these linear routes were primarily functional (McNab and Pryce, 1985). With the demise of steam trains the resource-intensive management of the vegetation was no longer essential for safety reasons and by the 1960s maintenance was reduced to the minimum required for the safety of trains and lineside workers. Local concern about apparent random felling of trees, and the visual impact this was having on the landscape, led to Hampshire County Council, Winchester City Council, British Rail and the Nature Conservancy Council commissioning the production of a lineside management plan for the area, which was rapidly followed by a guide to management of the vegetation for the rail network as a whole. More recently the 25 kilometre route of the Victoria to Gatwick Rail Corridor has been enhanced by a partnership which sought to address the issues of lineside management. New woodland was planted and guidelines were drawn up for new planting and management of the woody vegetation in the scheme. Objectives for this scheme included the involvement of local residents in environmental changes, the opening up of views and the reduction of the potential of leaves on the line (National Urban Forestry Unit, 2000b). More recently lineside felling of trees has been reported in other urban locations, such as Sheffield, with Railtrack giving 'leaves on the line' as the reason for a massive felling programme. This has met with local outrage

because of the extensive loss of the environmental benefits experienced by the community. Unlike the above example, there has been no attempt at an overall and agreed management plan for this stretch of railway in South Yorkshire.

The view from the road has been considered with respect to the fact that driving can be considered a stressful experience. A range of research reported by Parsons *et al.* (1998) has shown that not only is driving stressful but that commuting to and from work is also stressful. Such commuter stress has been recorded as increasing blood pressure, lowering job satisfaction, increasing the levels of absence due to illness and decreasing the ability to undertake certain cognitive tests. Thus research was undertaken to clarify whether drives dominated by views with nature or views of built-up areas would have a beneficial impact on stress, the hypothesis being that the former would be more beneficial than the latter (Parsons *et al.*, 1998). In order to try to create a more realistic sense of the environment the recorded drives included a relatively subtle distinction between the two types of roadside environments. Initially baseline recordings of six biological measures, including heart rate and blood pressure, were monitored during the experiment. Participants experienced a brief passive stressor by watching a film about workplace accidents. This was followed by an active stressor of a mathematical nature and finally participants were exposed to the 'drive'. Participants were recorded as being less stressed by the experience of the more natural view from the car than by the view of the urban landscape. In addition the nature-dominated view from the car increased the ability to recover from stress and increased the ability to cope with stress.

The opportunities that existing urban transport corridors provide both for improving the view from a vehicle and for sustaining wildlife have been acknowledged in some parts of the UK by the introduction of structural planting. The introduction of urban forests is addressing this opportunity by developing strategies for planting along both primary and secondary road and rail routes. The 'Woodlands by the Motorway Programme' in the West Midlands had three aims.

These were:

> To enhance environmental quality of the principal transport route through the urban West Midlands by maximising woodland cover on land within sight of the motorways; to improve the environment for people living and working close to the motorways and to demonstrate a strategic approach to urban forestry.

This programme took place from 1992 to 1996 and included a land use survey, negotiation with landowners, community consultation and participation, design and implementation, all underpinned by partnership funding. The project achievements included: 63 new hectares of woodland on a total of 56 different sites; 4,000 local people, including school pupils, being involved in planting operations and an increase in woodland cover from 7.2 per cent to 9.4 per cent in the area under consideration (National Urban Forestry Unit, 1998). The National Urban Forestry Unit suggests that this approach could be repeated wherever road and rail routes pass through urban Britain.

In addition, consideration of the route of a new road is important for visual and functional reasons. There may be times when it is appropriate for a route to align with other transport systems, such as a railway. If the road is to pass through an urban area the relationship that the proposed route may have on the urban grain should also be considered (Evans, 1986). A further consideration in many road schemes has been not only the route, but, once the route has been chosen technical issues such as the treatment of cuttings and embankments (Coppin and Richards, 1986). Missed oppor-tunities for scenic beauty through consideration of aesthetics in the design of roads in both rural and urban areas are identified by Pushkarev (1960), who discusses the fact that drivers see and perceive the road and the landscape differently, depending upon the speed at which they are travelling. The human eye of the driver or passenger does not see the road as an engineering problem, as many road designers do, but as an aesthetic entity. A large and wide road can be seen as a ribbon unwinding on the landscape and even taking the form of a three-dimensional sculpture as it moves across the land, vertically and horizontally. Pushkarev goes on to discuss how in order for a road not to look like a foreign body in the urban or rural landscape it should be carefully designed. Such design should take account of the cross-sectional and longitudinal impact that a road might have on the landscape.

So, many people experience the linear routes of road, rail and canals in their daily urban lives. The question that society needs to address is what is the quality of that experience? For many the experience is dominated by traffic, fumes and late-running trains and often people will give little consideration to the spaces within which these transport systems are set. Yet planting in such urban spaces can contribute significantly to the amelioration of the urban climate, as discussed in chapter three, and can also have a mental health impact, reducing the stress of life by providing a view of natural elements rather than urban elements, as discussed in chapter two and above. There are many possibilities for well-planned, designed and managed spaces for transport and waterway systems to provide these benefits in urban areas.

Recreational

Woodland

Several renowned authors have discussed the history of the British landscape and included in their discourse the situation with respect to woodlands (see Hoskins, 1955; Fairbrother, 1970; Rackham, 1986). It is apparent that from the end of the last ice age, at about 12000 BC, the British Isles were increasingly covered with forests except for some small areas of moorland, grassland on some mountains, coastal dunes and salt marsh areas (Rackham, 1986). The succession of tree species resulted in climax wood-land types including oak and ash (Fairbrother, 1970) until large-scale human activity began to have an impact on the landscape

(Rackham, 1986). Hunter-gatherer mankind may have begun to develop methods of management of the vegetation and the land upon which this grew but this impact was, overall, minimal. The greater impact began in about 4500 BC when farmers began to use crops and animals in their cultivation of food and the development of tools. Within 3,000 years large areas of woodland became farmland or heath (Rackham, 1986). Rackham reports that in Roman times wood was used for rods and poles and to supply timber for buildings, bridges, ships and for the development of baths, bricks, hypocausts, corn-drivers, iron, lead and glass. Thus the impact of wood products is not only on the landscape but also on the economy of the country at that time.

The Domesday Book is clear that the landscape of England was not fully wooded; indeed only 15 per cent of the country was recorded as being covered with woodland (Fairbrother, 1970; Rackham, 1986), as confirmed by evidence from Anglo-Saxon charters which also recorded information about economic uses of wood such as coppicing, the supply and transport of rods, charcoal and wood. Rackham concludes that the distribution of woodland at this time was not radically different from Roman times, despite the refinement in agricultural techniques. By 1350 only 7 per cent of England was covered with woodland, which had become valuable property with an economic return often greater than from agricultural land – one of the reasons that boundaries became important. Between 1350 and 1850 woodland was protected from other land uses partly because of its economic and social value (Rackham, 1986). The development of heavy manufacturing industries such as iron, glass, leather and shipbuilding over the next 200 years resulted in a high use of wood and timber products before technology changed, with the impact being felt particularly in the leather and shipbuilding industries. Rackham reports that during the nineteenth century wood became linked, to some extent, to the modern economy, with changes in coal prices and agriculture both impacting on woodland. In the twentieth century much timber was felled to meet the demands of the two world wars and in the social upheavals between the

wars. These fellings did not destroy woodlands and nearly all of the ancient woodlands of 1870 were still present in 1945 (Rackham, 1986). Coppicing and other underwood trades declined. At first the Forestry Commission had little impact on woodland areas, but after 1945 woods were treated as moorland and existing vegetation was destroyed and replaced by plantations for economic reasons. The growth of interest in woodland conservation, the recession in agriculture, and the approaches of Forest Enterprise, Forest Authority and the National Trust have all had a positive impact on woodland (Rackham, 1986).

There are many environmental, economic and social benefits that can be derived from woodlands and trees in urban areas, and the acceptance and realisation of some of these benefits is neither new nor untested. The Earl of Dudley, in about 1810, undertook land restoration projects at Wren's Nest and Castle Hill in Dudley and subsequently this inspired the Midland Reafforesting Association (MRA). The Black Country, an area of high levels of heavy industry to the north of Birmingham, England, had large expanses of land that were disfigured by mining and suffered from severe atmospheric pollution as a result of the industry. The MRA, founded in 1903, planted trees on its own land, and on private and publicly owned land, including within school grounds. These trees were often raised from seed in their own nurseries and planted by local volunteers. The association also produced educational and informative pamphlets and gave lantern slide lectures. Over the twenty-three years of the association's existence more than 40 hectares of new woodland was planted on thirty-two different sites (National Urban Forestry Unit, 2000a).

What might be called modern urban forestry seems to have originated in North America and Canada during the 1960s, and only moved to the UK some twenty or so years later (Johnston, 1997). The Motherwell Urban Woodland Project, initiated in 1982 close to Glasgow in Scotland, was a pilot scheme developed by a partnership. Variable support from the partners, together with the fact that the local community had not been

7.6 *Woodland – a good place to walk*

7.6

involved, resulted in the full potential of this urban woodland scheme never being realised. The next major urban forestry initiative was one pioneered in the London borough of Tower Hamlets. Five demonstration sites were planted but strained staff relationships, due to the use of contract labour, and a change of political control meant that this was not as successful as it might have been.

In 1986 the Forest of London project was conceived. This had three aims:

- To get Londoners working together to plant trees where they were most needed;
- To increase Londoners' awareness, appreciation and sense of responsibility to the capital's trees; and
- To encourage community involvement in the planting and care of trees on publicly owned land.

A partnership of local authorities, businesses, media and a variety of voluntary groups was set up and a series of high-profile media activities was successful in raising people's awareness of the project. Despite being beset with problems of funding, staffing and the results of the hurricane winds of October 1987 the Forest of London project planted over 50,000 trees, raised some sponsorship and involved tens of thousands of Londoners in events and activities before being wound up (Johnston, 1997).

In 1989 the Community Forests Initiative was launched with proposals to establish twelve new community forests on the 'outskirts of major cities in England and Wales' (Johnston, 1999). The main aim of this initiative was to help restore derelict land in urban fringe areas and to provide recreational and employment opportunities. Plans were also put in hand for a New National Forest in the Midlands, a larger version of the community forests to cover a more rural area. In 1990 the Black Country Urban Forestry Unit was established and supported by a wide range of financial sponsors. The aim was to 'promote extensive forestry planting throughout the industrial landscapes of the Black Country as a means of reclaiming dereliction, improving the public image of the area and encouraging inward investment'

(Johnston, 2000), an aim not too far from those of the Earl of Dudley and the Midland Reafforesting Association. Other urban forestry projects have developed, in one form or another, in a variety of locations including Cardiff, Middlesborough, Edinburgh and Glasgow. In addition the City of Oxford was an early supporter of the National Tree Warden Scheme. Their voluntary tree warden scheme provided opportunities for training in tree planting and maintenance as part of a policy of promoting care of existing trees and of community involvement in tree-related activities. The City of Leeds has fostered a scheme that exploited commercial opportunities of urban woodland by the use of a woodchip-fired boiler to 2 hectares of glasshouses and the production of seats and fencing for local parks (Johnston, 2000). Over the years conferences have provided opportunities for those involved in urban forestry to network and influence people.

The National Urban Forestry Unit was set up in 1995 as a charitable organisation working to raise awareness of the positive contribution that trees contribute to the quality of life in urban areas. The Unit works with partnerships across the UK to help people and communities understand the many benefits of urban trees and woodlands. The National Urban Forestry Unit defines urban trees and woodlands as including groups of trees, trees in people's gardens and street trees. The Unit provides support to those who work and teach in this subject area through a range of publications, case studies and conferences and seeks to encourage strategic approaches to the development of urban forestry, thus providing a focus within the UK for matters dealing with urban woodland. One of the most recent strategies that the Unit has inspired is that of the Green Gateway as part of an approach to create a greener Thames Gateway London using trees and woods and to realise some of the potential for tree cover in this part of the country (http://www.nufu.org.uk, last accessed 2 May 2002).

How do urban residents feel about woodlands and trees? Rollestone Wood in Sheffield, less than 5 kilometres from the city centre, and within easy reach of thousands of local residents, was the object of a research project and can provide an insight into one community's feelings about its local woodland. Observations, interviews and house-to-house interviews with local people identified that the wood was important to the local community for a variety of reasons. Daily life patterns were recorded as reflected in the use of the woods: a short cut to school or work in the morning, dog walking, leisurely walks, education and play activities at different times of the year. Children and young people showed distinct use patterns with girls playing at the edges or along paths and boys being more likely to wander away from the paths and deeper into the wood, especially with increasing age. In fact the local youth club leader acknowledged that the wood was fully used by young people and that they were able to undertake activities that were not acceptable elsewhere. Or as one boy stated 'Nobody chases us out of the wood' (Tartaglia-Kershaw, 1982). Some remem-bered using the wood as a child themselves, while accepting that grandchildren now enjoy the opportunities provided by the wood. It is clear that the wood was an important part of life to those involved in the research and that it contributes to the sense of place and history within the community (Tartaglia-Kershaw, 1982).

Because of the many benefits that woodlands have provided over thousands of years, woodlands, forests and even individual trees are embedded in Western culture, but often this is with negative connotations developed in early childhood. The experiences of Hansel and Gretel, Little Red Riding Hood, and even the baby in the tree top, as expressed in fairy stories and nursery rhymes, are all negative with bad things happening to people, which are repeated to children at the knee. Yet there are increasing moves to develop community forests across the country, with some of these linking in to existing urban woodland areas. It has been shown that woodland areas are valued as sites for countryside recreation (Burgess, 1996) and without further research it is possible to hypothesise that woodlands in urban areas are similarly valued, providing opportunities for experience of near nature, as discussed in

chapter two, as well as for walking – people and dogs – and play. However, the negative connotations of woodland are to some extent confirmed by the research of Burgess (1996) for a variety of people. Women were worried about being the victim of a sexually motivated crime by a man and additional concerns about getting lost or being out at dusk related to this main fear. Men were reported as being anxious about being the victim of a robbery with violence by either an individual or a gang, while teenage boys were fearful of the dark and being a victim of male rape. Asian and Afro-Caribbean women were frightened that even within a family group they would not be free from the threat of physical violence. Thus there are perceived fears of woodland areas and the extent to which individuals, families or groups will use a woodland within an urban area will depend upon a balance between the actual and perceived fear and the real benefits that can be experienced in such urban open spaces.

Golf courses

Golf courses are a specific sports facility that is usually not encompassed within a space – such as a park – but are a discrete open space in themselves.

It is generally accepted that the earliest reference to golf in the UK is a pictorial image in the form of a stained glass window in Gloucester Cathedral. This window, in the east wing, was commissioned by Sir Thomas Broadstone to commemorate his comrades who fell in battle against the French at Crécy. The window is believed to date from 1340, which is more than 100 years before the first written records for the game (Pitkin (2002). The origins of the word 'golf' are considered to be the German word *kolbe* and the Dutch word *kolf* meaning club. If these derivations are correct golf is in fact the 'game of club'. The earliest written records are those in Scotland, generally acknowledged as the home of golf. There are no clear records as to when the game was first played in either England or Scotland, but it is thought that it might have developed from a 'rustic pastime of the Romans'. It had apparently become popular by

7.7 *Golf is increasingly popular
in the urban context*

7.7

the middle of the fifteenth century, during the reign of James the Second, because statutes dated 1457 ban golf, 'lest it should interfere with the more important accomplishment of archery'. At this time the bow was one of the most important weapons of war in Europe, and anything detracting from its practice was frowned upon. (An earlier act of 1424 had banned football but did not mention golf, so it has been assumed that the popularity of golf developed during the early part of the fifteenth century.) The game was especially popular in the north of England and Scotland. During the reign of James the Third and James the Fourth Acts of Parliament again prohibited both golf and football (Clark, 1899).

With the development of gunpowder as a military weapon in Scotland the importance of the bow diminished, and the acts restricting the practice of golf fell into disuse. The game once again became popular and became 'the favourite amusement of the nobility and gentry in all parts of the country' (Clark, 1899). Indeed royalty now accepted the enjoyment of the game and King Charles the First was 'extremely fond of the exercise' (Clark, 1899). Evidence of the existence of the Blackheath Golf Club dates from 1766 and this is considered to be the first location for the game in England. The Old Manchester Club was the first of the modern era and during the first part of the nineteenth century many such clubs were formed (Cobham Resource Consultants, 1992).

As the popularity of the sport has developed, many golf courses have been constructed around the country. Common locations for such courses include coastal areas and rural locations, but golf courses have become significant open spaces in urban areas and are often positioned on the urban fringe of

7.8 *Cemeteries – places for remembering the dead*

a conurbation, as can be seen in the case study of Stockley Golf Course.

Ownership and control of golf clubs falls into a range of categories – course-owning, municipal, commercial and joint venture. Golf courses in England occupy about half a per cent of the land area of the country, with provision per head being higher in rural than in urban areas (Cobham Resource Consultants, 1992). About three-quarters of the estimated 1,450 number of 'full-length' nine and eighteen hole clubs are controlled by members' clubs, with the remaining 25 per cent evenly divided between municipal and commercial courses.

It seems reasonable to assume that the majority of the municipal courses are in urban areas and thus it is of interest to understand some of the patterns of use of these facilities. Most of the users of municipal courses are individual local people using the facility for exercise and relaxation. Between 1980 and 1990 the popularity of golf expanded, with the numbers of rounds increasing to 50,700 each year – significantly higher than the number of rounds at members' clubs. The time-consuming nature of the game is well known; the average playing time is three hours forty-five minutes, while total time, including travel, preparation and relaxation after a game is about six hours (Cobham Resource Consultants, 1992). Significant numbers of courses have been built and more are planned. This research was undertaken for the Sports Council and it seems reasonable to assume that the numbers of people playing golf, particularly in urban areas, has increased even more since 1992.

Thus golf courses provide a large number of city dwellers with opportunities for relaxation and exercise or mental and physical health improvement, as discussed in chapter two. In addition golf courses will contribute to the climatic and environmental improvement of an urban area to some extent, although the wildlife and environmental value of the large areas of closely cut grass are minimal. However, these spaces are important to the urban fabric, and although they may not be obvious to non-golfers, they can make a significant contribution to city life. Their location will not be within the city centre but in suburban areas, on the urban fringe and within the green belt, but nevertheless they are an important part of the urban fabric.

Cemeteries

Cemeteries are probably considered as important at the end of our earthly life when we die; but they are also important at other times. For some they are places of healing during the difficult bereavement period, for others they become places in which to play (Hoyles, 1994).

For thousands of years memorials to the dead, initially in the form of burial mounds, have been positioned in prominent positions within the landscape (Nielsen, 1989). In many countries burial mounds were superseded by other religious burial areas; in the UK and much of Europe this was the development of Christian burial grounds. Such landmarks increasingly included memorial monuments and the careful placing of vegetation, particularly trees. In the UK, churchyards were used for burials until the Victorian era when cemeteries were first developed and became places where families went for a weekend stroll (Weller, 1989). These early cemeteries were usually laid out in a geometric grid or on a series of geometric units, with the landform often terraced (Elliott, 1989). Later in the century this distinctive design was questioned as attempts were made to associate planting within cemeteries with the horticultural trends of contemporary gardening. In addition the introduction of non-denominational burial grounds took place during the nineteenth century (Nierop-Reading, 1989). The first of these non-denominational cemeteries in England was the Rosary Cemetery, in Norwich. A tranquil landscape garden design approach was adopted and enhanced by the provision of monuments and a preponderance of deciduous trees. During the last quarter of the nineteenth century deciduous planting dominated over the excessively gloomy conifers, generally used in the earlier part of the century.

The era of the churchyard being the dominant burial place in the UK ceased as cemeteries were increasingly provided on the edge of towns and cities, now well within city boundaries. This came about as a result of concern about health issues related to corpses, together with a lack of space for burial in inner cities (Rugg, 1998, 2000). During the twentieth century cemetery provision slowed and the increase in cremation supported a change in the desire and design of crematoria. Local authorities assumed responsibility for cemeteries, and the associated increase in cost was passed on to the ratepayer or taxpayer (Weller, 1989). The tightening of local authority budgets since the 1980s means that levels of maintenance have declined in many cemeteries across the UK (MacIntyre et al., 1989), although some argue that municipal cemeteries have been over-maintained during the last two decades of the twentieth century (Rugg, 1998). Perhaps the issue is, in fact, more to do with the style of maintenance and management and people's perceptions and expectations. More recently the design of spaces for the placing or keeping of ashes following cremation has become of importance. Designers of such commemorative landscapes may take different approaches, but the creation of spaces allowing for calm and quiet contemplation for the living are surely essential (MacIntyre et al., 1989).

Towards the end of the twentieth century a trend for woodland burials began to develop. In some cases people have wished to have non-religious events to commemorate the death of loved ones and where a family has environmental concerns these celebrations have increasingly taken the form of woodland burials. The first natural burial project in the UK was developed in Carlisle, within the existing Carlisle Cemetery, with the design being approved by the city council in 1995. The concept of woodland burial was explained in a leaflet made available to the public. Initially ninety-six double grave plots were laid out and trees, mainly oaks that had been grown by a local smallholder, were planted. Demand for this type of burial exceeded all expectations, and by the fourth year of operation 35 per cent of burials at the Carlisle Cemetery were undertaken in the woodland area. The total number of available woodland burial plots has been increased as a result of this demand. The woodland area has developed a spiritual significance that is now

reflected in some of the funeral services. In 1998 the cemetery received the UK Cemetery of the Year award (National Urban Forestry Unit, 1999b).

Cemeteries can play a crucial role in 'encapsulating the specific and unique memory and history of a place' (Worpole, 1997). This is also the case for the history of some individuals buried within cemeteries. The burial of famous people such as Karl Marx in Highgate Cemetery in London affords an opportunity for educational study in the subject area of history. Some local groups are keen to be involved with the maintenance of local cemeteries and churchyards (Parker, 1989) and their use for environmental education, while such spaces have also been identified as ideal locations for the conservation of wildlife (Wright, 1989). Indeed the many possible benefits of cemeteries, apart from the burial of the dead, were identified many years ago by Loudon when he claimed that properly founded cemeteries, 'might become a school of instruction in architecture, botany and in those important parts of general gardening, neatness, order and high keeping' (Loudon, [1843] 1981).

Cemeteries can provide opportunities for exploration around gravestones for local history interest, artistic interest or for tracing a family tree. In addition traditional churchyards can offer 'hints of a life, to be enriched by the imagination' (Dicker, 1986). But the regimented layout of many municipal cemeteries, often the result of limited space, does not necessarily provide for casual use. Cemeteries and crematoria should be places of tranquillity and provide opportunities for the casual visitor seeking serenity, as well as those seeking peace and solitude (Dicker, 1986). In addition opportunities are being taken for activities such as guided walks being provided in some historical cemeteries.

Although little empirical research has been undertaken to prove the importance of cemeteries or crematoria in the grieving process, such places can become a focus for grief where friends or relatives can talk to their loved ones or tend the grave or memorial (Clegg, 1989). A well-designed and maintained site can not only provide a good image but can also provide a sense

7.9   *Cemeteries – places for
enjoying drama*

7.9

of privacy and happiness, thus uplifting the spirit and morale of the grieving person (Flora, 1991). In these ways cemeteries and crematoria can act as a therapeutic landscapes and help to ease the pain of the loss felt by the death of the deceased. The importance of visiting a cemetery or a crematorium in order to pay respects to the dead is emphasised by Woudstra (1989), who states that about a third of the population of the Netherlands visits these once each year. The important role that cemeteries play as a place for quiet and contemplation while coping with grief is reiterated by others (e.g. Stockli, 1997). A further assertion that cemeteries are for the living and not the dead is given by the design of the recently developed burial ground in Columbia, Maryland. This project was designed in the

form of a sumptuous woodland park – the designer wanted people to feel that they are walking around an arboretum, not a cemetery. Design features of the scheme include human-scale space within the open fields, a complex method of siting the graves, rather than the standard grid format, the careful location of built forms in a screened manner and a meditation space with rustic seating. Overall the developer's aim is to help people 'forget that they are visiting a cemetery' (Nugent, 1991).

How bodies are dealt with after death, and how friends and relatives grieve with respect to bodies in the future, in the UK, may depend on a wide variety of factors. It may be that increasing numbers of people opt for green and woodland burials, whereas other will continue to require traditional burials and cremation. All of these options will require land to be planned, designed and managed, provision for which should be included in Unitary Development Plans and local authority strategies (Worpole, 1997).

Cemeteries, graveyards and woodland burial areas all provide many opportunities for climate and environmental amelioration, together with wildlife habitats, in the urban context because of the usually high level of vegetation that exists in such spaces. In addition it is clear that by providing opportunities for grieving and relaxation they can help with the mental health of individuals and families. Where old plans, gravestones and memorials exist these give opportunities for education and historical exploration. Thus cemeteries, graveyards and woodland burial areas are not only important at the end of life; for some, they are important places that help them cope with grieving and other areas of life.

CHAPTER EIGHT

A new deal for urban open spaces?

Quality of life – the challenge for sustainable cities

The government is calling for sustainable cities and 60 per cent of new housing requirements to be built on derelict or under-used land in urban areas, but what does this mean for the quality of life of urban people? High densities of housing can, of course, contribute to a sense of society and community and can therefore be a good thing. The concept of sustainable cities can give a nice warm feeling, but what are the realities of this idea? Does this just mean a very dense built form with no open spaces? What benefit would that be when we have clearly seen from chapters one to four of this book that there are many social, health, environmental and economic benefits available to individuals and communities by having open spaces in urban areas?

It has been claimed that development can result in a continuously expanding demand for shelter in the urban situation, and open space can be seen as an easy resource for development (Eckbo, 1987), with its intrinsic value being ignored. For some people the economic or potential economic value of a piece of land, depending on the category of planning permission it posesses, is more important than the befefits that open spaces can provide. But are they right? Have such people considered quality of life issues? I consider that it is in the most built up parts of cities, the central business districts and the inner city areas, where living and work stress levels are the greatest, that the need for open spaces to aid the quality of daily living is greatest.

Some of the benefits and opportunities discussed in the early chapters of this book are, generally, not new, although they may be to some individuals and organisations, and were some of the reasons that many open spaces were developed and retained during the industrialisation of the Western world. A summary of the benefits of parks – a supposition of agreed comments between a landscape architect, an advocate of public parks for environ-mental health reasons and a naturalist in the nineteenth century (Danzer, 1987) – can still be applied to many of the urban open spaces discussed in this book:

1. Human beings need contact with the natural environment in order to be healthy in a physical, emotional and spiritual sense.
2. The development of industrial cities has largely destroyed the natural environment, to the detriment of the populace.
3. It is the mission of public parks (public open spaces) to bring back to the cities the benefits of nature and to provide each citizen with the opportunity to walk through a natural landscape.
4. The extent to which a city provides these opportunities and the extent to which it develops open spaces to serve the needs of its citizens are ways of measuring the progress of democracy.

Despite their limitations these statements can help to us to understand that many of the benefits of open spaces have been accepted as truths for a long time.

The Prime Minister has talked about a 'virtuous circle of regeneration' (Social Exclusion Unit, 1998) and this circle must include the provision, planning, design and management of urban open spaces. Capacity building of such open spaces, to realise the many potential benefits and opportunities that they can afford, is important to accompany the capacity building of the communities to be involved in such regeneration. Thus the quality of life for individuals and communities can be enhanced in as many ways as possible.

Many of our open spaces are appreciated by many members of our communities – perhaps more so than by the decision-makers and funders of regeneration. It behoves us as a society to take seriously our responsibility towards open space in our urban areas – to return to the concept of stewardship or custodianship of our urban open spaces.

Urban open space is important to everyone's daily life, whether you are a child, teenager, young mother, father or carer looking after children, unemployed, working in a boring job, working in a stressful job, a patient in a hospital, retired, or in prison. At each of these times of life the benefits and opportunities that can be offered by the variety of open spaces, whether they be domestic, neighbourhood or civic, throughout the urban fabric can provide an opportunity to enhance the quality of life. Perhaps it is the garden, or school playground, the natural green space, park, local playing fields, the square by the office, the view from the hospital, office or prison window that can offer you these benefits. Whichever of these apply to your daily life there is no doubt, and research proves it, that your quality of life will be improved if you have access to, a view of, or even just know that a particular open space is there. In order that such open space can be well designed and maintained (there is not space here to debate what I mean by well designed or maintained), with the communities that will use such a space being carefully considered and consulted, resources are needed.

So what prevents this ideal to help our urban quality of life? I would suggest that it is mainly a lack of knowledge, or acknowledgement, or disinterest in the provision and maintenance of a good system or network of open spaces in our cities. There is no doubt that some cities, such as London, Bristol and Sheffield, do have existing formal and informal systems of open space. But what of their ongoing quality and appropriateness for the twenty-first century? What of the political priority, including finance, that is allocated to them? Of course housing and schools and hospitals are important, but so are open spaces. There has never been a research project to quantify how much factors such as truancy might drop, behaviour and crime improve and health improve when a comprehensive system of well-designed and managed urban open spaces is provided. But the research gathered together in this book, and it is not exhaustive of the topics discussed, clearly indicates that many elements of life for urban individuals and communities can be improved by the existence of open spaces.

Recently the government has called for research-led policies to be considered. In this book I have presented a selection of evidence from a variety of different academic and professional disciplines that discuss issues that affect the daily lives of many urban people. All of these discussions point to the important role that the provision, existence, good design and management of a range of different types of open spaces play in daily urban living.

Tools and methods for the way forward

So what is needed to help develop this potential of urban open spaces? What tools are needed?

Currently open space planning, design and management in urban areas is adressed, to some extent, through a range of regeneration sources such as the Single Regeneration Budget, the Heritage Lottery Fund (HLF) – in the form of the Urban Parks Programme, the HLF Revenue Programme, the Heritage Townscape Initiative and the New Opportunities Fund Green Spaces and Sustainable Communities theme. Money can also be obtained from the Landfill Tax Credit scheme and European funding sources. The government also provides finance, to a greater or lesser extent, to open space regeneration through the British Trust for Conservation Volunteers, the Civic Trust, the Rural Development Commission, the Groundwork Trusts and the National Federation of City Farms. We must not forget that in some parts of the country open space development, on a range of community scales, has taken place under the auspices of Agenda 21. In addition Housing Action Zones, Education Action Zones and Health Action Zones can all be considered as opportunities for funding the regeneration or management of open spaces.

But in many instances the finance that has become available for open spaces through such programmes has come only through the extremely hard work of project officers and chartered landscape architects who were creative and innovative in their approach to dealing with urban open spaces. It has not been the result of a cross-disciplinary strategic approach.

A review of the Standard Spending Assessment (SSA) – the money given by national government to local government – could help financial resources for urban open spaces. The SSA could be amended to include open spaces as a discrete category. Why on earth should highway maintenance be mentioned as a specific category in the SSA and open spaces not? The latter provide so many benefits to communities, whereas the former may allow for vehicular transport, but at what cost? A stressful life combined with pollution and accidents, many resulting in deaths.

There also needs to be an acknowledgement that there are qualified people who have the skills and experience to undertake and facilitate this work. Landscape architecture is a profession whose primary concern is that of the planning, design and management of open spaces that have much to offer to an interdisciplinary and integrated approach to urban regeneration. Project officers, park rangers, sports staff working in parks and open spaces and many others also contribute, or could contribute if adequate resources were made available, to the vitality and viability of many of our urban open spaces, thus realising many of the benefits available to our urban communities.

My plea then is that politicians, businesses, sport, health and educational establishments – to name a few – of all levels work together with communities and the relevant professionals to ensure that open space provision does provide for these quality of life issues in all our urban areas, from villages and market towns, through our coastal and historic towns to our metropolitan cities. Fund and facilitate projects for the design, development, regeneration and ongoing management and use of open spaces. Involve communities in these projects. Provide appropriate types of open spaces in appropriate locations, building on local distinctiveness as a theme. And as urban, and rural, areas begin to cope with the expansion deemed necessary in our housing stock, let us not become a nation that denies people the benefits and opportunities that a whole variety of good quality open spaces can provide for everyday urban living. We owe it to our children and our children's children not to ignore this issue as it is an essential part of a sustainable approach to regeneration which we, as a society, ignore at our peril.

So the overall challenge for government, communities and

society as a whole is to re-acknowledge the many benefits and opportunities that urban open spaces can provide – social, health, environmental and economic. Such an approach should also reaffirm the fact that individuals and communities value their urban open spaces for many reasons. In addition the quality of those spaces needs to be enhanced to make them suitable for the contemporary society that we currently live in.

In the weeks that I finalise the text for this book I find myself in an interesting situation as the government's Urban Green Spaces Taskforce publishes its final report *Green Spaces: Better Places* (Department of Transport, Local Government and the Regions, 2002). The report is the result of the hard work of the taskforce itself and its six working groups. The report also draws upon the research that was commissioned soon after the launch of the taskforce (Dunnett *et al.*, 2002). The report is a breath of fresh air – it acknowledges the importance of parks, play areas and green spaces for the many benefits and opportunities that they provide for urban life. The report also acknowledges that for many years urban parks and green spaces have been in decline and extremely under-funded. It then goes on to 'set out a programme for national and local government to work in partnership with local communities, businesses, voluntary organisations and other interested parties to create an urban renaissance with parks and green spaces' (Department of Transport, Local Government and the Regions, 2002).

Green Spaces: Better Places is divided into four parts. The first examines why parks and green spaces remain popular in urban areas, discussing some of the benefits that these spaces bring to neighbourhoods, towns and cities, and emphasising the important contribution that they make to the liveability of urban conurbations. Part two discusses current concerns about urban parks and some of the solutions to these concerns. This section discusses the value of partnerships as the way forward for providing the quality of spaces that communities desire. In this light it recommends that at least an extra £100 million capital funding should be made available for each of the next five years. It also suggests a new national agency to promote urban parks and green spaces and makes recommendations about training and skills development for relevant managers, staff, communities and people involved in partnerships. The third part of the report confirms that in order to enhance the status of green spaces political and strategic networks need to be put in place and that 'planners, designers and managers should recognise the definitions of the "ideal" green space by local communities' (Department of Transport, Local Government and the Regions, 2002). Finally the taskforce report presents parks and green spaces as part of a general vision of liveable sustainable conurbations. It proposes common criteria for issues such as excellence and conspicuous care and discusses the fact that links between local and national government are required.

These many issues, together with the revised PPG 17, now named Open Space, Sport and Recreation, are welcome, if long overdue, in the political arena.

The testing time for the Taskforce report is now underway. In October 2002 the government responded to the Green Space Taskforce report at the Urban Summit in Birmingham by the publication of *Living Spaces: Cleaner, Safer, Greener*. The response confirms that high-quality parks and green spaces are important to people's lives and that this should be acknowledged particularly in deprived areas by the Neighbourhood Renewal Strategies being developed by Local Strategic Partnerships. Recommendations for resources include consideration as to how lottery funds might be better used for green spaces, a review of the Landfill Tax Credit Scheme, support for increased use of Section 106 agreements under the revised PPG17 and the possibility of money being used for green spaces in Business Improvement Districts. As this book is published two other recommendations are about to be implemented which it is hoped will have a significant impact. First, a scheme of strategic enablers is being set up to help local authorities 'to develop integrated approaches to planning and managing green spaces'. Second, the government is initiating a new unit within the Commission for Architectue and the Built Environment (CABE) for urban spaces. This unit, known as CABE Space, and to be

set up in April 2003, has the remit to:

i) Champion the role of urban parks and green spaces in improving the quality of life and delivering urban renaissance.

ii) Work closely with relevant government departments and agencies, voluntary organisations and funding providers to improve co-ordination and delivery of programmes and initiatives.

iii) Advocate the need for higher priority and resources for parks and green spaces at national, regional and local levels and provide advise on funding issues.

iv) Strengthen existing and promote and stimulate new partnerships for improving green spaces involving the voluntary and private sectors and local groups.

v) Promote and develop skills and training needs for delivering and supporting improvements.

vi) Carry out research and develop information, quality standards and good practice.
(Office of the Deputy Prime Minister, 2002)

By the time you are reading this I hope that you will begin to see the results of these recommendations.

Perhaps at last the hope I expressed at the beginning of the book may be closer to being fulfilled. It is clear that people within communities do value their urban open spaces but we may now be approaching a time when politicians, funders and decision-makers will appreciate the utmost importance that urban open spaces are to people's daily lives and that resources, strategies and will power are needed to retain and enhance these spaces for the benefit of urban living.

Urban Open Spaces
Case Studies

Introduction

One of the aims of section three of this book is to provide case studies of urban open spaces where a key member of the design team has been a chartered landscape architect. This is partly to counter the belief that there is no good landscape design in this country. I do not claim that all of the case studies are good practice – it has not been the aim of this book to define guidelines for good practice. In addition, most of the project design teams may not have had the evidence that sections one and two of the book have discussed available to them; there is often a gap of knowledge between available research and practitioners in the landscape profession. But these projects have been produced to real budgets and client briefs and used professionals in this field to achieve high-quality schemes.

Because I wanted all of the case studies in the book to involve a chartered landscape architect, an early decision was taken that the major source for possible case studies would be the registered practices of the Landscape Institute, the professional institute for landscape designers, managers and scientists. To this end an initial questionnaire, requesting possible case study projects, was distributed by the Landscape Institute to all registered practices in the UK. This initial questionnaire asked whether practices had examples of projects that they thought would be suitable under the open spaces headings of section two of the book. Nearly 50 practices responded with over 200 possible case studies. A selection of these potential case studies were chosen, one in each type of open space, and a second questionnaire was sent to the chartered landscape architect, requiring more detailed information. Following an editorial decision that sixteen would be a practicable number to include the final selection was made . In each case the final text has been agreed with the relevant landscape practice.

Neighbourhood and recreational urban open spaces

Sherwood, Longsands and Cottam, Preston, Lancashire

Client	English Partnerships (formerly Commission for New Towns)
Landscape architect	Trevor Bridge Associates
Engineers	Howard Humphries and Company, Warrington
Archaeologist	Lancaster University Archaeological Unit, Lancaster
Contractor	Lanes Landscape Ltd, John Mallinson (Ormskirk) Ltd, Baldwins Landscaping Ltd, Randall's Landscapes Ltd, Roots and Shoots Ltd, William Pye and Son Ltd
Initial involvement	November 1993
Work started on site	March 1994
Practical completion	December 1997
Project value	£900,000 (hard works: £650,000, soft works £250,000)
Capital funding sources	Commission for the New Towns (CNT)

1

Project aims

To provide recreational facilities for residents and workers, a network of footpaths and bridleways to link facilities, landscape buffers between developments and to enhance existing wildlife habitats while creating new ones. A series of sites were identified as important locations such as adjacent to communication routes, the canal or at urban focal points.

Landscape architect's role

The landscape architect was involved from the inception of the work, through feasibility, design, production of contract documentation and tendering to monitoring the works on site up until completion.

1   Enjoying one of the ponds
2   Going for a walk
3   Bridge over a stream

2

3

Project constraints

The only real constraint was the need to start on site expedit-iously. Budgets and timescales were considered to be reasonable.

The unique opportunities of this project

These works formed part of a wider area of a new town devel-opment and a number of separate landscape architectural practices were chosen by the client to produce designs for different sites. In a number of instances a site designed by one practice would be set immediately adjacent to a site designed by another consultancy. This created the opportunity for different styles and design approaches to be adopted, but each practice had also to ensure that its design complemented the adjacent site.

The comprehensive master plan and brief provided for the retention of specified areas of land for public open space in this predominantly greenfield development. The series of linear open spaces within urban areas, utilising and improving existing landscape features, facilitated a major contribution to this new urban environment. In addition to providing areas for recreation, important wildlife corridors were retained and improved. Conservation and enhancement of a range of habitats, together with improved access for people and the provision of new recreational activities, resulted in the creation of an important asset for the community.

Project design

A series of linear open spaces and other publicly accessible areas were developed as part of new residential and business areas across the north end of Preston. The sites tended to follow streams, some of which were in steeply sided valleys that had remained relatively undeveloped and uncultivated, and contained extensive mature woodlands. Formal and informal paths, depending on their context, lead into these areas. Bridges span streams, some of which are wide, others of which have to accommodate maintenance vehicles. In order to reduce potential conflict between walkers and horses a separate system of bridleways has been provided in parallel with the footpath system. Extensive naturalistic planting, pond renovation, new pond creation and the introduction of wildflower meadows have enhanced areas both visually and in terms of wildlife conservation. A new village green, containing sports pitches, adjacent to existing ponds, provides a new focal point. Careful excavation of a previously filled mediaeval moat has created an interesting archaeological feature and signage at this point is an educational asset. Timber has been used for bridges, fences, gates, seats, signage and decking to protect the edge of ponds. This material reflects the more rural nature of some parts of the development. In more urban parts of the development painted steel has been used for railings and gates. Macadam, concrete block paving, stone and bark have all been used for surfacing according to the appropriateness of the situation. Stone has

4

5

been used for walling and drainage, while clay has been used for pond puddling. Native planting has been used in the more rural parts of the development, while exotic trees and shrubs have been used in the more urban context, especially at site entrances and focal points. Aquatic and marginal plants have been used around ponds and bulbs have been introduced to provide variety round the year. Two methods of wildflower planting were trialled. The most successful was the use of seed, with topsoil being removed. Less successful were areas where plug plants were placed into existing grass and topsoil.

Partnerships and community involvement

All liaison was undertaken by the client and the information was fed through to the landscape architects.

Current site users

The client was pleased that the briefs had been adhered to and that a high-quality project was provided. Preston Borough Council have commented that the sports fields within the project are the best drained ones within the town. The sites are well used for a wide range of recreational activites. From comments that have been received it is apparent that the series of open spaces are considered to be an important asset to the housing development.

Ongoing management of the project

Each site was initially managed for two years by the landscape contractor who had undertaken the capital works. During this time use of the sites was closely monitored in order to ascertain whether design improvements were required and feasible; if so these were incorporated into the scheme. Management plans were developed, for the different sites, by either English Partnerships (formerly CNT), Preston Borough Council or the Woodland Trust, with the aim of perpetuating the facility and further enhancing it by sympathetic management and ongoing monitoring. Issues covered in these plans included woodland management, tree maintenance, wildflower woodland management, shrub bed maintenance, grass-cutting regimes, pond and water course management, sports pitch, footpath, bridleway, bridge, fencing and gates maintenance. In addition trim trail equipment maintenance, signage maintenance and litter picking were covered.

4   *A wooded area*
5   *Wildflower meadow*

Northwestern Gardens, Llandudno

Client	Conwy County Borough Council (CCBC) Tourism and Leisure Department
Landscape architect	Bridget Snaith Landscape Design, Chester
Engineers	Department of Highways and Technical Services, CCBC
Architect	Ideas Illustrated
Contractor	Direct Services Organisation, CCBC
Initial involvement	August 1996
Work started on site	January 1999
Practical completion	May Bank Holiday 1999
Project value	£420,000 (£400,000 for hard works and £20,000 for soft works)
Capital funding sources	The Heritage Lottery Fund (75%), Conwy County Borough Council, Wales Tourist Board, Llandudno Town Council, The Welsh Office
Revenue funding sources	Conwy County Borough Council, Llandudno Town Council

1

Project aims

To re-establish the importance of the Northwestern Gardens as a public open space, rather than an island isolated at the junction of the two main roads into Llandudno, a Victorian era seaside resort. Conwy County Borough Council and the Mostyn Estates (owner of the town centre properties) hoped restoration of the gardens, which were in a state of decline, would act as a catalyst for further improvements to the area.

Landscape architect's role

The landscape architects were initially appointed to prepare an application to the Heritage Lottery Fund's Urban Parks Programme for two listed parks on the periphery of Llandudno. They recommended that the client adopt a more strategic view to the town's Conservation Area as a threatened historic landscape in its entirety. This resulted in an enlarged scope

1 *Northwestern Gardens*

2

including proposals for North Western Gardens with other open spaces in the centre of the town, in addition to schemes for the original listed parks. The bid successfully secured over £900,000 from the HLF by linking matched funding to coastal protection measures and traffic engineering work being undertaken by the Council. The landscape architects were then appointed to develop their proposals, with technical assistance provided by the council highways' civil, traffic management and lighting engineers. The landscape architects met with community groups, led all aspects of the design process (including road layout and hard works), maintained project meeting records, developed briefs for the architectural sub-consultant and sculptor and were responsible for the tender process and contract administration for the soft works.

Project constraints
The historic nature of the gardens, set in a conservation area, resulted in historical detailing and HLF approval being required

at each stage of the project. The seaside location meant that the importance of tourists in the summer months could not be ignored, and together with a desire to minimise disruption to traders in the Christmas period this resulted in a shorter contract period than would have been desirable. Traders' fears about loss of income and the impact of tree planting obscuring CCTV were dealt with carefully.

The unique opportunities of this project
The broader project provided the unique opportunity to create a new landmark and urban landscape for the town: a major avenue terminating in an attractive open space.

Project design
When the gardens opened in the 1920s the park consisted of a simple triangle of lawn, underground toilets, a low perimeter wall in decorative concrete and elm saplings. In recent years the use of the park had diminished due to the encircling traffic. This project

directed the traffic to one side, thus linking the park to the adjacent row of shops, while opening up views into the conservation area from the main road. Additional zebra crossings allow for improved pedestrian movement in all directions. A period style canopy over the toilet entrances, together with a new lift, make the toilet facilities accessible to all.

The shape of the regenerated park reflects its original shape, although it has doubled in size and thus has more room for planting, seating and wider paths. Flowering shrubs and perennials around the perimeter emphasise the garden character of the park and separate it from the traffic. Increased seating (twenty-eight long benches, grouped), new lighting and trees are located along the spine of the pedestrianised road, now an urban square, with a transit stop at one end and a sculpture at the other. Paved areas in the square use high-quality concrete pavers, complemented in the garden areas with coloured chippings. Stone was not an option due to its higher capital cost.

The park's heritage was retained by using the central lawn concept and replacing diseased and senescent trees on the periphery. Lighting, walling and furniture in cast iron and concrete were restored or replicated through use of historic photographs from the 1920s and involved the reuse of salvaged materials. Some modification was required to ensure layout and furniture complied with modern safety standards.

Partnerships and community involvement

Initial support for the project was given by interested residents and business people at two public meetings. In addition letters of support were provided by some local businesses and civic groups. Comments received resulted in a keyed service access for the shops adjacent to the park, interpretative signs including Welsh, English and braille and more seasonal bedding in order to help the city's annual bid for 'Wales in Bloom'. Seven artists presented models of sculptures in the town centre shopping precinct, and these were voted on by the public.

3

Current site users

An increased number of shoppers now use the park, while routes to the town centre from the beach and the railway station have resulted in increased numbers of visitors using the park. In addition the refurbished toilets attract people. Sitting and walking around the gardens are now popular activities with all ages and types of people.

Ongoing management of the project

A management plan was drawn up by the landscape architects and adopted by the local authority. The ten-year plan, required by the Heritage Lottery Fund, addresses issues such as maintenance of the trees to encourage growth to maturity and dappled shade. In the garden areas shrubs will be allowed to grow to their natural form in order to provide a border separating different areas and to provide a sense of enclosure from traffic. Daily maintenance issues such as litter picking, cleaning, painting and renewal of broken paving are also addressed.

4   5

2   *View down the gardens*
3   *Historic elements: ballustrading and lighting*
4   *Enjoying the gardens*
5   *Walking to the centre*

Stormont Estate Playpark, Belfast, Northern Ireland

Client	Department of Finance and Personnel, Northern Ireland
Landscape architect	Department of Finance and Personnel, Northern Ireland Construction Service, Landscape Architects Branch
Engineers	Department of Finance and Personnel, Construction Service, Civil Engineers Branch
Quantity surveyor	Department of Finance and Personnel, Construction Service, Civil Engineers Branch
Contractor	Henry Brothers, Magherafelt, Northern Ireland
Initial involvement	1996
Work started on site	December 1998
Practical completion	July 1999
Project value	£380,000 (£120,000: play equipment, £16,000: live willow wall)
Capital funding sources	Department of Finance and Personnel, Northern Ireland
Revenue funding sources	Department of Finance and Personnel, Northern Ireland

1

1 *Overall view of the playground*

Project aims

To provide a sensitively designed and located supervised play facility, not just with standard equipment, but with a unique character developing imaginitive and environmental themes. Options for future development were important. To help, as part of a broader programme, alter the image of the Stormont Estate from that of a formal setting for the former parliament building, to an area that can be actively used by all of the community.

Landscape architect's role

To liaise with the client at the inception stage to decide the siting of facilities, access and to discuss planning considerations. Initial concept sketches were refined and a report produced to outline the anticipated costings and advice on other professional input that would be required. Good working relationships with the civil engineers began and continued throughout the project.

Advice was given for the appointment of other disciplines, such as artists. Local workshops, organised and facilitated by the landscape architects were held in the grounds of the Stormont estate. Following the workshops and further design development the master plan was drawn up in collaboration with the civil engineers. Other information prepared by the landscape architects included schedules of play equipment, materials for tender purposes, input to the Health and Safety Plan, as required by the Construction, Design and Management Regulations, the specification for the willow wall structure and sculptural features. The landscape architects also arranged for inspections and certification by the Royal Society for the Prevention of Accidents (ROSPA).

Project constraints

The site was perceived as being sensitive both environmentally and due to its political history. The visual integrity of the parkland was to be retained and not compromised by the playground. Car parking was not to be intrusive in the landscape. Adjacent jogging areas were not to be disturbed. Other constraints related to the budget for the initial phase and the timescale.

The unique opportunities of this project

The site provided a unique opportunity to enhance the play experience through the use of the existing topography and a setting that would allow an environmental theme to prevail.

Project design

From 1931 until 1972, when the local parliament was suspended, Stormont House was the parliament building, with access restricted to government employees and residents in the immediate vicinity. With the changing political scene in Northern Ireland a desire to broaden and change the use of the site was initiated by the Secretary of State for Northern Ireland, Mo Mowlam. Thus the concept for the inclusion of a playground, of approximately 5000 square metres, set within the 100 hectares of parkland was developed. The aim was to provide a welcoming and useful facility, signalling greater community involvement. The planning authority had particular concerns about the possibility that play structures might be visible from the nearby housing. In addition the planners were also committed to minimising the visual intrusion of the scheme in the historic parkland setting. The possible disturbance of wildlife was also an issue that the planners highlighted and known badger setts were identified and checked throughout the project.

There was an opportunity to engage schoolchildren with local artists and the local conservation volunteers in the construction of a live willow wall. The play equipment chosen for the project was made of treated softwood, where structurally viable, in order to complement the parkland setting as much as possible. Wet-pour synthetic surfacing – in some locations coloured – and bark chippings were used as the surfacing for the playground to provide some protection from the impact of possible falls for children, to provide variety and to blend in with the character of the park as much as practicable. The car park, which is remote from the play area and with an access through the trees, has a bitmac surface. Footpaths and compound areas were constructed from stone and blinded with quarry dust, which was a preferred surface for wheelchair users. Edgings were made of wood with stakes and flexible board.

Planting within the newly designed scheme is dominated by the presence of the live willow wall which provides for different types of play – rough, mystery, creative – and which visually links the different elements of the play area together. In addition the willow wall provides opportunities for environmental education.

Partnerships and community involvement

Several local schools were involved in an initial workshop, held on the Stormont estate. This enabled the young people to be involved in the project from an early stage and generated some imaginative concepts, which were later translated into the design. Output from this workshop in the form of drawings was exhibited within the parliament building. Many animal themes

3

4

emerged from this process, as well as the idea of including speaking tubes in the design. The theme of the Irish elk was introduced at the beginning of the workshop and this, together with the large parkland setting, no doubt influenced the emergent animal themes.

Current site users

The site is now predominantly used by children aged 5 to 12 years old. The levels of use vary with time of day, school holidays and weekends, with an overall acceptance by everyone that the playground is a great success.

Ongoing management of the project

A management plan has been prepared for this site with the aim of ensuring the effective continued use of the play area and the safety of the users and the equipment. This will be facilitated by monitoring the use of the play area. Detailed issues covered in the management plan include the supervision of children, the frequency of inspection of the play equipment, the play and path surfaces, and the maintenance of paths and the willow wall. The management plan will be implemented by the Stormont Estate.

3   *Watching the world go by*
4   *Enjoying the willow wall*

Redgates School Sensory Garden for Children with Special Educational Needs, Croydon

Client Redgates School, Croydon	
Landscape architect	Robert Petrow Associates, New Malden, Surrey
Artist carpenter	Clwyd Oak, Llangwm, Corwen, Clwyd, Wales
Mosaic artist	Mosaic Workshop Unit, London
Instrument maker	Kevin Renton, Leamington Spa
Contractor	Beechings, Redlands Farm, Farnham, Surrey
Initial involvement	April 1999
Work started on site	August 1999
Practical completion	September 2000
Project value	£35,000 (£34,000 for hard works and £1,000 for soft works)
Capital funding sources	Redgates School, Croydon and sponsorship from local businesses

1

1 *Overview of playground*

Project aims

To provide and extend outdoor play and sensory experiences for children with special educational needs. To enhance opportunities for use of the school grounds for National Curriculum subjects such as art, science and geography. To provide opportunities for the development of physical and social skills as well as interactive play. To create a beautiful space for everyone at the school to enjoy.

Landscape architect's role

The landscape architect was the lead design professional on this project, co-ordinating the work of all the others involved. Workshops and consultations were undertaken with the school, and following the completion of a survey outline proposals were drawn up.

An important aspect of the project was not only to understand the existing site but also to explore needs of the people who were going to use the completed project. In order to help with this the landscape architect attended meetings with therapists and teachers. A great deal of time was spent observing the children and developing unique anthropometric data. This was to ensure that access, reach and user characteristics of the children were incorporated into the design. It was found that the application of averages as a criterion would effectively exclude about half of the school community from safely using the space. It was therefore essential that dimensional characteristics for all end-users were properly understood to produce design solutions which were equally efficient for all the children.

Ideas and alternative solutions were presented and a sketch scheme with outline costs prepared. Information from specialist suppliers was collected and a shortlist of artists drawn up. These were interviewed by the landscape architect and client group and the successful candidates were employed directly by the school.

The development of detailed design proposals was proposed and once agreed tender documents were prepared using the JCLI form of agreement for the construction phase of the project. The landscape architect administered the contract and project managed the practical on-site issues relating to the main contractor and artists.

Project constraints

The main constraints related to a tight timescale (all works had to be finished during the school summer holidays) and poor site access, which was through the main building. The desire to create a unique and interesting project was inevitably constrained by the need to produce a safe environment which also had to be challenging and stimulating to a range of children with differing disabilities and needs.

The unique opportunities of this project

The unique opportunity of this project was to provide a stimulating environment for 66 pupils from the age of 4 to 14 with severe learning difficulties and autism. For the designers this was an opportunity to understand how such children respond to their environment.

Project design

The existing site comprised a courtyard approximately 200 square metres in size, entirely paved with concrete units and contained on all sides by the school building. An internal corridor flanked by windows around the site allows good views into it from the main school building. A small pergola and some seating had been installed but overall the site was barren, very hot in summer and under-used.

The design took inspiration from the five senses: sight, sound, smell, touch and taste. Overall it is fluid and curvilinear in form. The main features include a bridge which crosses the site at an angle to the surrounding building. This is constructed from green oak and has set into it swinging chimes, xylophone bars and guiros. The bridge is accessed by steps and ramps and crosses over a sinuous band of blue recycled glass paving which forms a virtual river. This is surrounded by resin-bound gravel to represent a beach. At one end a raised sandpit has been designed in the shape of a boat with a fabric sail to provide shade and shelter, while at the other end a granite bubble fountain has been incorporated. Within the blue glass-fish mosaics which swim under the bridge and around the fountain have been incorporated. A musical path is formed by the bridge and three large musical instruments (swinging chimes, gong and slap tubes) all of which are hung from green oak timber frames.

One corner of the site is a work area which is enclosed by raised beds and a pergola. The hard paved surface is formed from Tegula concrete blocks. The raised beds contain tactile and scented plants such as lavender, sage, rosemary and lamb's ear. A grapevine has been planted to scramble over the pergola to provide shade and shelter. An art area has been incorporated within the design and utilises vertical art boards fixed to timber uprights, shaped to emulate pencils. Within the school building a variety of games, mosaics and mirrors have been fixed.

2

3

4

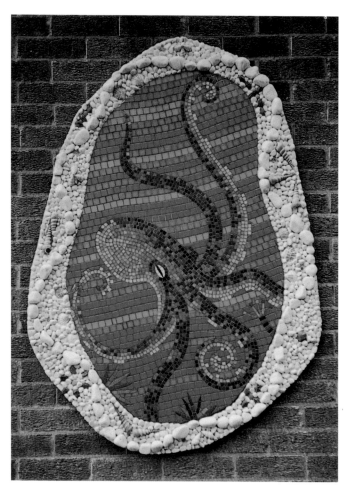

5

Partnerships and community involvement

Outline proposals, ideas and alternative solutions were discussed with the school. In order to facilitate discussions between the landscape architect and the school a steering group was formed. This comprised the head teacher, a governor, interested teachers and therapists. This group effectively became the client with whom the landscape architect worked.

Current site users

Since the outdoor space had been redesigned the level of use has dramatically increased and it is now used every day by the school. Uses include musical therapy, outdoor classrooms, art classes and informal play. A gardening club has been started and vegetables and flowers are grown in pots. Visitors, parents, teachers and most of all the children greatly enjoy the sensory experiences contained within the garden. A recent Ofsted report commended the school for its vision in creating a now well-used and much-loved garden.

4   *Enjoying the water*
5   *Octopus on the wall*

Spring Gardens, Buxton, Derbyshire

Client	High Peak Borough Council
Landscape architect	Landscape Design Associates, Peterborough
Quantity surveyor	Henry Riley and Son, Peterborough
Engineers	Stirling Maynard and Partners, Peterborough
Contractor	SOL Civil Engineering
Initial involvement	1992
Work started on site	1996
Practical completion	1997
Project value	£1.2 million (approximately)
Capital funding sources	High Peak Borough Council
Special funding	Spring Gardens Shopping Centre funded a new entrance canopy to the centre
Revenue funding sources	High Peak Borough Council, Derbyshire County Council

1

1 *Pedestrian route defined by stone cubes*

Project aims

The aims of this project were to assist the regeneration of Buxton's principal retail street, to provide a pedestrian priority environment, and to improve the east–west pedestrian link from the east side of the town centre via the Crescent to the Pavilion Gardens. The project was to provide a setting for the town centre, conservation area and important listed buildings. In addition the scheme aimed to boost tourism – both visitors on a daily basis and to the annual festival.

Landscape architect's role

Landscape Design Associates were project manager, design team leader, landscape architect and contract administrator, with the support of a full-time clerk of works. They co-ordinated the design team, managed the programme, provided materials for and arranged the public consultation, co-ordinated planning

2

3

applications, undertook negotiations with statutory authorities and researched the views of the retailers. They also undertook liaison between the client and design team and guided the direction of work and actions of the team, as well as preparing sketch designs, outline designs, detailed designs, selecting the contractors and managing the tender process.

Project constraints

It was not possible to achieve the full pedestrianisation desired because the street was constrained by the requirement of premises requiring access throughout the day. This resulted in a pedestrian priority scheme with special dispensation for an office and a garage. Traffic had to continue using the A6, which ran across the western end of Spring Gardens and was allowed to access the eastern end of Spring Gardens. Localised flooding to properties on one road also had to be addressed. The existence of services, which were not adequately recorded, restricted the possible positioning of trees. There was a financial constraint in that the original master plan included a series of water features and canopies that could not be included.

4   5

2 *Sitting and lolling on cubes*
3 *Evening on the street*
4 *Walking on the cubes*
5 *Inspecting the drainage system*

The unique opportunities of this project

Buxton is a Georgian/Victorian spa town set high within the Peak District and its history, location and nature as a spa town provided aspects of local character that were built upon in this project. The fine architecture is enhanced by the use of stone from local quarries, reflecting the rugged countryside.

Project design

The requirement for vehicular access to service shops on the southern side of the street before 10 am and after 4 pm and permanent access to two commercial properties meant that a separate vehicular/pedestrian surface and protected pedestrian areas had to be defined. This was done physically by a line of stone cube bollards that ran down the middle of the street. The combined vehicular/pedestrian surface was identified in a repro- duction sett with a flush footway of York stone against the buildings that vehicles could also run on. The pedestrian northern, and therefore sunnier side of the street, was defined by a more intricate paving pattern of stone and setts and was also the location for seating, lighting, litter bins, telephone kiosks, trader electricity points and stone sculptures. Their locations were ordered and related to the central line of stone cubes, so that by providing clear order to the design it was possible to make the street easily usable by visitors with visual and mobility disabilities.

Hard materials were carefully chosen to enhance the concept of local distinctiveness. Stone was used in different forms: paving, ashlar for retaining walls and bollards, rubble walls and rough-hewn quarry-cut rocks as sculpture. The use of stone complemented the fine buildings and was of an appropriate quality for the setting within a conservation area. A reproduction sett was used in vehicular areas to visually complement the York stone pedestrian paving. Limited areas of concrete slabs and asphalt were used for a short vehicular service area. Street furniture consists of modern designs for cast iron bollards and seats, with a robust feel to complement the rugged countryside surrounding Buxton. Planting took the form of street trees of Pyrus Chanticleer. These were chosen for their upright habit, size and ability to tolerate the hard winters of one of England's highest towns, retaining their leaves for a substantial part of the year.

Partnerships and community involvement

Considerable research was undertaken with the retailers and meetings were held with them during the design development and during the works on site. Wider ranging consultations took place with particular individual retailers, the local Civic Society, the emergency services, various disability groups, the County Council, the Environment Agency, Severn Trent Water and the highway authority, especially lighting engineers. Extensive public consultation was undertaken in the form of public exhibitions at different stages of the design process. These were attended by local authority officers and the design team and held in the shopping centre or in empty retail units within Spring Gardens. Exhibitions, leaflets and questionnaires were prepared and samples of all materials and street furniture were included in the exhibitions.

Current site users

The project was well received by the client, who acknowledged that the scheme would have been improved by the inclusion of the proposed water features. The response of retailers has also been generally positive; Spring Gardens Shopping Centre is now fully let and there are almost no vacant shops in the street.

Ongoing management of the project

Ongoing management is undertaken by the High Peak Borough Council. A management plan was not produced because it was felt that most of the skills required already existed within the local authority team. The Borough Council intend to appoint a Town Centre Manager.

Stockley Golf Course, London

Client	Stanhope Plc, Stockley Park Consortium Ltd, London Borough of Hillingdon
Landscape architect	Bernard Ede Assoicates/Ede Griffiths Partnership, Warminster
Golf architect	Robert Trent Jones, Fort Lauderdale, Florida
Clubhouse architect	Architects' Department, London Borough of Hillingdon
Master plan architects	Arup Associates, London
Quantity surveyor	Ove Arup and Partners, London
Engineers	Ove Arup and Partners, London and Grontmij, De Bilt, Holland and Haslemere Surrey
Contractors (some)	Nuttalls, Bernhards, Davidson International, Southern Golf
Initial involvement	June 1984
Work started on site	April 1985
Practical completion	June 1993
Project value	Approximately £19m for the golf course, park and country park
Capital funding sources	Stockley Park Consortium Limited/Universities' Superannuation Scheme
Revenue funding sources	Golf course fees

I *Aerial view of Stockley Park*

I

Project aims

To recycle hazardous and polluted land to create open space and resources in an area deprived of open space. The golf course is part of a larger complex including a business park and country park. To provide opportunities for play for novices, players and tournaments and to allow for possible future extension of the course. Land features were to be created, while maintaining public routes such as footpaths, cycleways and bridlepaths through and around the golf course.

Landscape architect's role

Production of master plan (with Arup Associates) and reclamation strategy (with Ove Arup and Partners). Co-ordination of the country park and golf course projects, integrating the golf course layout and routing, undertaken by the golf course architects, into the overall design for the new business park open space infrastructure. Concept, outline proposals and detailed design of the new landform and innovative drainage system in conjunction with Ove Arup and Partners. Responsibility for the concept, outline and detailed design of all the country park elements, including golf course planting, paths and secondary drainage system. Constant on-site monitoring of the works with the golf design and construction contractor.

Project constraints

A ten-year period was allowed in order to remove the landfill hazards and pollution and create a large public open space and golf course, to strict environmental requirements. The golf course integrated with the surrounding urban area and business park open spaces. The use of site-won land-making materials, such as clay and gravel, was also a constraint.

The unique opportunities of this project

A unique opportunity for the total transformation of a derelict and polluted site into an entirely man-made landscape for the benefit of the local community, while providing commercial opportunities. The project involved innovative recycling of materials on site. The partnership between the local authority and the private developer was also ground breaking.

Project design

The 160 hectare site lies within the London green belt, north of Heathrow airport. In 1690 the area of this project was enclosed as part of the Dawley Estate with formal gardens and avenues. From 1866 the site was excavated for gravel and backfilling with domestic rubbish began in 1912. The landfill had risen up to 12 metres above the surrounding ground level by 1961 and in 1972 there was a severe underground fire. Tipping ceased in 1985 and the land was capped with clay and returned to grazing by horses, which restricted the development of woody vegetation. The complex transformation of this site, from 1984 to 1993, resulted in a 36 hectare business park, to the south within easy access of the M4 motorway and Heathrow

airport, while 100 hectares were transformed into a golf course, playing fields and park land. Stormwater attentuation features were developed as a system of ditches, swales and linear lakes. Rubbish had been deposited to a depth of 16 metres during the lifetime of the landfill site and the problem of methane generation was dealt with by a unique transition of layers of landfill material and clay subsoil from the site. A manufactured topsoil of sewage cake and clay forms a semi permeable top layer for drainage and soil development. A total of 4.6 million cubic metres of rubbish and clay were moved in order to develop the landform, intended as an outlier of the the Chiltern Hills, to the north. This landform has created landmarks and viewpoints and a varied pattern of drainage features and landforms, such as terraces, ramps and circular mounts. These enhance golf play and the experience of paths and trails. The landform of the golf course was based upon the concept of a pre-existing overall large, rounded hill which had been subsequently dissected by a major road, with terraces, sinuous fairways and tee and green platforms cut into it. A fifth of the land area of the entire complex was planted with forestry-type planting of trees and shrubs, with species such as alder and birch and blocks of oak, ash and hornbeam and native underplanting of shrubs. The planting structure of the golf course is seen as having been cut into this woodland mass. Some of the birch pioneer or nurse trees are to remain. Dense planting of small stock trees and shrubs in a bare earth regime to reduce grass and weed competition has been spectacularly successful. The initial nurse trees and shrub fringes have been thinned and remaining tree canopies lifted to produce excellent play conditions. The golf course accommodates strategic public paths, linking different parts of the park and serving features such as viewpoints and the clubhouse. Finally a unique planting system was developed, with Cobham Resource Consultants, which had a two-fold approach of successional and shot-gun planting.

2

3

4

Partnerships and community involvement

The local community was involved throughout the design and construction period using a series of methods. There was a constant open information system. Meetings were held regularly and throughout the process exhibitions were held indicating the stage that the project had reached and the design decisions being taken. A newsletter was produced by Stockley Park Consortium Limited. There was also collaboration with a local interest group.

Current site users

The 18-hole golf course was opened in June 1993 and is a Professional Golf Association European Tour Course. The course is used by novices, independent players and for competitions. It is estimated that 40,000 people a year play there.

Ongoing management of the project

The landscape architects drew up an integrated management plan for the golf course, business park and country park which addressed the aims of short-, medium- and long-term vegetation development, public safety, quality and appearance of the park. The plan includes drainage, mowing regimes, forestry and paths, and is implemented by Stockley Park Golf Limited and paid for by the proceeds from the golf course.

2   *Footpath and bridleway*
3   *Planting five years on*
4   *Nick Faldo opens the golf course*

Civic urban open spaces
Victoria Square, Birmingham

Client	Birmingham City Council
Landscape architect	The Landscape Practice Group, Birmingham City Council with input from Eachus Huckson, consultant Landscape Architects
Artists	Dhruva Mistry, Principal Artist; The Carving Workshop, Cambridge; Rory Coonan, Arts Council (public arts advisory role), Bettina Furnée (letter carver) and Marc Neale (artist)
Quantity surveyor	City Building Finance Division, Corporate Services Division, Birmingham City Council
Engineers	Civil, structural, mechanical, electrical and lighting: City Engineers Department, Birmingham City Council
Specialist fountain engineer	Ford Water Engineering Limited, Birmingham

Specialist lighting engineer	Imagination Limited, London
Specialist hydraulic engineer	Dr Peter Hedges, Aston University
Contractor	Impresa Castelli UK Limited
Landscape subcontractor	Whiting Landscape Limited
Initial involvement	1991
Work started on site	January 1992
Practical completion	February 1993
Project value	£3.7 million for works and fees (£3.25 million contract): Hard works – £2.0 million; soft works – £150,000
Capital funding sources	Birmingham City Council Main Programme Capital, European Regional Development Fund (ERDF)
Revenue funding sources	Birmingham City Council, (£75,000–90,000 per annum)

1

Project aims

To create a new civic square, of high quality and modern character, for the centre of Birmingham in place of a busy traffic junction, following the Hilderbrandt Pedestrian Movement and Open Space Framework study, undertaken in 1988, while making a pedestrian-friendly environment easily accessible by disabled people. To create a large space in front of the Council House, linking it with the Town Hall, central library and retail areas of New Street and Corporation Street. To maintain the character of the area by the choice of hard materials with low maintenance requirements and by introducing large trees and colourful bedding displays.

1   *Pedestrian route to the Town Hall*

2

Landscape architect's role

The Landscape Practice Group led the design team throughout the pre-contract stages of the project and then had an advisory role to the civil engineers during the post-contract stages. In addition the landscape architects led the design throughout the project.

Project constraints

The main project constraints were of time and budget.

The unique opportunities of this project

This project provided a unique opportunity to create a civic space in front of the Grade II listed Council House and adjacent to the Grade I listed Town Hall, while carefully dealing with the changes of level and providing access for disabled people.

Project Design

During the 1960s, development in the centre of Birmingham was dominated by extensive road building. The advantages, such as easy access to New Street Railway Station, were increasingly felt to be outweighed by the dominance of engineering structures and unpleasant and disorienting subways, resulting in a

poor image and experience for pedestrians. A City Centre Enhancement Programme, supported by significant amounts of city council capital funding, was developed.

Victoria Square was never really a square – it was more a traffic junction, dominated by cars, with pedestrian access becoming increasingly difficult over the years. The new scheme sought to change this and give priority to pedestrians, as part of a pedestrian spine for the city centre. A large fountain makes use of the significant change of level from the 'top' to the 'bottom' of the square. The fountain acts as a focal point, a meeting place and a resting space. The fountain is dominated by the statue of a bronze river goddess and young adults, while guardians and obelisks are made of stone. The sound from the fountain provides opportunities for relaxation and meditation at the heart of the city.

The top space is open, providing opportunities for civic events associated with the Grade I Listed Town Hall and the Council House. The lower space is more of an oasis and is at the head of the pedestrianised New Street. This forms a small amphitheatre which can hold street events, while the steps and edges of the fountain provide many opportunities for seating.

The water features and planters are clad in fine-grained

3

4

Derbyshire sandstone, from the same quarry that the stone for the Council House came from 100 years earlier. Much of the paving has been designed to take heavy traffic, for events, and uses brindled clay pavers. The street furniture is robust and yet in sympathy with the surrounding Victorian buildings. Semi-mature trees, bedding displays and hanging baskets on the lighting standards provide the greenery for the space. Lighting highlights the features of the overall design.

Partnerships and community involvement

The business community in the city centre were very supportive and enthusiastic about the project. All interested parties were invited to a series of open meetings where information about the progress of the project was disseminated. The contractor had daily contact with those businesses with shop frontages facing onto the site and with members of the public. Access for All, a body representing disabled groups, was consulted during the design and thoughout the construction phase and provided an exchange of ideas.

Current site users

The business community, visitors, residents and people working in the city have been overwhelmingly appreciative of the scheme and the improvement over the previous road junction. Many people use the spaces not just as a through route from one part of the city to another, but as somewhere for lunch, relaxing or meeting friends in the evening. The upper part of the square

is used for cultural and musical events and a Christmas Carousel, while the lower part of the square is used by flower sellers and for carol singing.

Ongoing management of the project

The overall aim is to maintain the civic square to a very high standard, consistent with its city centre location. A simple management plan was produced by the Landscape Practice Group which indicates the parties involved, the materials, contractors, suppliers and key contacts. It includes recommendations for maintenance requirements including weekly or monthly cleaning of elements, touching up of paint work, daily and weekly maintenance issues for the fountain, and daily, annual and long-term requirements for the maintenance of the bronze and stone statues.

2 *Victoria Square and the Council House*
3 *Central water feature*
4 *Evening view towards the Town Hall*
5 *The bronze river goddess*

5

The Peace Gardens, Sheffield

Client	Sheffield City Council, Department of Planning, Transport and Highways
Landscape architect	Sheffield City Council, Design and Property
Architect	Sheffield City Council, Design and Property
Quantity surveyor	Sheffield City Council, Design and Property
Engineers	Sheffield City Council, Design and Property
Lighting designers	Equation, London
Metalwork artist	Brian Asquith, Youlgreave, Derbyshire
Stonework artist	Richard Perry, Nottingham
Ceramics artist	Tracey Heyes, Sheffield

Contractor	Management Contractor: Tilbury Douglas
Initial involvement	May 1995
Work started on site	August 1997
Practical completion	November 1998
Project value	Heart of the City Public Realm approximately £12 million, with approximately £5 million for the Peace Gardens – £4.85 million for hard works and £150,000 for soft works
Capital funding sources	Lottery Millennium Fund, Single Regeneration Budget and European Regional Development Fund (ERDF)
Revenue funding sources	£120,000 per annum, (plus cost of 24-hour security) Sheffield City Council

Project aims

To change the public perception of the city centre and provide a civic garden with a setting for the existing Grade 1 listed Town Hall, existing retail premises and £120 million commercial regeneration project including a hotel, Millennium Gallery, Winter Gardens, shops and offices. To provide a visitor attraction displaying the highest standards of craftsmanship, horticulture and public art to complement the Millennium Gallery and Winter Gardens.

1   *Picnicking in the gardens*
2   *The Peace Gardens and the Town Hall*

1

2

Landscape architect's role

The larger Heart of the City Public Realm project was managed by Sheffield City Council's Chief Architect. Within this project there were three elements – Hallam Square, Town Hall Square and the Peace Gardens. The team leader for the Peace Gardens was one of the city council's principal landscape architects. Their responsibilities included the master plan, design, community consultation, liaison with all the artists, drawing up general construction and soft landscape design and specification packages for tender and monitoring of works on site.

Project constraints

The project was delivered by a fast-track management contract in order to spend the ERDF money within the set timescale. Thirty-six separate works contracts were let, being designed in sequence in order to achieve an early start on site.

The unique opportunities of this project

Two unique opportunities were provided by this project. First, this was the setting for the largest city centre regeneration project since the post war reconstruction of the 1950s. Second, this was a unique opportunity because the setting is adjacent to Sheffield's premier Grade 1 listed building – the Town Hall.

Project design

The site was originally a largely grassed area with concrete slab paths, bench seats and horticultural floral displays, which often had visual low spots at key times of the year, such as the summer. The space was used, particularly at lunchtimes. The redesign of the site took into account the strong relationship with the Grade 1 listed Town Hall and the existing and proposed commercial sites on the other three sides of the space. Access points into the gardens are provided in five places (two providing a through route for people with disabilities), while the external side of the gardens has provided an area for a street café served by an

4

5

adjoining commercial property and for occasional art and craft markets. Provision is also made for an open space for bus stops and general pedestrian access.

Wide pathways with water rills, lined with ceramics, lead one to the focal point of the 80 jets of water that create the interactive fountain display. Planting and grassed areas are raised two feet above the level of the paths to prevent pedestrians taking short cuts across soft landscaped areas and to provide sitting lawns.

Hard materials were chosen to be in character with the Sheffield setting and to be robust. Stoke Hall gritstone to match the Town Hall was used for walls, balustrades and relief carving, while Rockingstone slab paving and granite setts were used to maintain the local character.

The planting was inspired by English gardeners such as Gertrude Jekyll and Graham Stuart Thomas, along with the contemporary gardeners Beth Chatto and Christopher Lloyd. The planting has a structure of shrubs underplanted with herbaceous perennials and bulbs. This gives a botanically rich mixture with interest all through the year. Bold foliage and strong architectural form complement the robust stone masonry.

Partnerships and community involvement

An initial exhibition was held for the Heart of the City Public Realm project in January 1995. This was followed by an exhibition specifically for the Peace Gardens in November 1995. Over 1000 people attended the exhibition and 800 people filled in questionnaires. This exercise established the public desire for a civic garden, rather than a civic square. There had been regular liaison with the city centre traders about the design and the impact of traffic during construction. Liaison with city centre residents related to construction issues such as noise and night-time working.

Current site users

The use of the area has vastly increased since it was redesigned. It has become a place where people bring their visitors. The scheme has been a great success with families, young people and children. Children love to play in the interactive fountains in fine weather and in some school holidays children take their towels, expecting to become pleasantly wet. Lunchtime and Saturday use is very high throughout the year.

Ongoing management of the project

The site is part of an enhanced city centre maintenance regime which includes regular litter clearance, high-pressure jetting of paving to remove chewing gum and dirt, a rapid response for graffiti removal, a 24-hour security guard and city centre CCTV. The dedicated gardener, with considerable horticultural knowledge, played a major role in the planting of the site and is supervised by a City Centre Horticultural Manager who also acts as client manager for the adjoining Winter Gardens project. The landscape architect, horticultural manager and gardener review the management plan, which was originally developed by the landscape architect, at least once a year.

3 *Water and stone reflect Sheffield's location*
4 *A peaceful night-time*
5 *Chatting over a water rill*

Edinburgh Park, Edinburgh

Client	New Edinburgh Limited
Landscape architect	Ian White Associates
Architect	Richard Meier and Partners, New York
Quantity surveyor	Various
Engineers	Halcrow, Edinburgh
Contractor	Various companies
Initial involvement	1988
Work started on site	1990
Practical completion	In stages – to be completed about 2015
Management started	1992
Project value	£120 million: £4 million for hard works; £4 million for soft works
Capital funding sources	New Edinburgh Limited (joint venture company between EDI Group (Edinburgh City Council) and the Miller Group
Revenue funding sources	Management charges through Edinburgh Park Management Limited (£53,000 annually for common areas and £60,000 for individual sites)

1 Marginal planting on the eastern edge
2 Landscape structure provided by a lochan
3 Nesting swans

1

Project aims

The aims of the landscape strategy were to create an ordered, high-quality environment as the setting for a business park. To create a landscape setting in advance of development. To create a landscape structure using a controlled range of materials. To control implementation and management standards in order to achieve a high-quality environment.

Landscape architect's role

The landscape architect has been an integral pat of the development process since 1988 through the master planning, implementation and management stages of this phased development. The landscape architect is responsible for the design and co-ordination of all external spaces, implementation of hard and soft landscape works and continues to provide advice to Edinburgh Park Management Limited. The landscape architect is

2

3

also a member of the design review committee, which controls all aspects of existing and proposed developments.

Project constraints

There were no major constraints to the project, but there was an increasing requirement to implement best practice in water management for attenuation and treatment of the water.

The unique opportunities of this project

The developer's decision to provide landscape infrastructure in advance of the building development as a means of establishing development standards on a cost-effective basis early in the development process and as a marketing aid. The site is a phased development over 20 years and therefore consists of completed occupied sites, major construction sites and sites awaiting development.

Project design

Edinburgh Park is located on a site that was recorded in 1400 as being Redheughs Farm. More recently the farm was extensively farmed, growing grain and winter feed for animals. In the early ninteenth century the area was developed as country houses and parkland for wealthy families.

Edinburgh Park, on the western edge of the city, is a 138 acre business park adjacent to the Edinburgh city bypass. The site is surrounded by a retail park, the bypass with green belt on the opposite side, a shopping centre, private housing and finance offices. It is planned on a strict Cartesian grid of 8 metres, to create an ordered environment, in accordance with the modernist principles of Richard Meier.

The central feature of the park is a series of lochans – small lochs – which follow the north–south route of the Gogar Burn. This feature opens up views towards the Pentland Hills. When the scheme is finished there will be four lochans in the water system. Water weeds provide food for ducks, while water lilies and reeds give way to flowers, shrubs and trees in the landscape at the side of the lochans. The lochans provide structure to the landscape and support a communal amenity area through the centre of the site. Wildlife supported by the lochans include a pair of nesting swans, coots, sticklebacks, tadpoles and frogs and a visiting heron.

The western edge, adjacent to the bypass into the city, is formal. The eastern edge, in contrast, consists of marginal planting. Other types of planting within the park hierarchy consist of peripheral woodland blocks, avenue/boulevard tree planting, and detailed gardens within individual development plots. Trees include willow, birch, rowan, alder hazel and beech and support over 200 types of insect. Chestnut and lime trees provide structure to the amenity area, while Scots pine and sessile oak are among the trees of the woodland planting. This selection of planting provides interest all the year round.

Current site users

Although the site is primarily intended for business users, the central amenity zone is enjoyed by residents of the surrounding community. The developer has encouraged interest in the parks' environment by publishing a brochure, *A Walk in the Park*, which provides information about plant and animal systems within the park. It describes two walks and discusses the ever-changing landscape.

Ongoing management of the project

Once common areas are complete they pass to Edinburgh Park Management Limited, a separate company in which occupiers are represented. A management plan was produced by the landscape architects and the plan includes issues relating to maintenance operations and water quality.

4

4   *An ordered environment*
5   *The western edge is formal in design*

5

Mold Community Hospital

Client	Clwydian Community Healthcare Trust (now North East Wales NHS Trust)
Landscape architect	Capita Property Services Limited, Cardiff (formerly Welsh Health Common Services Authority, WHCSA)
Architect	Capita Property Services Limited, Cardiff (formerly WHCSA)
Quantity surveyor	Cragg Patterson Partnership
Mechanical and electrical engineers	Capita Property Services Limited (formerly WHCSA)
Structural engineers	Grove and Wright
Contractor	Norwest Holst
Initial involvement	1980
Work started on site	1982
Practical completion	1984
Project value	£1,286,990 (£200,000 for hard works and £12,000 for soft works)
Capital funding sources	Welsh Office, Hospital League of Friends funded the courtyards (£100,000)
Revenue funding sources	North East Wales NHS Trust

1

Project aims
To provide an external environment appropriate to health care which is reassuring, restful, caring and sensitive to patients' passive and active needs.

Landscape architect's role
The landscape architect worked on this project as part of the design team and was involved from the outset of the initial planning of the site through the design stages, preparation of tender documentation, providing relevant information to the quantity surveyor and monitoring of the landscape works until completion of works on site. In addition the landscape architect prepared the grounds maintenance strategy.

1 *Amenity courtyard*
2 *Taking the air*

2

Project constraints

The compact nature of the site and the requirement for significant car parking resulted in only a small percentage of the site being available for external works.

The unique opportunities of this project

As this was the first community hospital to be developed in Wales it was essential that the landscape design reflected the needs of the patients, staff and visitors and this was achieved by meetings with them. The original hospital was on a tight, cramped site and had little in the way of external amenities. The project provided a unique opportunity to provide better standards of design and external environment and was a pioneer of this approach in Wales.

This community hospital provides an integrated local community and hospital nursing service in association with local general practitioners. A variety of patients are served, including the elderly, chronically ill, outpatients and with those requiring physiotherapy, day care and accident treatment.

Project design

Mold Community Hospital is located in the grounds of a former cottage hospital on the edge of the town. Most of the original buildings were retained and converted into a Community Mental Health Resource Centre. The site is small, low lying and rises steeply on the eastern side. The east of the site comprises housing, while to the north there are a series of playing fields. The small, eighty-bed hospital is constructed of brick with a red clay tiled roof.

The footprint of the building is rectangular with two courtyards separated by a pavilion meeting area. One of the courtyards contains a water and general amenity garden, while the other has a physiotherapy garden with a ramped exercise area. In addition there is a greenhouse and small occupational therapy garden outside the occupational and physiotherapy departments. First-floor ward windows have integral window boxes. Many flowers and plants are donated and the boxes are looked after by staff, the League of Friends and a local gardening club. Echelon arrangement of the wards allows for supervision of each patient from the nurse base while also providing each

3   4

patient with their own individual space. This arrangement also provides for both near and distant views of window box planting from each patient's bed.

Access to the site is via an adjacent housing access road, while access to the courtyards is from an access corridor. Paved areas are built of locally sourced Ruabon tiled pavers. The perimeter of the site is reinforced by the use of hedges, while the eastern slope stabilisation is aided by mass planting of shrubs and ground cover planting including hebe and cotoneaster. Amenity shrub and tree planting within the site helps to screen and integrate the car parking for the many cars into the landscape. Softly contoured areas of grass complement the other elements of the external environment.

Partnerships and community involvement

The local hospital League of Friends were involved with the project during the design process and financed the courtyard development through voluntary fundraising efforts.

Current site users

Views of the users of this hospital were gathered by a research project for the six years following the opening of the hospital (Singleton, 1990) and some of those views are summarised here, in order to help us understand how the people who use the hospital feel about the landscape associated with this bulilding. The manager of the hospital has found the landscape to provide a pleasant working environment, and feels that there are therapeutic benefits for the patients associated with the hospital environment.

Nursing staff have reported that they consider there are benefits to the landscape of the hospital. They happily recount taking patients outside for fresh air, walks and the seasonal changes of the plant material. Both occupational therapists and physiotherapists have stated that they like 'the gardens, the setting and the work environment' (Singleton, 1990).

Patients referred to several aspects of the environment that they value. Those most consistently mentioned are the views to the planting and courtyards from beds, day rooms and outdoor seating spaces. Access to the outside spaces are also valued and the overall atmosphere is considered to be warm and friendly.

Ongoing management of the project

A maintenance plan was drawn up by the landscape architects and implemented by the North East Wales NHS Trust. A local gardening club has taken over the responsibility of maintaining the two internal courtyards.

3 *View from a window*

4 *Exercising on the steps*

Heriot-Watt University, Riccarton Campus, Edinburgh

Client	Heriot-Watt University, Edingurgh
Landscape architect	Weddle Landscape Design, Sheffield
Architect	Reiach & Hall, Merrylees and Robertson and others
Quantity surveyor	Thomas and Adamson, James Gentles and others
Engineers	Blyth and Blyth and others
Ecologist	Weddle Landscape Design
Contractor	Various
Initial involvement	1968
Work started on site	1968
Practical completion	Ongoing
Project value	£100 million over 30 years (£30 million for hard works and over £5 million for soft works)
Capital funding sources	University Grants Committee and sale of university properties
Revenue funding sources	University annual budgets

1

1 *The Loch and student village*

Project aims

To create a university campus within the grounds of a central Scotland historic estate, dating from the seventeenth century, within the green belt of Edinburgh. The retention of woodlands, a loch and gardens while creating a new landscape for 5,000 students has been the overall aim of the project.

Landscape architect's role

For more than thirty years the landscape architect has had a wide-ranging set of responsibilities on this site. These have included master planning, to establish a sustainable land use framework and detailed site planning and design for individual development projects such as halls of residence, car parks and new academic buildings. The landscape architect identified areas of ecological risk and importance and has ensured adequate protection and reinstatement at the end of each phase of

2

2 *The lime avenue*
3 *Wildflower meadows and ponds, West Student Village*

construction. After twenty-five years a follow-up Wildlife and Ecology Study (environmental audit) was carried out and concluded that there had been an improvement in the landscape quality and diversity. The landscape architect has developed a master plan to expand the campus capacity to 10,000 students. In addition the landscape architect sits on the Site Conservation Committee.

Project constraints

Two main constraints have existed throughout the duration of this project. First, this has been a long-term development which has evolved over the years. The second main constraint has been the desire to minimise the impact of construction works, both on the landscape itself and also on the life of the students. Each construction site has been rigorously protected with fencing and access routes have been clearly designated.

The unique opportunities of this project

The relocation of Heriot-Watt University to this historic landscape in the green belt of Edinburgh provided constraints with respect to the manner in which the landscape was treated, with protection and management of the woodlands, ancient trees, historic landscape and gardens being of utmost priority. These provide an enhanced quality of life for the academic campus and habitat opportunities for wildlife.

Project design

The Riccarton Campus at Heriot-Watt University, of 150 hectares, was previously the Riccarton Estate, home to the Gibson-Craig family who had a deep interest in trees. The prestigious tree collection on the estate was initiated in 1823 and has been constantly added to. Many of the trees are thus more than 150 years old but unfortunately some of the trees that had been recorded in 1884 were removed by gales of 1968 and 1972. In 1969 Heriot-Watt University took over the site and has continued the tradition of tree planting, together with the aim of landscape protection, of the site. The layout of the historic

3

gardens has been researched with the assistance of Scottish Natural Heritage and a management plan for restoration has been drawn up.

The overall concept of the campus is of a car-free core with segregation of pedestrian and vehicular service routes. In various parts of the campus ponds and a stream corridor have been designed in order to take the surface run off water from existing and future buildings to a loch. A zone of conserved landscape, consisting of the loch, historic gardens and central woodlands, which is 'bridged' by footpaths, runs through the heart of the site. The campus is buffered from surrounding roads by 30 hectares of perimeter woodlands. To the south there are extensive playing fields, while to the north and the east is the first Research Park to be developed in the UK.

There are eight different settings within the landscape – the academic campus, student villages, playing fields and sports centre, core and students union with entrance hall and conference centre, woodlands, research park, central woodlands with gardens and loch, and future development areas that are in agricultural use. Within the central core area it is possible to move from building to building along internal corridors and bridges allowing people to avoid the worst of the winter weather while enjoying and benefiting from the views of the landscape.

Throughout the campus desire line footpaths and cycleways link these different elements and allow for exploration of the environment and jogging. A sculpture trail has been developed, while a tree trail makes use of some of the fine collection of native, exotic and old trees.

Partnerships and community involvement

There has been systematic community involvement through the Site Conservation Committee that meets to discuss all aspects of wildlife, campus protection and landscape development. Wider consultation of the master-plan has been a planning requirement of the Rural West Edinburgh Plan.

4

4 *Path to West Student Village*
5 *The lawn within the formal garden*

5

Current site users

A range of academic departments, administrative services and student accommodation are based on this campus, resulting in large numbers of potential site users. These include 5000 students who live and study on the campus during the academic year and 1700 academic and administrative staff. In addition there are 1500 Research Park staff together with conference guests and members of the community who use the facilities of the campus.

Ongoing management of the project

A management plan was drawn up by the landscape architects in 1978. This document covers issues of general estate management. This plan is implemented by the Heriot-Watt Estates Office with ongoing advice from the landscape architect and a twice yearly review through the Site Conservation Committee.

Curzon Street Courtyard, London

Client	Waterbridge Group Limited
Landscape architect	The Terra Firma Consultancy, Petersfield, Hampshire
Quantity surveyor	Burke Collis Partnership, Reading
Engineers	Ian Gledsdale, Sevenoaks
Contractor	Clifton – with specialist input on water features from Fountains Direct and waterproofing from Alumasc
Initial involvement	August 1996
Work started on site	August 1997
Practical completion	January 1998
Project value	£130,000 (£115,000 for hard works and £15,000 for soft works)
Capital funding sources	Waterbridge Group Limited
Revenue funding sources	Waterbridge Group Limited (approximately £2,000 per annum)

I

I *Seating walls*

Project aims

To bring life in to an otherwise dull office courtyard by the introduction of a strongly designed theme for enclosure, colour, water, planting and lighting for semi-public use of the space.

Landscape architect's role

The landscape architect was the project co-ordinator and liaised with the client throughout the entirety of the project. As lead designer the landscape architect co-ordinated the work of other professionals – engineers and quantity surveyors. Following the development of concepts for the courtyard the landscape architect developed sketch designs into a final design. The planning process revealed no problems and in fact the planners welcomed the scheme. Working drawings and other tender documentation was prepared, with the quantity surveyor preparing the specifications and bills of quantities. The landscape architect also administered the JCLI form of contract on site.

2

3

Project constraints

The courtyard is the roof of a car park and offices, so weight constraints had to be considered and sub-surface services and waterproofing carefully co-ordinated. Working offices and through access had to be maintained throughout the duration of the contract, so working space and programming were severely confined for the contractor.

The unique opportunities of this project

The project offered the possibility of designing a sheltered, protected and well-maintained site with the opportunity of using high-quality materials and features without fear of vandalism.

Project design

Prior to this project being undertaken this 250 square metres of courtyard was paved from wall to wall and was a much under-used open space. The buildings on either side of the courtyard are occupied by different businesses, with a church nearby, and thus the symmetrical design would not be seen to favour one set of occupants or the other. There is a formal processional entrance with a central circulation route. The design has created an outdoor room providing an ethereal roof of light tree canopy, a floor carpeted with a strong paving pattern and planted, seating walls. Raised beds provide seating opportunities as well as provision for planting.

In order to give life and a feeling of movement to the space a variety of high-quality materials have been used. Natural stone and brick provide contrast in colour and texture. Water has been used as a visual and aural feature. Lighting highlights the water features, the paved route and the trees. In the summer canopy uplighters are used, while in the winter festoon tree lighting is used. The lighting is controlled by a time switch.

A planting structure is provided by a formal framework of evergreen box. The tree framework is provided by gleditsias, which provide light shade in the confined space. Liriope, heuchera, zandtedeschia, hosta, ferns, bulbs and rhododendron

5

yakushimanum give year-round colour and texture in the semi-shade planting beds. Specimen trees of yew and laurel are used in pots to provide accents and emphasis at the entrances and exits to the courtyards.

Partnerships and community involvement

Office users and the church were consulted with the sketch design in informal meetings to discuss the scheme prior to finalisation.

Current site users

Since the completion of the refurbishment, use of the courtyard has increased significantly. The most popular times of use are coffee breaks and lunchtimes and occasionally meetings are held in the courtyard. The use is somewhat weather-dependent, but there is access through the courtyard all the time. The space is considered to be a good experience to move through because of the sound, light and colour. Significant visual amenity is also provided to people in the church, offices and apartments.

Ongoing management of the project

A management plan was produced by the landscape architect with the aim of maintaining and nurturing the scheme to the highest possible standard. Details covered in the plan included a full record of the scheme as built and the materials used. A specification of the maintenance of the paving, planting and other elements, such as the water feature, within the scheme were also included in the plan. After three years small sections of the original planting have been replaced, at the suggestion of the landscape architect, by more shade-loving species due to the success of the gleditsias, which form a canopy of semi-shade in the summer.

2 *View down Curzon Street courtyard*
3 *Lush planting*
4 *The courtyard illuminated*
5 *Detail of water feature*

Marie Curie 'Garden of Hope', Finchley, London

Client	Highways Agency
Landscape architect	David Huskisson Associates, Tunbridge Wells, Kent
Quantity surveyor	Gifford Graham and Partners, Southampton
Engineers	Gifford Graham and Partners, Southampton
Contractor	Hard works: Edmund Nutall Limited, Soft works: Brophy Landscape, then English Landscape
Initial involvement	1989
Work started on site	January 1993
Practical completion	June 1999
Project value	£4 million (including engineering works for underpass) (£55,000 for soft works)
Capital funding sources	Highways Agency
Revenue funding sources	Transport for London (formerly Highways Agency)

1 *Gravel paths wander through the planting*

1

Project aims

The project consisted of a cut and cover tunnel to maintain an existing link across the North Circular road (A406) of a local road. The aim was to create a pocket park on the underpass roof, providing an informal village green for the local community.

Landscape architect's role

Project co-ordination and liaison with the client throughout the entirety of the project. As part of the design team, led by the engineer, the landscape architect had to provide information relating to all hard and soft works as required. Following the development of concepts for the roof pocket park the landscape architect developed sketch designs into a final design. The roof garden was part of a major civil engineering project and there was close liaison with the project engineers through-out the process. Hard landscape details were designed by the

2 *Marie-Curie daffodils*

landscape architects and brought together in the tender documentation put together by the quantity surveyor. The landscape architects prepared all detailed design drawings and specifications for the soft works, and monitored the progress of works on site for both the hard and soft landscape contracts.

Project constraints

The project was predominantly an engineering one and thus the constraints for the landscape element of the scheme related to matters such as weight loading on the roof of the underpass and the geometry of the engineering design. Drainage and associated water storage and topsoil specifications were matters that required careful consideration due to the nature of the scheme. Safety parapets at the portals of the tunnel were required.

The unique opportunities of this project

The entire project was somewhat unique for the UK in providing an opportunity to create a roof garden above a dual carriageway – often the sort of space that is dominated by other cars and vehicles or just wasted. Other opportunities afforded by this project include the use of innovative drainage and water retention layers in order to create a suitable growing environment for the soft works.

Project design

The interchange of the East End Road and the A406 was a roundabout that was frequently congested with heavy traffic, causing noise and air pollution for local residents and pedestrians. The roundabout was a hazard to children walking to the local school and detracted from the visual amenity of the area.

As part of a larger London North Circular Highway Improvement scheme the main design concept, for this interchange, was to segregate the A406 from the local community by a deep cutting for the main road. The surface-level vehicular circulation remained for local traffic only. The concept was to develop the cover of the road underpass into a small pocket park – to provide a pleasant space for people to enjoy and to improve the safety for pedestrians.

Innovative engineering and landscape design techniques have been used to enable the road underpass to function as a roof garden, supporting and sustaining tree, shrub and grass planting without the need for expensive irrigation. A waterproofing layer was covered by a system of reservoir cells filled with light expanded clay aggregate carefully designed to balance the need for water storage while also allowing drainage to prevent waterlogging at times of prolonged heavy rain. A layer of geotextile prevents this reservoir system from silting up, while the subsoil and topsoil meet the requirements of a precise specification.

Due to the requirements for headroom for the A406 on bridging over the London Underground line to the east, together with headroom requirements of the underpass itself, it was necessary for the roof of the underpass to rise above the ground level at the eastern end. In order to ameliorate the visual impact of this the sides of the structure were clad in brick with an upstand to retain topsoil and facilitate planting to green the view.

A coherent palette of high-quality, robust, vandal-proof materials and furniture has been used to give the space a sense of place. Planting provides colour all year round and has been chosen for its ability to survive drought in this roof garden situation. The establishment of these species was achieved without excessive watering. Paths are of gravel-dressed bitmac and granite setts. Litter bins, lighting and seating are of a modern design in metal. Generous swathes of daffodils, adding another interest in spring, represent the emblem of Marie Curie Cancer Care.

Partnerships and community involvement

No partnerships or community involvement took place through the design and construction periods of the project. However, the Marie Curie Cancer Care charity adopted the pocket park at a daffodil bulb planting ceremony in November 1998. The site was chosen by the charity because of its visual accessibility to many people, both park users and those travelling past the site. The garden was named the Marie Curie 'Garden of Hope' and a plaque on the site acknowledges the charity's involvement in the project.

Urban Open Spaces – Case Studies

3

4

5

Current site users

Since the completion of the site in June 1999 it has become used increasingly by local residents for sitting, walking, reading and other passive recreational activities. The children from the local school enjoy the space on their way to and from home.

Ongoing management of the project

The ongoing management of the project is the responsibility of Transport for London and was undertaken by English Landscapes Limited until May 2002 when the Highway Authority's term maintenance contractor took over the responsibility.

3 *General view of roof garden*
4 *High-quality materials have been used*
5 *Eastern end: entrance to underpass*

Dockside Regeneration at Chatham Maritime

Client	English Partnerships
Landscape architect	Gibberd Landscape Design, London
Quantity surveyor	Gardiner and Thebald, London
Engineers	Parkman, Chatham
Contractor	Tarmac Construction
Initial involvement	April 1991
Work started on site	November 1991
Practical completion	July 1992
Project value	£398,000 (£350,000 for hard works and £48,000 for soft works)
Capital funding sources	English Partnerships
Revenue funding sources	Chatham Maritime Trust

1

Project aims

To establish a strong sense of place which would be an important focal point for informal recreation within the Chatham Maritime development area. To provide a design solution which established a performance space for the benefit of the local community. To adopt materials of the highest quality which recognised the historic setting and the need to maintain a coherent and co-ordinated approach to the treatment of the new townscape within the development area.

1 *Bollards echo the maritime past*

2 *Raised lawn*
3 *Performance area at dockside*

Landscape architect's role

The landscape architect was appointed as the lead consultant for this project. Following the development of several design options the scheme most favoured by English Partnerships was taken forward to detailed design, tender documentation and through the tender process. The landscape architect also acted as the contract administrator while the works were on-site.

Project constraints

Unlike the majority of projects the dockside regeneration initiative provided very few constraints. Possibly the greatest constraint was the need to produce a contemporary design within an area of historic importance.

The unique opportunities of this project

The historic nature of the site and association with the broader Chatham Maritime development was a unique aspect of this project, as was the recognition that the design should embody purpose-designed features such as lighting and railing details.

Project design

The master plan for the redevelopment of the former Royal Naval Dockyard at Chatham was conceived in 1985. This master plan, developed by Frederick Gibberd Partnership in association with Leslie Ginsburg, emphasised the importance of urban design and the value of robust, high-quality hard and soft landscape infrastructure and the need to establish a strong sense of place. Dock Square itself comprises some 3,640 square metres of what was derelict dockside. There are several main elements to the landscape of Dock Square: hard landscape, boundary walls, performance area, lighting, lawns and tree planting.

In keeping with the former dockyard site the hard landscape is dominated by the Yorkstone paving and granite setts that define the perimeter of the new square. Red clay pavers are used in the square and provide unity with the same paving material used alongside one of the water basins. The boundary walls have been constructed from 'Chatham mix' bricks which

have been selected to match the predominantly red brick used extensively within the existing dockyard – one way of respecting the historic nature of the site.

A performance area has been designed at the edge of the dock. This takes the form of a raised area, covered by a tent-like structure. Lighting units were specifically designed for this site and were developed to emphasise its character.

This predominantly hard landscape is complemented by the use of semi-mature London plane trees which provide a significant visual impact from the completion of the project. They are planted on a seven metre grid either side of the raised lawns. Simple robust planting in the form of ivy has been used at the base of the trees. There are four lawns, constructed of high-quality turf, arranged in two levels to provide valuable green space.

Partnerships and community involvement

All design and implementation stages of the project were progressed with an open dialogue with English Partnerships, Kent County Council, Rochester Upon Medway City Council and Gillingham Borough Council, in order to realise the true potential of the site development. Considerable emphasis was placed upon the importance of the Chatham Maritime infrastructure as a catalyst for future development and the need to establish a close working partnership between all parties.

Current site users

English Partnerships regard the Chatham Maritime area as one of its flagship developments. The dock square is used extensively, especially in good weather by employees of commercial tenants in their lunchtimes. The site is regarded as an important venue, especially in the summer months, when events for Navy Day are held. In addition the venue is popular for small orchestral concerts and modern dance events. About six events are held each year.

2

3

4

Ongoing management of the project

A management plan was produced by the landscape architects which addresses the issues of the day-to-day management of the land and soft landscape, replacement of failed plant stock and the cleaning of pavements. A long-term contractor has been appointed to execute the management plan. The Chatham Maritime Trust manages the Chatham Maritime Estate, of which this site is a part. In addition the estate covers the sea defence walls, open landscape areas and dock basins. Finance for future maintenance is thus secured within the trust and cannot be spent on other external projects. As a charity the trust enjoys certain tax advantages for its investments.

4   *Good quality materials have been used*
5   *Robust planting has been used*

5

Black Country Route Sculptures

Client	Wolverhampton City Council
Landscape architect	Wolverhampton City Council Regeneration and Transportation Landscape and Environment Section
Engineers	Ove Arup and Partners for *Tower of Light*, L.V. Ingram and Partners for *Tower of Light* and foundation design to various other sculptures, Wolverhampton City Council for Wall Grills by Richard Criddle, W.S. Atkins for patterned walls by Jane Kelly
Contractor	Cowley Structural Timberwork, Waddington: *House of Birds* and *Bilston Oak*; David Ables Boatbuilders, Bristol: *Tower of Light*; Arden Fabrications, Knowle: *Beth's Arch* and *Horse and Rider*
Public art consultants	Public Art Commissions Agency, Birmingham
Initial involvement	1989
Work started on site	1992
Practical completion	1998
Project value	Approx £0.5 million
Capital funding sources	Transport Supplementary Grant, European Regional Development Fund

1

1   *Ponies: use of scrap and fabricated wrought steel reflects the local history*

Project aims

The route of the road was chosen to link the A4123, Birmingham New Road, and M6, while opening up access to derelict land for development. The sculptures provide an identity and a series of landmarks and points of interest for users and local residents.

Landscape architect's role

The sculptures were formally commissioned by the Highways and Transportation Committee of the Council advised by a panel comprising councillors, local community representatives and a representative from the university. The panel was serviced by the landscape architects, who provided shortlists of artists for the various projects in conjunction with the public art consultants. The landscape architects also worked with an artist in residence (Jamie McCullough) on the proposals for the artworks in the vicinity of the footpath and cycleway.

2

The landscape architect designed the soft landscape to the road and detailed and specified items such as salt splash strips, bridge finishes, street furniture and railings, paint finishes and acoustic barriers. They managed the commissioning of the art works, administered some of the individual contracts, and liaised with the artists on their designs and on the fabrication and installation of the sculptures, in conjunction with the public art consultants.

Project constraints

Extensive contamination of the land was dealt with by the engineers and one of the sculptures is positioned on a mound where contaminated material was not removed – thus the *Bilston Oak* sculpture will flex as the mound changes shape. Artists were given a fixed budget for a project.

The unique opportunities of this project

To provide a new road serving regenerated industrial areas with the local character and history of the area reflected in a series of sculptures visible from the road and the footpath/cycleway. Some of the sculptures, produced by nineteen artists, provide interactive opportunities for people.

Project design

The area of Bilston developed from a small farming village of 1000 people in 1700 through to becoming a significant coal and steel producing area by the early 1900s. It has been famous for producing small decorative enamelled boxes since the 1700s. Canal, railway and roads have all been methods of transportation in this heavily industrial area, but with the closure of the steel works in 1979 and the closure of the GKN Sankey car component factories in the 1980s came mass unemployment. Large tracts of land became derelict and obsolete from their previous land use. The Black Country Route was developed to provide access to sites for regeneration and to relieve congestion from the centre of Bilston. This has been complemented by new metro links to Birmingham.

The Route is 7 kilometres in length, 4 of which are within Wolverhampton; the artworks are confined to the part of the route lying within Wolverhampton City's boundaries. There are footpaths running parallel with the route for much of its length, and access by foot and bicycle is provided on a footpath and cycleway running through a landscaped area adjacent to the route for 1 km in the part of Bilston known as the Lunt.

3

The overall design of the footpath/cycleway and sculpture programme was planned in conjunction with the artist Jamie McCullough and includes two major works by him. The footpath/cycleway is 5 metres wide and made of red and black bitumen macadam with concrete kerbs and colour-coated steel fencing and bollards. Three-metre wide grass strips adjacent to the footpath and cycleway ensure long sight lines so users feel safe. There is largely native tree and shrub planting and wildflower meadow to the central reservation between the carriageways.

Many of the sculptures reflect the history of the area in their design, name or the material from which they are constructed. *The Bilston Oak*, *Giant Oak Seat*, *Carved Oak Seat* and *Roller Seats* include oak in their construction as a representation of the old forest of Bilston. The *House of Birds* is tree-like in its form. The *Steel Monoliths*, *Beth's Arch*, *Steel Columns* (made of sweet chestnut), *Tower of Light*, *Horse and Rider* and *Ponies* reflect the steel-making industry that for so long sustained the population. The *Stone Seat* is made from Portland Stone and was inspired by the enamel boxes that have been made in Bilston for over two centuries.

Partnerships and community involvement
Lunt Community Centre and Scout Group, Villiers Primary School, Mosley Park School and Colton Hills Community School were all involved during the project. Three large, local exhibitions showing proposals were held, three in Bilston Craft Gallery and one in a disused supermarket in Bilston town centre.

Current site users
Local residents are the most frequent pedestrian and cycle users of the route with dog walking and play being popular activities. Commuters using the road to work daily have the visual experience of the sculptures and the growing vegetation, and for many visitors to the area their first view of the city is from the Sculpture Route.

Ongoing management of the project
The soft works are maintained under contract supervised by horticultural staff in Lifelong Learning, while periodic maintenance work to the sculptures is organised by the landscape and environment section using highway maintenance funds.

4

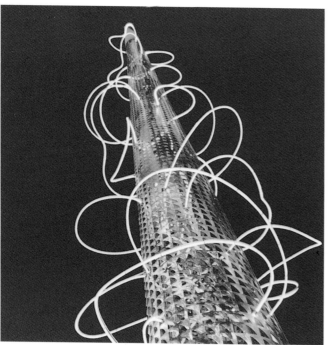

2 *Horse and Rider: travelling through the centuries to the future*
3 *Steel Columns: 15, 6-metre high, sweet chestnut carvings*
4 *Beth's Arch: 8 metres high, fabricated and painted steel –
named after the main blast furnace*
5 *Tower of Light: a futuristic tower of steel mesh and
fibre-optic cables*

5

Victoria Quays, Sheffield Canal Basin

Client	British Waterways and Sheffield Development Corporation
Landscape architect	British Waterways, Rugby
Architect	British Waterways (Basin Master's building) and Alan Johnson and Partners, Warwick (Straddle building)
Quantity surveyor	Bucknall Austin, Sheffield
Engineers	Cameron Taylor Bedford, Coventry (Straddle building); British Waterways Technical Services, Leeds (canal works)
Developers	Tom Cobleigh Brewery, Wilson Bowden Developers, British Waterways and others
Contractor	Hallamshire Contractors for the landscape works; Jarvale Construction (Basin Master's building); Mowlem Construction Limited (Straddle building)
Initial involvement	Early 1993
Work started on site	April 1994
Practical completion	May 1995
Project value	£35 million – total basin developments including warehouses; £1 million for hard works, £300 for soft works
Capital funding sources	Landscape works were grant aided by the Sheffield Development Corporation
Revenue funding sources	British Waterways

I

I *Victoria Quays in the city centre context*

Project aims
This regeneration project, in the centre of the City of Sheffield, aimed to provide a destination for boaters and to create a vibrant events' space for boat festivals and music concerts. While regenerating the area the project aimed to retain existing canal artefacts such as a coal staithe and bridge abutments. In addition the scheme was designed to create different areas and spaces catering for differing boating needs, visitors, trip boats and restaurant boats.

Landscape architect's role
The landscape architects developed the master plan for the site and liaised with the client about the design of surrounding sites. They also prepared the contract drawings and other contract documentation and were contract administrator for the landscape works.

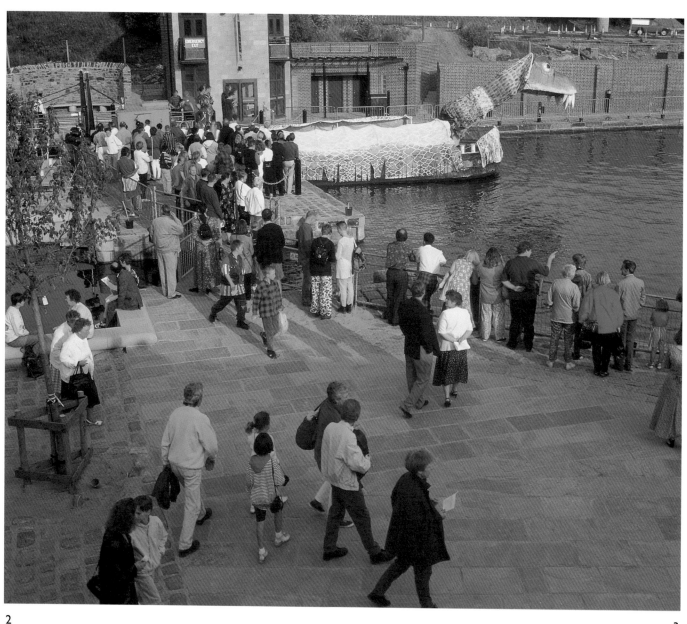

2

3

Project constraints

The main project constraint was the tight deadline determined by the different developers involved in the individual sites and buildings. In addition the budget was tight and the landscape budget was only determined once the engineering works were complete.

The unique opportunities of this project

This project provided the unique opportunity to restore an old stepped dry dock that had been long buried. An old slipway was converted into a wet dock to house a restaurant/hotel boat. The project also involved the refurbishment of a unique straddle warehouse and the creation of a Basin Master's building.

Project design

Sheffield canal basin, a 30 acre site close to the city centre, contains a number of historic and listed buildings. It last saw freight in 1970 and had steadily become derelict over the years. A number of attempts to revive the area failed until in 1993 British Waterways and Sheffield Development Corporation joined forces to enable redevelopment to take place.

The scheme involved the regeneration of a range of buildings: the Sheaf Works initially into a pub; the Terminal and Grain warehouse into residential units and a bar/pub; the South Quay Development into offices; and the Straddle Warehouse into office accommodation. Associated with the regeneration of the buildings was the development of a high-quality external environment. The

4

north side of the basin remains open in character in order to maximise the south-facing aspect for events and festivals

It was essential to maintain a 4 metre smooth route for people with disabilities around the basin with a 1 metre tactile strip adjacent to the water's edge. Many York stone setts had been reclaimed from the site and stored before being reused on the site. These were complemented by additional York stone pavings and copings. Seats were made from reconstituted concrete.

In order to retain the urban industrial nature of the site there was only a small amount of soft landscape works and this was mainly in the form of ash trees.

Partnerships and community involvement

Partnerships were an essential part of this regeneration project. British Waterways leased the Grain and Terminal warehouses to Sheffield Development Corporation and retained the historic Straddle warehouse. The Straddle refurbishment was helped by a £1.5 million grant from the Sheffield Development Corporation, while British Waterways financed the rest and restored the canal basin to provide improved boating facilities.

Current site users

Sheffield Development Corporation saw this project as one of its landmark sites, as did British Waterways. The Basin Master's building provides a base for a Basin Master to manage the boating operations from and visitor facilities and exhibition space.

5

There are a variety of people who visit the site from office workers and visitors to the hotel to the general public using shops in the arches and the public house. In addition there are residential craft in the basin, trip boats and visitors to boats and people attending events. Many events take place including activites during Sheffield's annual Children's Festival.

2 *Victoria Quays festival*
3 *Fun at the canal basin*
4 *Coffee by the waterside*
5 *Arches developed for retail units*

References

Abercrombie, S. (1981) 'The entire city should be seen as a playground', in L. Taylor (ed.) *Urban Open Spaces*, London: Academy Editions.

Abrams, R. and Ozdil, T. R. (2000) Sharing the civic realm: pedestrian adaptation in the post modern city, in J. Benson and M. Roe (eds) *Urban Lifestyles: Spaces, Places, People*, Rotterdam: A. A. Balkema.

Adams, E. (1989) 'Learning Through Landscapes', *Landscape Design* 181: 16–19.

Anderson, L. M. and Cordell, H. K. (1988) 'Influence of Trees on Residential Property Values in Athens, Georgia (USA): A Survey based on Actual Sales Prices', *Landscape and Urban Planning* 15: 153–164.

Appleton, J. (1996) *The Experience of Landscape*, 2nd edn, Chichester: Wiley.

Appleyard, D. and Lintell, M. (1972) 'The Environmental Quality of City Streets: The Residents' Viewpoint', *American Institute of Planners Journal* 38: 84–101.

Armstrong, N. (1993) 'Promoting Physical Activity in Schools', *Health Visitor* 66, 10: 362–364.

Baines, C. and Smart, J. (1984) *A Guide to Habitat Creation*, London: Greater London Council.

Baird, C. and Bell, P. B. (1995) 'Place Attachment, Isolation and the Power of a Window in a Hospital Environment: A Case Study', *Psychological Reports* 76: 847–850.

Barber, A. (1994) *Law, Money and Management, The Future of Urban Parks and Open Spaces*, Working Paper number 2, London and Gloucester: Comedia and Demos.

Barnhart, S. K., Perkins, N. H. and Fitzsimonds, J. (1998) 'Behaviour and Outdoor Setting Preferences at a Psychiatric Hospital', *Landscape and Urban Planning* 42: 147–157.

Barton, H., Davis, G. and Guise, R. (1995) *Sustainable Settlements: A guide for planners, designers and developers*, Bristol: Local Government Management Board and University of the West of England.

Beer, A. and Higgins, C. (2000) *Environmental Planning for Site Development*, London: E. and F. N. Spon.

Bengtsson, A. (1974) *The Child's Right to Play*, Sheffield, England: International Playground Association.

Benjamen, J. (1974) *Grounds for Play*, London: Bedford Square Press.

Beveridge, C. E. and Rocheleau, P. (1995) *Frederick Law Olmsted: Designing the American Lansdcape*, New York: Rizzoli.

Bishop, J. C. and Curtis, M. (eds) (2001) *Play Today in the Primary School Playground*, Buckingham: Open University Press.

Borhidi, A. (1988) 'Some ecological and social features of big cities' in *Cities and Ecology (2)*, Moscow: UNESCO Man and Biosphere Program.

Bortz, W. (1990) 'Breaking the Age Barrier', *Running Magazine* (December) 8: 38–39.

Box, J. and Harrison, C. (1993) 'Urban Greenspace: Natural Spaces in Urban Places', *Town and Country Planning* 62, 9: 231–235.

Bradley, C. and Millward, A. (1986) 'Successful Green Space – Do we know it when we see it?', *Landscape Research* 11, 2: 2–9

British Heart Foundation (2000a) *Couch Kids: The growing epidemic – looking at physical activity in children in the United Kingdom*, London: British Heart Foundation.

British Heart Foundation (2000b) *Get Kids on the Go!*, London: British Heart Foundation.

British Waterways (no date) *General Information Sheets*, Watford: British Waterways.

British Waterways (2000a) *Annual Report and Accounts 1999–2000*, Watford: British Waterways.

British Waterways Map (2000b) *British Waterways Map and Information 2000–2001*, Watford: British Waterways.

Broadmeadow, M. and Freer-Smith, P. (1996) 'Urban Woodlands and the Benefits for Local Air Quality', *Research for amenity trees No 5*, Forestry Commission Research Division and Department of the Environment, London: The Stationery Office.

Bundred, P., Kitchiner, D. and Buchan, I. (2001) 'Prevalence of Overweight and Obese children Between 1989 and 1998: Population Based Series of Cross Sectional Studies', *British Medical Journal*, 322, 7282: 326–328.

Burgess, J. (1996) 'Focusing on Fear: The use of Focus Groups in a Project for the Community Forest Unit, Countryside Commission', *Area* 28, 2: 130–135.

Burke, G. (1971) *Towns in the Making*, London: Edward Arnold.

Burnett, J. D. (1997) 'Therapeutic effects of landscape architecture', in S. O. Marberry, *Healthcare Design*, New York: Wiley.

Butler, K. (1989) 'Environmental Education at St Luke's', *Landscape Design* 181: 22–23.

Carr, S., Francis, M., Rivlin, R. and Stone, A. (1992) *Public Space*, Cambridge: Cambridge University Press.

Cary-Elwes, G. (1996) 'A Precious Asset', *Landscape Design* 252: 11–12.

Chandler, T. (1974) 'Urban climates and environmental management', in *Nature in Cities*, Annual Symposium of Landscape Research Group in conjunction with the North West Chapter of the Institute of Landscape Architects.

Chandler, T. (1978) 'The man-modified climate of towns', in Lenihan, J. and Fletcher, W. W. (eds) *The Built Environment*, Environment and Man, Volume 8, London: Blackie.

Chidister, M. (1986) 'The Effect of Context on the Use of Urban Plazas', *Landscape Journal* 5: 115–127.

Chidumayo, E. (1988) 'Conservation problems of urban growth in a developing country: the example of Chipata in eastern Zambia', in *Cities and Ecology (2)*, Moscow: UNESCO Man and Biosphere Program.

Chilean National Committee on Recreation (1986) 'Recreation and the Elderly', *World Leisure and Recreation Association* 28, 2: 15–17.

Churchman, C. and Fieldhouse, K. (1990) 'HLM Practice Profile and a Sympathetic Response', *Landscape Design* 174: 35–41.

Clark, R. (1899) *Golf: A Royal and Ancient Game*, 3rd edn, London: Macmillan and Company.

Clegg, F. (1989) 'Cemeteries for the Living', *Landscape Design* 184: 15–17.

Cobham Resource Consultants (1992) *Study of Golf in England: A Report to the Sports Council*, London: Sports Council.

Coffin, G. M. (1989) *Children's Outdoor Play in the Built Environment: a Handbook*, London: National Children's Play and Recreation Unit.

Collins, M. F. (1994) *The Sporting life: Sport, Health and Recreation in Urban Parks*, Working Paper 11, London and Gloucester: Comedia and Demos.

Coppin, N. and Richards, I. (1986) 'Edge of the Road', *Landscape Design* 159: 51–53.

Corbishley, M. (1995) *The Legacy of the Ancient World: Greece and Rome*, Hemel Hempstead: Macdonald Young Books.

Correll, A., Converse, P. E. and Rodgers, W. L. (1978) *The Quality of American Life*, New York: Russell Sage Foundation.

Cotton, W. R. and Pielke, P. A. (1995) *Human Impacts on Weather and Climate*, Cambridge: Cambridge University Press.

Council of Europe (1986) *Recommendation No. R(86) 11* of the Committee of Ministers to Member States on Urban Open Space, Strasbourg: Council of Europe.

Cranz, G. (1982) *The Politics of Park Design: A history of urban parks in America*, London: MIT Press.

Crompton, J. L. (1999) *Financing and Acquiring Park and Recreation Resources*, Champaign, USA: Human Kinetics.

Danzer, G. A. (1987) *Public Places: Exploring Their History*, The Nearby History Series, Nashville, Tennessee: American Association for State and Local History.

Day, K. (2000) 'The Ethic of Care and Women's Experiences of Public Space', *Journal of Environmental Psychology* 20: 103–124.

Day, M. (1995) *Keep Out! The story of castles and forts through the ages*, Hemel Hempsted: Macdonald Young Books.

De Potter, J. C. (1981) 'Sport for the Handicapped', *FIEP Bulletin*, 50, 1: 22–27.

Denton-Thompson, M. (1989) 'New Horizons for Education', *Landscape Design* 181: 11.

Department of Education and Science (1990) *The Outdoor Classroom* – Building Bulletin, 71, London: Her Majesty's Stationery Office.

Department of the Environment (1973) *Children at Play*, London: Her Majesty's Stationery Office.

Department of the Environment (1996) *Greening the City: A Guide to Good Practice*, London: The Stationery Office.

Department of the Environment, Transport and the Regions (2000) *Our Towns and Cities: The future delivering an urban renaissance*, London: The Stationery Office.

Department of Transport; Local Government and the Regions (2001) *Green Spaces: Better Places (Interim report of the Greenspaces Taskforce)*, London: The Stationery Office.

Department of Transport, Local Government and the Regions (2002) *Green Spaces: Better Places Final Report*, London: The Stationery Office.

Diallo, B. (1986) 'Leisure in the Context of the World Assembly on Aging', *World Leisure and Recreation Association* 28, 2: 11–14.

Dicker, E. A. (1986) 'Cemeteries Should be Living Places of Peace and Serenity', *Memorial Advisory Bureau Bulletin*, June 1986: 6–7.

DiGilio, D. A. and Howze, E. H. (1984) 'Fitness and Full Living for Older Adults', *Parks and Recreation*, 12, 19: 32–37 and 66.

Dodd, J. S. (ed.) (1988a) *Energy Saving through Landscape Planning (1): The Background*, Property Services Agency, Croydon: Her Majesty's Stationery Office.

Dodd, J. S. (ed.) (1988b) *Energy Saving through Landscape Planning (3): The Contribution of Shelter Planting*, Property Services Agency, Croydon: Her Majesty's Stationery Office.

Dodd, J. S. (ed.) (1988c) *Energy Saving through Landscape Planning (6): A Study of the Urban Edge*, Property Services Agency, Croydon: Her Majesty's Stationery Office.

Dreyfuss, J. A. (1981) 'The possibilities never stop', in L. Taylor (ed.) *Urban Open Spaces*, London: Academy Editions.

Driver, B. L. and Rosenthal, D. (1978) 'Social Benefits of Urban Forests and Related Green Spaces in Cities', *First National Urban Forestry Conference Proceedings*, 98–113, USDA, State University of New York.

Dunnett, N. and Qasim, M. (2000) 'Perceived Benefits to Human Well-being of Urban Gardens', *HortTechnology* 10, 1: 40–45.

Dunnett, N., Swanwick, C. and Woolley, H. (2002) *Improving Urban Parks, Play Areas and Green Spaces*, London: The Stationery Office.

Eckbo, G. (1969) *The Landscape that We See*, New York: McGraw-Hill.

Eckbo, G. (1987) 'The City and Nature', *Ekistics* 327: 323–325.

Elkin, T., McLaren, D. and Hillman, M. (1991) *Reviving the City: Towards sustainable urban development*, London: Friends of the Earth with Policy Studies Institute.

Elliott, B. (1989) 'The Landscape of the English Cemetery', *Landscape Design* 184: 13–14.

English Sports Council (1997a) *Policy Briefing 7: Local authority support for sports participation in the younger and older age groups*, London: English Sports Council.

English Sports Council (1997b) *Policy Briefing 2: The economic impact of sport in England*, London: English Sports Council.

English Sports Council (1997c) *Policy Briefing 5: Local authority support for national sports policy*, London: English Sports Council.

Epstein, G. (1978) 'University Landscapes', *Landscape Design* 121: 13–17.

Evans, J. (1986) 'Follow the Grain', *Landscape Design* 159: 44–45.

Fairbrother, N. (1970) *New Lives, New Landscapes*, Harmondsworth: Penguin Books.

Fairclough, S. and Stratton, G. (1997) 'Physical Education Curriculum and Extra-curriculum Time: A Survey of Secondary Schools in the North-West of England', *British Journal of Physical Education* 28, 3: 21–24.

Federation of City Farms and Community Gardens (1998) *A Selection of Current Areas of Work*, Bristol: Federation of City Farms and Community Gardens.

Federation of City Farms and Community Gardens (1999) *City Farming and Community Gardening*, Bristol: Federation of City Farms and Community Gardens.

Federer, C. A. (1976) 'Trees Modify the Urban Climate', *Journal of Arboriculture* 2, 7: 121–127.

Flora, T. (1991) 'In Cemeteries and all Around Wildlife is Part of us', *Memorial Advisory Bureau Bulletin* August: 6–7.

Francis, M. (1995) 'Childhood's Garden: Memory and Meaning of Gardens', *Children's Environments* 12, 2: 182–191.

Francis, M., Cashdan, L. and Paxson, L. (1984) *Community Open Spaces*, Washington, DC: Island Press.

Freeman, C. (1996) *The Ancient Greeks*, Abingdon: Andromeda Oxford.

Frommes, B. and Eng, H. C. (1978) *Applied Climatology: Better and cheaper building and living*, pp.24–29, Luxembourg: Standing Committee Urban and Building Climatology.

Ganapathy, R. S. (1988) 'Urban Agriculture, Urban Planning and the Ahmedabad Experience', in *Cities and Ecology (2)*, Moscow: UNESCO Man and Biosphere Program.

Gaster, S. (1992) 'Historical Changes in Children's Access to U. S. Cities: A Critical Review', *Children's Environments* 9, 2: 23–36.

Gehl, J. (1987) *Life Between Buildings: Using public spaces*, New York: Van Nostrand Reinhold.

Gilbert, O. (1991) *The Ecology of Urban Habitats*, London: Chapman and Hall.

Girardet, H. (1996) *The Gaia Atlas of Cities*, 2nd edn, London: Gaia Books.

Girouard, M. (1985) *Cities and People: A Social and Architectural History*, New Haven and London: Yale University Press.

Gold, S. M. (1973) *Urban Recreation Planning*, Philadelphia: Lea and Febiger.

Gold, S. M. (1980) *Recreation Planning and Development*, New York: McGraw-Hill.

Goldstein, E. L., Gross, M. and Martin A. L. (1985) 'A Biogeographic Approach to the Design of Greenspaces', *Landscape Research* 10, 1: 14–17.

Goode, D. (1997) 'The Nature of Cities', *Landscape Design* 263: 14–18.

Goode, D. (1989) 'Urban Nature Conservation in Britain', *Journal of Applied Ecology* 26: 859–873.

Goodman, P. and Goodman, P. (1960) *Communitas*.

Government's Response to the Environment, Transport and Regional Affairs Committee's Report (1998), *The Future of Allotments,* London: Department of the Environment, Transport and the Regions.

Great Britain, Committee on Land Utilisation in Rural Areas (1942) *Report of the Committee on Land Utilisation in Rural Areas*, London: Her Majesty's Stationery Office.

Greenhalgh, L. and Worpole, K. (1995) *Park Life: Urban parks and social renewal*, London: Comedia and Demos.

Gregory, K. J. and Walling, D. E. (eds) (1981) *Man and Environmental Processes*, London: Butterworths.

Halcrow Fox and Associates, Cobham Resource Consultant and Anderson, P. (1987) *Planning for Wildlife in Metropolitan Areas*, Peterborough: Nature Conservancy Council.

Hall, P. and Ward, C. (1998) *Sociable Cities: The Legacy of Ebeneezer Howard*, Chichester: John Wiley and Sons.

Hanson-Kahn, C. (2000) *Home Zone News*, Issue 1, London: National Children's Bureau Enterprises.

Harrison, C. and Burgess, J. (1988) 'Qualitative Research and Open Space Policy', *The Planner* November: 16–18.

Harrison, C. and Burgess, J. (1989) 'Living Spaces', *Landscape Design* 183: 14–16.

Harrison, C. Limb, M. and Burgess, J. (1987) Nature in the City: Popular Values for a Living World, *Journal of Environmental Management*, 25, 4: 347–362.

Harrison, C., Burgess, J., Millward, A. and Dawe, G. (1995) *Accessible Natural Greenspace in Towns and Cities*, London: English Nature Research Report, Number 153.

Hart, R. (1979) *Children's Experience of Place*, New York: Irvington Publishers Incorporated.

Harvey, M. (1989) 'Children's Experiences with Vegetation', *Children's Environments Quarterly* 6, 1: 36–43.

Heckscher, A. (1977) *Open Spaces: The life of American cities*, New York: Harper and Row.

Heisler, G. M. (1977) 'Trees Modify Metropolitan Climate and Noise', *Journal of Arboriculture* 3, 11: 201–207.

Heisler, G. M. (1986) 'Energy Savings with Trees' *Journal of Arboriculture* 12, 5: 113–125.

Herzog, T. R. (1985) 'A Cognitive Analysis of Preference for Waterscapes', *Journal of Environmental Psychology* 5: 225–241.

Herzog, T. R., Kaplan, S. and Kaplan, R. (1982) 'The Prediction of Preference for Unfamiliar Urban Places', *Population and Environment: Behavioural and Social Issues*, 5: 43–59.

Herzog, T. R., Black, A. M., Fountaine, K. A. and Knotts, D. J. (1997) 'Reflection and Attentional Recovery as Distinctive Benefits of Restorative Environments', *Journal of Environmental Psychology* 17: 165–170.

Heseltine, P. and Holborn, J. (1987) *Playgrounds: The planning, design and construction of play environments*, London: Mitchell Publishing Company.

Hitchmough, J. and Bonguli, A. M. (1997) 'Attitudes of Residents of a Medium Sized Town in South West Scotland to Street Trees', *Landscape Research* 22, 3: 327–337.

Holden, R. (1988) 'Parks of the Future', *Landscape Design* 171: 11–12.

Holden, R., Merrivale, J. and Turner, T. (1992) *Urban Parks: A discussion paper*, London: The Landscape Institute.

Hole, V. (1966) *Children's Play on Housing Estates*, National Building Studies, Research Paper 39, Ministry of Technology, Building Research Station, London: Her Majesty's Stationery Office.

Holme, A. and Massie, P. (1970) *Children's Play: A Study of Needs and Opportunities*, London: Michael Joseph.

Hosking, S. and Haggard, L. (1999) *Healing the Hospital Environment: Design Management and Maintenance of Healthcare Premises*, London, E. & F. N. Spon.

Hoskins, W. G. (1955) *The Making of the English Landscape*, Harmondsworth: Penguin Books.

Hough, M. (1995) *City Form and Natural Process: Towards a new urban vernacular*, 2nd edn London: Routledge.

House of Commons (1999) *Environment Sub-committee Inquiry into Town and Country Parks*, London: Department of the Environment, Transport and the Regions.

Hoyles, M. (1994) *Lost Connections and New Directions: The private garden and the public park*, Working Paper number 6, London and Gloucester: Comedia and Demos.

Hughes, B. (1994) *Lost Childhoods: The case for children's play*, Working Paper number 3, London and Gloucester: Comedia and Demos.

Humphries, S. and Rowe, S. (1989) 'A Landscape for Life: The Coombes County Infant School', *Landscape Design* 181: 25–28.

Hurtwood, Lady Allen (1958) *Play Parks for Housing, New Towns and Parks*, London: Holloway Press Company Limited.

Hurtwood, Lady Allen (1968) *Planning for Play*, London: Thames and Hudson.

Hutchison, R. (1987) 'Ethnicity and Urban Recreation: Whites, Blacks and Hispanics in Chicago's Public Parks', *Journal of Leisure Research* 19, 3: 205–222.

ILAM (Institute of Leisure and Amenity Management) (1996) *Policy Position Statement No. 15 Nature Conservation and Urban Green Space*, Reading: Institute of Leisure and Amenity Management.

Institute of Civil Engineers (2000) *Designing Streets for People: An inquiry into the design, management and improvement of streets*, London: Institute of Civil Engineering in co-operation with the Urban Design Alliance.

Jackson, T. (1991) 'Sport for All!', *County Council Gazette* 83, 11: 318–319.

Jacobs, J. (1961) *The Death and Life of Great American Cities*, Harmondsworth: Pelican.

Jacobson, B. H. and Kulling, F. A. (1989) 'Exercise and Aging: The Role Model,' *Physical Educator* 2, 46: 86–89.

Jensen, R. (1981) 'Dreaming of Urban Plazas', in L. Taylor (ed.) *Urban Open Spaces*, London: Academy Editions.

Johnston, M. (1997) 'The Early Development of Urban Forestry in Britain: Part 1', *Arboricultural Journal* 21: 107–126.

Johnston, M. (1999) 'The Springtime of Urban Forestry in Britain – Developments Between the First and Third Conferences, 1988–1993, Part I', *Arboricultural Journal* 23: 233–260.

Johnston, M. (2000) 'The Springtime of Urban Forestry in Britain – Developments Between the First and Third Conferences, 1988–1993, Part II', *Arboricultural Journal* 23: 313–341.

Johnston, J. and Newton, J. (1996) *Building Green: A guide to using plants on roofs, walls and pavements*, London: London Ecology Unit.

Kaplan, R. (1980) 'Citizen Participation in the Design and Evaluation of a Park', *Environment and Behavior* 12: 494–507.

Kaplan, R. (1993) 'The Role of Nature in the Context of the Workplace', *Landscape and Urban Planning* 26: 193–201.

Kaplan, S. (1995) 'The Restorative Benefits of Nature: Toward an Integrative Framework', *Journal of Environmental Psychology* 15: 169–182.

Kaplan, R. and Kaplan, S. (1989) *The Experience of Nature: A psychological experience*, Cambridge: Cambridge University Press.

Kaplan, S. and Wendt, J. S. (1972) *Preference and the Visual Environment: Complexity and some alternatives*, EDRA Conference Proceedings, University of California: Environmental Design Research Association.

Kelly, (2000) unpublished paper, Warwick workshop.

Kirkby, M. (1989) 'Nature as Refuge in Children's Environments', *Children's Environments Quarterly* 6, 1: 7–12.

Korpela, K. and Hartig, T. (1996) 'Restorative Qualities of Favorite Places', *Journal of Environmental Psychology* 16: 221–233.

Kuo, F. E., Bacaicoa, M. and Sullivan, W.C. (1998) 'Transforming Inner City Landscapes: Trees, Sense of Safety and Preference', *Environment and Behavior* 30, 1: 28–59.

Kweon, B.-S., Sullivan, W. C. and Wiley, A. R. (1998) 'Green Common Spaces and the Social Integration of Inner-City Older Adults', *Environment and Behavior* 30, 6: 832–858.

Lambert, J. (1974) *Adventure Playgrounds: A personal account of a play-leader's work*, Harmondsworth: Penguin.

Laurie, I. (1979) *Nature in Cities: The natural environment in the design and development of cities*, Chichester, New York: Wiley.

Leather, P., Pyrgas, M., Beale, D. and Lawrence, C. (1998) 'Windows in the Workplace: Sunlight, View and Occupational Stress', *Environment and Behavior* 30, 6: 739–762.

Lenihan, J. and Fletcher, W. W. (eds) (1978) *The Built Environment*, Environment and Man, Volume 8, London: Blackie.

Lennard, H. L. and Lennard, S. H. C. (1992) 'Children in Public Places: Some Lessons from European Cities', *Children's Environments* 9, 2: 37–47.

Llewelyn-Davies Planning (1992) *Open Spaces Planning in London*, London: London Planning Advisory Committee.

Loudon, J. C. ([1843]1981) *On the Laying Out, Planting and Managing Cemeteries and on the Improvement of Churchyards*, new edn, Redhill: Ivelet Books.

Loukaitou-Sideris, A. (1995) 'Urban Form and Social Context: Cultural Differentiation in the Use of Parks', *Journal of Planning Education and Research* 14: 89–102.

Loukaitou-Sideris, A. and Banerjee, T. (1998) *Urban Design Downtown: Poetics and politics of form*, Berkeley, Los Angeles and London: University of California Press.

Lowry, W. P. (1967) 'The climate of cities', in *Cities: Their Origin, Growth and Human Impact*, Readings from *Scientific American*. San Francisco: W. H. Freeman and Company.

Lucas, B. (1995) 'Playgrounds of the Mind', *Landscape Design* 245: 19–21.

Lucas, B. and Russell. L, (1997) 'Grounds for Alarm', *Landscape Design* 260: 46–48.

Ludeman, H. (1988) 'Ecological Aspects of Urban Planning Illustrated by the Cases of GDR Cities', in *Cities and Ecology (2)*, Moscow: UNESCO Man and Biosphere Program.

Luttik, J. (2000) 'The Value of Trees, Water and Open Space as Reflected by House Prices in the Netherlands', *Landscape and Urban Planning* 48: 161–167.

Lynch, K. (1981) *A Theory of Good City Form*, Cambridge, MA: MIT Press.

MacDougall, E. B. (1994) *Fountains, Statues and Flowers: Studies in Italian Gardens of the Sixteenth and Seventeenth Centuries*, Washington, DC: Dumbarton Oaks.

MacIntyre, J., Pardey, J. and Yee, R. (1989) 'Phoenix Winners', *Landscape Design* 184: 26–27.

McLellan, G. (1984) 'Elcho Gardens – A Neighbourhood Landscape', *Landscape Design* 150: 33–36.

McNab, A. and Pryce, S. (1985) 'Lineside Landscape', *Landscape Design* 158: 14–15.

McNeish, D. and Roberts H. (1995) *Playing it Safe*, Ilford, Essex: Barnardo's.

Marans, R. and Mohai, P. (1991) 'Leisure Resources, Recreation and the Quality of Life', in Driver, B. L., Brown, P. J. and

Peterson, G. L. (eds) *Benefits of Leisure*, State College: Venture Publishing.

Maslow, A. (1954) *Motivation and Personality*, New York: Harper and Row.

Matthews, H. (1994) 'Living on the Edge: Children as Outsiders', *Tijdschrift voor economische en sociale geografie*, 86, 5: 456–466.

Miller, P. L. (1972) *Creative Outdoor Areas*, Englewood Cliffs: Prentice-Hall.

Milmo, C. (2001) ''Quick-fix'' Britain neglects its horticultural heritage', *Independent*, 1 May 2001.

Moore, R. C. (1995) 'Children Gardening: First Steps Towards a Sustainable Future', *Children's Environments* 12, 2: 222–232.

Morales, D., Boyce, B. N. and Favretti, R. J. (1976) 'The Contribution of Trees to Residential Property Value: Manchester, Connecticut', *Valuation* 23, 2: 26–43.

Morcos-Asaad, F. (1978) 'Design and building for a tropical environment', in Lenihan, J. and Fletcher, W. W. (eds) *The Built Environment*, Environment and Man, Volume 8, London: Blackie.

More, T. A. (1985) *Central City Parks: A behavioural perspective*, Burlington: School of Natural Resources, University of Vermont.

More, T. A. (1988) 'The Positive Values of Urban Parks', *Trends* 25, 3: 13–17.

More, T. A., Stevens, T. and Allen, G. P. (1988) 'Valuation of Urban Parks', *Landscape and Urban Planning* 15: 139–152.

Morgan, G. (1991) *A Strategic Approach to the Planning and Management of Parks and Open Spaces*, Reading: Institute of Leisure and Amenities Management.

Morgan, R. (1974) 'The educational value of nature to urban schools', in *Nature in Cities*, Annual Symposium of Landscape Research Group in conjunction with the North West Chapter of the Institute of Landscape Architects, March 1974, Manchester: University of Manchester.

Mumford, L. (1966) *The City as History: Its origins, transformations and its prospects*, Harmondsworth: Penguin.

Nakamura, R. and Fujii, E. (1992) 'A Comparative Study on the Characteristics of Electroencephalogram Inspecting a Hedge and a Concrete Block Fence', *Journal of the Japanese Institute of Landscape Architects* 55, 5: 139–144.

National Federation of City Farms (1998) *Annual Review and Accounts, 1997/8*, Bristol: National Federation of City Farms.

National Playing Fields Association (1992) *The Six Acre Standard: Minimum standards for outdoor playing space*, 2nd edn, London: National Playing Fields Association.

National Playing Fields Association (2000) *Best Play*, London: National Playing Fields Association.

National Urban Forestry Unit (1998) *Urban Forestry in Practice, Case Study 2: Greening of strategic urban transport corridors*, Wolverhampton: National Urban Forestry Unit.

National Urban Forestry Unit (1999a) *Urban Forestry in Practice, Case Study 9: Community orchards in towns*, Wolverhampton: National Urban Forestry Unit.

National Urban Forestry Unit (1999b) *Urban Forestry in Practice, Case Study 12: Woodlands burial*, Wolverhampton: National Urban Forestry Unit.

National Urban Forestry Unit (2000a) *Urban Forestry in Practice, Case Study 20: Historic urban forestry*, Wolverhampton: National Urban Forestry Unit.

National Urban Forestry Unit (2000b) *Urban Forestry in Practice, Case Study 14: Rail corridor enhancement through lineside vegetation management*, Wolverhampton: National Urban Forestry Unit.

Newman, O. (1972) *Defensible Space: People and Design in the Violent City*, London: Architectural Press.

Nichols, G. and Taylor, P. (1996) *West Yorkshire Sports Counselling: Final Evaluation Report*, Sheffield: Leisure Management Unit, University of Sheffield.

Nicholson-Lord, D. (1987) *The Greening of Cities*, London: Routledge and Kegan Paul.

Nielsen, E. H. (1989) 'The Danish Churchyard', *Landscape Design* 184: 33–36.

Nierop-Reading, B. (1989) 'The Rosary Cemetery', *Landscape Design* 184: 48–50.

Noble, D. G., Bashford, R. I. and Baillie, S. R. (2000) *The Breeding Bird Survey 1999*, Thetford: British Trust for Ornithology, Joint Nature Conservation Committee and the Royal Society for the Protection of Birds.

Nohl, W. (1981) 'The Role of Natural Beauty in the Concept of Urban Open Space Planning', *Garten und Landschaft* 11, 81: 885–891.

Noschis, K. (1992) 'Child Development Theory and Planning for Neighbourhood Play', *Children's Environments* 9, 2: 3–9.

Nugent, T. (1991) 'A Cemetery for the Living', *Landscape Architecture 81*: 73–75.

Oberlander, C. H. and Nadel, I. B. (1978) 'Historical perspectives on children's play', in Otter, M. (ed.) *Play in Human Settlements*, Sheffield International Playground Association.

OECD (Organisation for Economic Co-operation and Development) (1990) *Environmental Policies for Cities in the 1990s*, Paris: Organisation for Economic Co-operation and Development.

Office of the Deputy Prime Minister (2002) 'Living Places: Cleaner, Safer, Greener', London: Office of the Deputy Prime Minister.

Olds, A. R. (1989) 'Nature as Healer', *Children's Environments Quarterly* 6, 1: 27–32.

OPCS (Office of Population Censuses and Surveys) (1993) *Census 1981: The National Report*, London: Her Majesty's Stationery Office.

Opie, I. (1993) *The People in the Playground*, Oxford: Oxford University Press.

Opie, I. and Opie, P. (1969) *Children's Games in Street and Playground*, Oxford: Clarendon Press.

Owens, P. E. (1994) 'Teen Places in Sunshine, Australia: Then and Now', *Children's Environments* 11, 4: 292–299.

Ozsoy, A., Atlas, N. E., Ok, V. and Pulat, G. (1996) 'Quality Assessment Model for Housing: A Case Study on Outdoor Spaces in Istanbul', *Habitat International* 20, 2: 163–173.

Parker, M. (1989) 'Churchyard and Community', *Landscape Design* 184: 24–25.

Parks, P. and Jenkins, M. (unpublished) *The Value of Open Space in Urbanizing Areas: Benefits and Costs of the Eno River Corridor*, Rutgers University and the Freshwater Institute, United States of America: Department of Agricultural Economics and Marketing.

Parsons, R., Ulrich, R. S. and Tassinary, L. G. (1994) 'Experimental Approaches to the Study of People-Plant Relationships', *Journal of Consumer Horticulture* 1: 347–372.

Parsons, R., Tassinary, L. G., Ulrich, R. S., Hebl. M. R. and Grossman-Alexander, M. (1998) 'The View from the Road: Implications for Stress Recovery and Immunization', *Journal of Environmental Psychology* 18: 113–140.

Paxton, A. (1997) 'Farming the City', *Landscape Design* 263: 53–55.

Payne, B. R. and Strom, S. (1975) 'The Contribution of Trees to the Appraised Value of Unimproved Residential Land', *Valuation* 22, 2: 36–45.

Penning-Rowsell, A. (1999) 'New Landscapes of Learning', *Landscape Design* 280: 32–34.

Peterson, J. T. (1969) *The Climate of Cities: Survey of Recent Literature*, Raleigh: United States Department of Health, Education and Welfare, National Air Pollution Control Administration, AP-59.

Pinder, S. (1991) 'And Cricket: A conversation with Ian Fell', Director for British Blind Sport, *Sport and Leisure*, May/June: 26.

Pitkin (2002) *Guidebook to Gloucester Cathedral*, Pitkin.

Portland House (ed.) (1988) *The World Atlas of Architecture*, New York: Portland House.

Powe, N. A., Garrod, G. D. and Willis, K. G. (1995) 'Valuation of Urban Amenities Using an Hedonic Price Model', *Journal of Property Research*, 12: 137–147.

Purcell, A. T., Lamb, R. J., Mainardi, E. and Falchero, S. (1994) 'Preference or Preferences for Landscape', *Journal of Environmental Psychology*, 14: 195–209.

Pushkarev, B. (1960) 'The Esthetics of Freeway Design', *Landscape*, 10, 2: 7–14.

Rackham, O. (1986) *History of the Countryside*, London: Dent.

Rayner, S. and Malone, E. (eds) (1998a) *Human Choice and Climate Change* (Vol. 2), Columbus, Ohio: Batelle Press.

Rayner, S. and Malone, E. (eds) (1998b) *Human Choice and Climate Change* (Vol. 4), Columbus, Ohio: Batelle Press.

Reilly. J. J., Dorosty, A. R. and Emmett, P. M. (1999) 'Prevalence of Overweight and Obesity in British Children: Cohort Study', *British Medical Journal*, 319: 1039.

Rishbeth, C. (2001) 'Ethnic Minority Groups and the Design of Public Open Space: An Inclusive Landscape?' *Landscape Research*, 26, 4: 351–366.

Rouse, W. (1981) 'Man-modified climates', in Gregory, K. J. and Walling D. E. (eds) *Man and Environmental Processes*, London: Butterworths.

Rowntree, R. and Nowak, D. J. (1991) 'Quantifying the Role of Urban Forests in Removing Atmospheric Carbon Dioxide', *Journal of Arboriculture* 17, 10: 269–275.

Rudie, R. J. and Dewers, R. S. (1984) 'Effects of Tree Shade on Home Cooling Requirements', *Journal of Arboriculture*, 10, 12: 320–322.

Ruff, A. R. (1979) 'An ecological approach to landscape design', in Ruff, A. R. and Tregay, R., (eds) *An Ecological Approach to Urban Landscape Design*, Occasional Paper No. 8, Manchester: Department of Town and Country Planning, University of Manchester.

Rugg, J. (1998) 'A Few Remarks on Modern Sculpture: Current trends and new directions in cemetery research', *Mortality*, 3, 2: 111–128.

Rugg, J. (2000) 'Defining the Place of Burial: What Makes a Cemetery a Cemetery?', Mortality, 5, 3: 259–275.

Sainsbury, T. (1987) 'Urban Outdoor Activities: A New Tradition in the Use of Open Space', *The Leisure Manager* 6, 2: 9–10.

Schmelzkopf, K. (1995) 'Urban Community Gardens as Contested Space', *The Geographical Review*, 85, 3: 364–381.

Schroeder, H. W. and Anderson, L. M. (1984) 'Perception of Personal Safety in Urban Recreation Sites', *Journal of Leisure Research* 16, 2: 174–194.

Scott, D. (1997) 'Exploring the Time Patterns in People's Use of a Metropolitan Park District', *Leisure Sciences*, 19: 159–174.

Seila, A. F. and Anderson, L. M. (1982) 'Estimating Costs of Tree Preservation on Residential Lots', *Journal of Arboriculture*, 8: 182–185.

Sheffield City Council (2000) *Leisure Service Plan: 2000/2001*, Sheffield: Sheffield City Council.

Sheffield City Council (2001) *Estimated Annual Visits to Sheffield's Parks and Woodlands: Analysis of the Citizen's Panel Talkback Survey 2000*, Sheffield: Sheffield City Council.

Sies, M. C. (1987) 'The City Transformed: Nature, Technology and the Suburban Ideal, 1877–1917', *Journal of Urban History* 14, 1: 81–111.

Simmons, S. A. (1990) *Nature Conservation in Towns and Cities*, Peterborough: Nature Conservancy Council.

Singleton, D.M. (1990) *Health Bulletin No. 45 Appendix II: Case Study on Therapeutic Benefits*, London: Her Majesty's Stationery Office.

Social Exclusion Unit (1998) *Bringing the United Kingdom Together: A national strategy for neighbourhood renewal*, Cm 4045, presented to Parliament by the Prime Minister, September 1998, London: The Cabinet Office.

Somper, J. P. (2001) *Market Research: Property Values and Trees Feasibility Study*, Gloucestershire: National Urban Forestry Unit.

Spellerberg, I. and Gaywood, M. (1993) 'Linear Landscape Features', *Landscape Design* 223: 19–21.

Spirn, A. W. (1984) *The Granite Garden: Urban Nature and Human Design*, New York: Basic Books.

Sport England (2000a) *Positive Futures*, London: Sport England. (Available online – http://www.english.sports.gov.uk/about/about_1.htm).

Sport England (2000b) *Young People in Sport in England 1999*, London: Sport England.

Sports Council (1994) *Trends in Sports Participation Fact Sheet*, London: Sports Council.

Sports Council and Health Education Authority (1992) *Allied Dunbar National Fitness Survey – Main Findings*, London: Sports Council.

Spronken-Smith, R.A. and Oke, T.R. (1998) 'The thermal regime of urban parks in two cities with different summer climates', *International Journal of Remote Sensing*, 19(11): 2085-2104.

Stockli, P. P. (1997) 'Nature and Culture in Public Open Spaces', *Anthos* 2, 94:35-38.

Stoneham, J. (1996) *Grounds for Sharing*, Winchester: Learning Through Landscapes.

Sukopp, H. and Henke, H. (1988) 'Nature in towns: a dimension necessary for urban planning today', in *Cities and Ecology (2)* Moscow: UNESCO Man and Biosphere.

Sukopp, H. and Werner, P. (1982) *Nature in Cities – Nature and Environment Series No. 28*, Strasbourg: Council of Europe.

Talbot, J. (1989) 'Designing Plants into Play', *Children's Environments Quarterly*, 6, 1: 55.

Tankel, S. (1963) 'The importance of open spaces in the urban pattern', in Wing, L. (ed.) *Cities and Spaces: The future use of urban spaces*, Baltimore: Hopkins.

Tartaglia-Kershaw, M. (1982) 'The Recreational and Aesthetic Significance of Urban Woodland', *Landscape Research* 7, 3: 22–25.

Taylor, A. F., Wiley, A., Kuo, F. E. and Sullivan, W. C. (1998) 'Growing up in the Inner City: Green Spaces as Places to Grow', *Environment and Behavior*, 30, 1: 3–27.

Taylor, H. A. (1994) *Age and Order: The public park as a metaphor for a civilised society*, Working paper No. 10, London and Gloucester: Comedia and Demos.

Taylor, J. (ed.) (1998) *Early Childhood Studies: An Holisitc Introduction*, London: Arnold.

Teagle, W. (1974) 'The urban environment', in *Nature in Cities*, Annual Symposium of Landscape Research Group in conjunction with the North West Chapter of the Institute of Landscape Architects, Manchester: Manchester University Press.

Tennessen. C. M. and Crimprich, B. (1995) 'Views to Nature: Effects on Attention', *Journal of Environmental Psychology*, 15: 77–85.

Thayer, R. L. and Maeda, B. T. (1985) 'Measuring Street Tree Impact on Solar Performance: A Five Climate Computer Modeling Study', *Journal of Arboriculture*, 11, 1: 1–12.

Thorpe, H. (1969) *The Report of the Departmental Committee of Inquiry into Allotments*, London: Her Majesty's Stationery Office.

Thorpe, H., Galloway, E. and Evans, L. (1976) *From Allotments to Leisure Gardens: A case study of Birmingham*, Birmingham: Leisure Gardens Research Unit, University of Birmingham.

Titman, W. (1994) *Special Places, Special People*, London: World Wildlife Fund.

Tregay, R. and Gustavsson, R. (1983) *Oakwood's New Landscape: Designing for nature in the residential environment*, Uppsala: Swedish University of Agricultural Sciences/Warrington and Runcorn New Development Corporation.

Turner, T. (1996a) *City as Landscape: A post-modern view of design and planning*, London: E. & F. N. Spon.

Turner, T. (1996b) 'From No Way to Greenway', *Landscape Design* 254: 17–20.

Ulrich, R. S. (1979) 'Visual Landscapes and Psychological Well-Being', *Landscape Research* 4: 17–23.

Ulrich, R. S. (1981) 'Natural Versus Urban Scenes. Some Psychophysiological Effects', *Environment and Behavior*, 13: 523–556.

Ulrich, R. S. (1984) 'View Through a Window may Influence Recovery from Surgery', *Science* 224: 420–421.

Ulrich, R. and D. L Addoms (1981) 'Psychological and Recreational Benefits of a Residential Park', *Journal of Leisure Research* 13 1:43–65.

Ulrich, R. S., Simons, R. F., Losito, B. D., Fiorito, E., Miles, M. A. and Zelson, M. (1991) 'Stress Recovery During Exposure to Natural and Urban Environments', *Journal of Environmental Psychology* 11: 201–230.

UNCHS (United Nations, Centre for Human Settlements) (1996) *An Urbanising World: Global Report on Human*

Settlements, Oxford: Oxford University Press for the UNCHS.

Urban Parks Forum (2001) *Public Park Assessment: A survey of local authority owned parks focusing on parks of historic interest*, Caversham: Department of Transport, Local Government and the Regions, the Heritage Lottery Fund, the Countryside Agency and English Heritage.

Urban Task Force Final Report (1999) *Towards an Urban Renaissance*, London: E. & F. N. Spon.

Verderber, S. (1986) 'Dimensions of Person–Window Transactions in the Hospital Environment', *Environment and Behavior* 18: 450–466.

Von Stulpnagel, A., Horbert, M. and Sukopp, H. (1990) 'The importance of vegetation for the urban climate', in Sukopp, H. (ed.) *Urban Ecology*, The Hague: SPB Academic Publishing.

Waddell, P., Berry, B. J. L. and Hooch, I. (1993) 'Residential Property Values in Multinodal Urban Areas: New Evidence on the Implicit Price of Location', *Journal of Real Estimate Finance and Economics* 7: 117–141.

Wakeman, R. (1996) 'What is a Sustainable Port? The Relationship between Ports and Their Regions', *The Journal of Urban Technology* 3, 2: 65–80.

Walker, S. and Duffield, B. (1983) 'Urban parks and open spaces – an overview', *Landscape Research* 8, 2: 2–11.

Walzer, M. (1986) 'Public Space: Pleasures and Costs of Urbanity', *Dissent* 33, 4: 470–475.

Ward, C. (1978) *The Child in the City*, London: Architectural Press.

Warren, B. (2000) *Viewing and Audience Figures for Ground Force*, e-mail communication with Helen Woolley.

Warrington Borough Council (2001) *What's On in Warrington's Parks: January – June 2001*, Warrington: Warrington Borough Council.

Weller, S. (1989) 'Cemeteries – Designing for the Public', *Landscape Design* 184: 10–11.

Westphal, J. M. (2000) 'Hype, hyperbole and health: Therapeutic site design', in Benson, J. and Roe, M. (eds) *Urban Lifestyles: Spaces, Places, People*, Rotterdam: A. A. Balkema.

Whalley, J. M. (1978) 'The Landscape of the Roof', *Landscape Design* 122: 7–24.

White, I. (1999) 'Setting the Standard – The Development of Landscape Design and the Contribution it has made in Improving the Quality of Life in Scotland', *Landscape Design* 282: 19–22.

Whyatt, H. G. (1923) *Streets, Roads and Pavements*, London: Sir Isaac Pitman and Son.

Whyte, W. H. (1980) *The Social Life of Small Urban Spaces*, Washington DV: Conservation Foundation.

Wildlife Trusts (The) (2000) *Media Information: Who we are, a brief history of the wildlife trusts and key facts and figures*, London: The Wildlife Trusts.

Williams, R., Bidlack, C. and Brinson, B. (1994) 'The Rivers Curriculum Project: a Cooperative Interdisciplinary Model', *Children's Environments* 11, 3: 251–254.

Wilson, J. (1997) 'Making a Garden: A Place for Horticultural Therapy', *Streetwise* 31, (8:3) 14.

Winter, R. (1992) 'The Miracle Medium', *Landscape Design* 208: 8.

Wolschke-Bulmahn, J. and Groning, G. (1994) 'Children's Comics: An Opportunity for Education to Know and Care for Nature?', *Children's Environments* 11, 3: 232–242.

Wood, R. (1994) *Legacies: Architecture*, Hove: Wayland Publishers.

Woolley, H. (2002) 'Inclusive open spaces', *Landscape Design* 310: 43–45.

Woolley, H. and Amin, N. (1995) 'Pakistani Children in Sheffield and their Perception and use of Public Open Spaces', *Children's Environments* 121, 4: 479–488.

Woolley, H. and Johns, R. (2001) 'Skateboarding: The City as Playground', *Journal of Urban Design* 6, 2: 211–230.

Woolley, H., Rowley, G., Spencer, C. and Dunn, J. (1997) *Young People and their Town Centres*, London: Association of Town Centre Management.

Woolley, H., Spencer, C., Dunn, J. and Rowley, G. (1999) 'The Child as Citizen: Experiences of British Towns and City Centres', *Journal of Urban Design* 4, 3: 255–282.

Woolley, H., Gathorne-Hardy, F. and Stringfellow, S. (2001) 'The listening game', in Jefferson, C., Rowe, J. and Brebbia, C. (eds) *The Sustainable Street: The environmental, human and economic aspects of street design and management*, Southampton: Wessex Institute of Technology Press.

Worpole, K. (1997) *The Cemetery in the City*, Stroud: Comedia.

Worpole, K. (1999) *The Richness of Cities: Working paper number 2 – Nothing to Fear? Trust and Respect in Urban Communities*: London: Comedia and Demos.

Worpole, K. and Greenhalgh, L. (1996) *The Freedom of the City*, London and Gloucester: Demos.

Woudstra, J. (1989) 'The European Cemetery', *Landscape Design* 184: 19–21.

Wright, G. (1989) 'Bats in the Belfry', *Landscape Design* 184: 22–23.

Young, M. and Wilmott, P. (1973) *The Symmetrical Family*, New York: Pantheon.

Yuen, B. (1996) 'Use and Experience of Neighbourhood Parks in Singapore', *Journal of Leisure Research* 28, 4: 293–311.

Zhang, T. and Gobster, P. H. (1998) 'Leisure Preferences and Open Space Needs in an Urban Chinese American Community', *Journal of Architecture and Planning Research* 15, 4: 338–355.

Index

Index

Index

Index